HOTEL MANAGEMENT

Contents

Preface

"Hotel Managment" as a paper is being taught at Hotel Management Courses at various universities and institutions. This book is designed as an introductory text to the above paper, encompassing vital information on all pertinent aspects. Thus the material presented here would be of interest as well as of great use to the students, teachers and professionals of Tourism Courses. This book will provide complete knowledge of objectives and policies of hotel industry, history of hotel management, hotel organization, housekeeping, safety and sanitation, front office management, maintenance of accounts, room occupancy management, marketing functions, purchasing and stores management, arrangement of kitchen and dining room, role of services, meanus and menu planning, food services, equipments in kitchen, problems and prospects of hotel industry to the students.

The major topics dealt in this book are—Evolution of Hotel Industry; Objectives and Policies; Introduction to Hotel Groups; History of Hotel Management; Organization of Hotel; Housekeeping, Safety and Sanitation; Front Office Management; Maintenance of Accounts; Room Occupancy Rate Management; Marketing Functions; Purchasing and Stores Management; Restaurant Development; Arrangement of Kitchen and Dining Room; Role of Supporting Services; Meanus and Menu Planning; Guidelines for Room and Food Services; Equipments in Kitchen; Problems and Prospects of Hotel Industry etc.

It is hoped that all those will benefit from the contents of this book for whom it is meant. The author will feel amply rewarded, if motive is achieved.

Editor

1

Evolution of Hotel Industry

EARLY HISTORY

Accommodation for travellers may be conveniently viewed in two ways. The traveller who left his home required accommodation at his destination and for journeys which cannot be completed in a single day. For this he needed overnight accommodation. Inns were perhaps the first such accommodation units which catered to the needs of travellers in early times. Inn keeping has been a very ancient profession. In ancient times and during the Roman Empire many such inns were established which provided food, drink and also entertainment to weary travellers. However with the decline of the Roman Empire by about 500 AD., the institution of inn keeping lost its importance and for many years there was not much development. Since people travelled very infrequently and there being not much trading activity, there was not much need felt for inn keeping.

Later, it was the Church which came to the rescue of the travellers. Travel grew again for religious pilgrimage purposes. Travellers in thousands visited religious centres. Many monasteries and cathedrals welcomed the travellers and made their stay a comfortable experience. The accommodation provided was free. By the fifteenth century, inns had developed in several countries of Europe, specially in England and France. During the seventeenth and the eighteenth centuries, the facilities provided in the inns were expanded. Some of the inns had as many as 30 or more rooms. English common law declared the inn to be a public house and imposed social responsibility on the inn-keeper for the well-being of the traveller. Even today a hundred old coaching and posting inns are still operating in England as hotels as part of Trust House Limited. Some of these were built about four hundred years ago.

In the United States of America another type of accommodation unit known as the 'tavern' was opened in the year 1634 by a man called Samuel Coles. Coles had come to the New World in search of a fortune in the year 1630 by a ship. By 1780, taverns were popular meeting places where people used to come for eating, drinking and entertainment. Many important events were associated with taverns. In the year 1783, General George Washington bid farewell to his top ranking officers at the Fraunces Tavern in New York city. The famous Boston Tea Party was planned in a tavern called Green Dragon.

In India the concept of shelter for travellers is not new. In fact it is as old as its recorded history. The historical records are replete with mention/references of viharas, dharamsalas, sarais, musafirkhanas, etc. These establishments provided a home to all wayfarers, be they pilgrims, scholars, adventurers or merchants. The shelter under various names have always been a part of India's culture as a valuable institution providing a vital service.

The ancient Buddhist monks were probably the first to institutionalise the concept of a shelter in India. The cave temples scattered all over the south-western region of India have both a Chaitya (sanctuary) for worship and prayer and a Vihara (monastery). These monks, although living in their quiet retreats, away from towns and villages, were nevertheless mindful of the needs of travellers and pilgrims who found sheltter and food at these monasteries. It is interesting to note that these monasteries are located on the ancient trade routes between important deities of the region. It is gathered from some inscriptions that merchants gave liberal donations for the construction and maintenance of these establishments. Mere charity was obviously not the motivation in these displays of generosity. The trader travelled with their merchandise and money on these routes and the Viharas were their 'hotels'.

In the medieval period this ancient institution gradualtly assumed a more secular character. Although religious centres invariably had 'dharamsalas' and 'musafirkhanas' attached to them the caravan 'sarai' appeared as an exclusive traveller's lodge with a 'Nanbai' or the cook attached with it. Sher Shah Suri, the Great Afghan Emperor and the builder of the Grand Trunk Road, is credited with having built caravan sarais at regular intervals all along this highway creating favourable conditions for commerce and travel. However, he was not alone in this venture. The Mughals built such facilities all over their empire. Later kings, Rajàs, Nawabs, rich businessmen and philanthropists built sarais making travel less arduous. At approximately the same point in time, the inn was the western counterpart of India's sarais. With the expansion of commerce, travelling became profitable and with it emerged the business of providing comfortable shelter and good food to the growing number of travellers. The sarais in India like inns in Europe or the stagecoach stations in the USA of the 18th and 19th centuries stood all along the well-travelled routes. They provided food and shelter to the travellers and fodder to their horses. The amenities these early hotels offered would seem to us to be primitive but they conformed to the life style of that age.

With the passage of time the age-old institution of the sarai or the inn adapted itself to the ever changing and constantly growing requirements of the market and has evolved into the modern hotel. From the age of the bullock cart and horses through the age of the rail road into the era of the jumbo jet and supersonic aircraft, the hotel industry developed with the simultaneous development of transportation systems. It also reflects the standard of living and the life style of the society in which it operates.

With the growth of travel in the eighteenth century there appeared in London the prototype of the modern hotel with the opening by one David Low in 1774. The next fifty years saw a gradual increase in the recognizable ancestors of the modern hotel in London and in resorts such as Brighton and Buxton and also certain other places. In the United States of America, hotels emerged from taverns by the simple expedient of a change of name. By about 1800, the terms tavern and hotel were used to describe the same thing. By the year 1820, 'hotel' became the accepted term to describe a place where people stayed for the night and, took their meals on payment. In the 1820s the first tourist hotel appeared in Switzerland.

The demand for some kind of accommodation away from home is an important function of travel. It is therefore not surprising that the main influence on the development of accommodation facilities has been developments in the mode of passenger transport. In the field of mass passenger transport, railways could perhaps be credited with being the pioneers. The evolution of the railway system in the eighteenth century greatly affected the quality and the quantity of accommodation used in conjunction with travel. The growth of the railways also brought to a speedy network of stage coach services. By the mid-nineteenth century the use of the stage coach as a means of travel had almost ceased. The industrialization in its wake brought increased urbanisation. The great number of people who flocked to various urban towns in search of employment and also entertainment needed some kind of accommodation. This need for accommodation enabled promising and enterprising people to build hotels and inns in many such urban towns to cater for an increasingly local market and also to serve the large number of travellers carried by the railways.

Until about the middle of the nineteenth century the bulk of the journeys were undertaken for business and vocational reasons, by road and within the boundaries of the individual countries. The volume of travel was relatively small and was confined to a fraction of the rich segments of the population in any country. Inns and similar establishments along the main highways and in the principal towns grew to become the hallmark of the accommodation for the travellers. The traveller could reasonably expect at most inns a clean and comfortable accommodation when he wished to eat or spend the night. It provided the bulk of accommodation en route. This trend continued until the end of the nineteenth century, as most of those who did travel did so by coach.

EMERGENCE OF THE HOTEL

Although the earliest hotels date to the eighteenth century, their growth on any scale occurred only in the following century when the railways created sufficiently large markets to help make large hotels possible. During this period a large number of hotels grew up at important destinations. The hotels were developed along the main railways and highway routes in major towns. Substantial development of the hotels thus awaited the volume and the type of traffic only the railways could bring. With the development if railway systems in many other countries within and outside Europe, the number of hotels also increased. These hotels catered to the increasing volume of traffic.

The 1960s also saw the introduction of Thomas Cook's railway and hotel coupons. Starting in 1868, Cook arranged regular circular tours of Switzerland and Northern Italy from England. By the 1890s, 1,200 hotels throughout the world accepted hotel coupons. Thus we find that railways greatly influenced the development of hotels during the early twentieth century.

The demand for accommodation of tourists was thus met by a variety of facilities ranging from inns, taverns, private houses and hotels. The main changes in the demand for tourist accommodation have come about from changes in tourist transportation and in the popularity of different forms of holidays. After the introduction of the motor car and the aircraft, a large number of hotels sprang up at various tourist areas and destinations. The growth of hotels continued until the 1950s. Hotels as a unit of accommodation dominated the scene all over the world.

Hotels provide dccommodation, meals and refreshments for irregular periods of time for those who may reserve their accommodation either in advance or on the premises. In broad terms hotels provide facilities to meet the needs of the modern traveller. The dictionaries define hotel in several ways: 'a place which supplies board and lodging', 'a place for the entertainment of the travellers', 'large city house of distinction', and 'a public building'.

The common law states that a hotel is "A place where all who conduct themselves properly, and who, being able and ready to pay for their entertainment, are received, if there be accommodation for them, and who without any stipulated engagement as to the duration of their stay or as to the rate of compensation, are, while there, supplied at a reasonable cost with their meals, lodging, and such services and attention as are necessarily incident to the use of the house as a temporary home".

A definition of the hotel as a business entity worthy of study was presented by hotel operators during the consideration of the hotel business to authorities of the National Recovery Administration, in Washington in 1933. This definition, as formulated by Stuart McNamara, was:

"Primarily and fundamentally an hotel is an establishment which supplies board and lodging, not engaged in interstate commerce, or in any interstate commerce, competitive with or affecting, interstate commerce (or so related thereto that the regulation of the one involves the control of the other), but is a quasi domestic institution retaining from its ancient origin certain traditional, and acquiring, in its modern development, certain statutory rights and obligations to the public, where all, persons, not disqualified by condition or conduct, prepared to pay for their accommodation are to be received and furnished with a room of place to sleep or occupy if such accommodations are available and with such services and attention as are incident to their use of the hotel as a home, and/or with food, at stipulated prices, and with or without contract as to duration of visit, and which conducts within the confines of its physical locations, this business of supplying personal services of individuals for profit. Incidental to such fundamental and principal business, the hotel may furnish quarters and facilities for the assemblage of people for social, business or entertainment purposes, and may engage in renting portions of its premises for shops and business whdse contiguity is deemed appropriate to an hotel".

TYPES OF HOTELS

Over the years the concept and the format of hotels have changed a great deal. There are various types of hotels catering to the increasing demands of tourists. The size, the facade architectural features and the facilities and amenities provided differ from one establishment to another. In addition the land scape in a particular destination area also greatly influences the architectural features of a hotel. Following are the main types of hotels.

(1) International Hotels. International hotels are the modern western style hotels in almost all metropolitan and other large cities as well as principal tourist centres. These hotels are luxury hotels and are classified on the basis of internationally accepted system of classification. The hotels are placed in various star categories. There are five such categories ranging from 5 star to 1 star depending upon the facilities and services provided. These hotels provide in addition to accommodation all the other facilities which make the stay a very comfortable and interesting experience. Various facilities provided include well appointed eception and information counter, banquet halls, conference facilities, etc. There are also a number of shops, travel agency, money changing and safe deposit facilities. Restaurant facilities, bars and banqueting are an integral part of the business of a hotel. The various services provided. In these hotels include international and the local cuisine, food and beverage service and speciality restaurant service. These hotels also provide entertainment for the guests in the form of various dance and music programmes, sports and games.

A number of these hotels belong to the luxury category. There are some international chains which own a large number of such luxury hotels. Hotels belonging to international chains are mostly owned by public companies and controlled by a Board of Directors. These hotels have various departments which are managed by persons qualified and experienced in the field of hoteliering. The chief of the hotel designated as General Manager is responsible for the overall management and operation of the hotel through his departmental heads. International hotels are suitable for metropolitan cities and for other large business and commercial towns and principal tourist centres. The potential of these hotels is therefore limited to these areas: A number of this type of hotels have conference/convention facilities and are suitable for holding meetings, conventions and conferences.

(2) Resort Hotels. Resort hotels cater to the needs of holiday-maker, the tourist and those who by reasons of health desire a change of atmosphere. Resort hotels are located near the sea, mountain and other areas abounding in natural beauty. Rest, elaxation and entertainment are the key factors around which 'resorts are built. The primary motive of a person visiting resort hotels is rest and relaxation which he is looking far away from his routine busy work life. The resort hotels in order to provide special services to the visitors are built with a view to give a visitor special welcome and atmosphere of informality. The type of services and amenities located in resort property include recreation facilities such as swimming pool, golf course, tennis courts, skiing, boating, surf-riding and other various indcor sports. Other important amenities include coffee shops, restaurants, conference rooms, lounge, shopping arcade and entertainment. Emphasis on resort hotels however, is on recreational facilities. The clientele of resort hotels is mostly persons with considerable income looking for relaxation and recreation. Resort hotels rarely attract commercial patronage.

Resorts can be of various types and can be classified on the basis of climate and also topography. Broadly they fall in the following categories: *(i)* Summer resorts, *(ii)* Winter resorts, *(iii)* Hill resorts, *(iv)* All season resorts, and *(v)* Health resorts.

Majority of the resort hotels are seasonal establishments which work to capacity during the high tourist season. Generally the high tourist season is the period when there are holidays at educational institutions. However, in recent years many of the resort hotels with a view to extend the season provide certain special facilities and offer various concessions to the guests. The concessions provided include reduced tariffs, free entertainment, sight seeing, gifts, etc.

(3) Commercial Hotels. The commercial hotels direct their appeal primarily to the individual traveller as compared to international or resort hotel where the focus is on the group travel. Most of the commercial hotels receive the guests who are on business although some have permanent guests. As the hotel caters primarily to people who are visiting a place for commerce or business, these are located in important commercial and industrial centres of large towns and cities. These hotels are generally run by the owners and their success depends on their efficient running and the comforts and facilities they provide. In some of the large industria! towns, fully licenced commercial hotels exist Complete with restaurants, grill room, functional accommodation and a garage for those travelling by automobile.

(4) Residential Hotels. These hotels can be described as apartment house complete with hotel service. These are often referred to as apartment hotels. The tariff of rooms in these hotels is charged on monthly, half yearly or yearly basis and is charged for either furnished or unfurnished accommodation. These hotels which are located mostly in big cities operate exclusively under the European plan where no meals are provided to the guists. These hotels were developed in the United States of America, where people discovered that permanent living in hotels offers many advantages. Services and amenities provided in these hotels are comparable to those of an average well regulated home. These are very popular in the United States and western Europe where these are also known popularly as Pension.

(3) Floating Hotels. As the name suggests, these hotels are located on the surface of the water. It may be on sea water, river water or on a lake. All the facilities and services of a hotel are provided in these hotels. These hotels are very popular in many countries. In many countries old luxury ships have been converted into floating hotels and are proving very popular among tourists. The atmosphere they provide is exclusive and exotic. In India, floating hotels in the form of house boats are very popular with tourists.

Supplementary Accommodation

Although hotels have been and still are the principal form of accommodation, there' has been a growth and development of some other forms of accommodation over the years. It can be of various types and can be classified on the basis of its location type of construction, type of property, type of management, etc. It is therefore difficult to classify. Different terms have been used to indicate similar functions of various accommodation units. It is not possible to give clear cut definition of various types of accommodation. The various accommodation units differ in a number of respects. A study of the different types of accommodation indicates that their diversity is a reflection of the specific nature of each one and their names simply indicate various ways in which one and the same function can be fulfilled or the need can be satisfied.

Hotels although a very important part of the tourism infra-structure are not the only type of accommodation available for the tourists. Tourist accommodation need not be viewed from the point of view of hotel industry alone. In addition to hotels, the demand for tourist accommodation is met by a variety of facilities. There are a series of other installations able to offer to the tourists lodging, food and corresponding services. This is popularly known as supplementary accommodation and is in fact an important segment of tourism.

Supplementary accommodation consists of various types of accommodation other than the conventional hotel type. It may be described as premises which offer accommodation but not the services of a hotel. All the establishments under the heading of supplementary accommodation are designed to offer accommodation in the broad sense of the term, namely, the possibility of stay overnight and meals in return of cash payment per day and on the basis of services provided. In supplementary accommodation the standard of comforts is modest compared to that of an hotel. On the other hand however, there are certain inherent advantages in this type of accommodation. The biggest advantage is that of price. The supplementary accommodation as compared to the conventional type of accommodation is moderately priced. In addition the atmosphere in the accommodation is informal and there is more freedom with regard to dress, etc. There is also more emphasis on entertainment and sports resulting in increased social contact among the guests.

Supplementary accommodation plays a very important role in the total available tourist accommodation in a country. This type of accommodation can cater to both international as well as domestic tourist traffic. In fact in some countries more tourists utilize this type of accommodation than in hotels. In France and Italy as also in some other countries in Europe and elsewhere there are more campers than there are hotel clients. Following are some of the principal forms of supplementary accommodation.

(1) Motel. The concept of motel and motel-hotel originated in the United States of America. Model was meant for local motorists and foreign tourists travelling by road. Primarily designed to serve the needs of motorists, motel almost exclusively meet the demand for transit accommodation. They serve the function of a transit hotel except that they are geared to accommodate motor travelling guests for overnight stay.

The important services provided by motels include parking, garage facilities, accommodation, restaurant facilities, public catering and recreational facilities. With a view to provide the above services to the motorists, all the motels are equipped with filling stations, repair services, accessories, garages, parking space, elevator service to the automobile entrance, restaurants, etc. There is also equipment and tools available which the guest can used himself if he wishes to repair his vehicle. The price charged for accommodation and meals/ refreshments is much cheaper as compared to that in hotels. Motels are mostly located outside the city limits in the countryside along with the main highway and preferably at an important road junction. Since these establishments cater mainly for persons travelling by road, their development is linked with the development of new motor ways along which these are necessarily located. Motels are of different types. Some motels provide just the minimum services while others are well furnished with comfortable accommodation and excellent facilities. The accommodation provided in a motel is of Chalet type which is furnished having a dining hall with fixed menu. Shopping facilities for travelling public are also provided for in a motel.

(2) Youth Hostel. In the form of a movement, youth hostels made their first appearance in Germany in about the year 1900. The movement which spread rapidly allover the world was based on the educational principles emphasising the need by youth of large cities to travel on foot throughout the country. In order to provide some sort of accommodation and services the dormitories in the inns were equipped with cots, mattresses, sheets and blankets. Large rooms in inns were used as dining and living areas providing full board at low cost to the guests. There was also provision of additional kitchen where travellers could themselves prepare their own meals. Since the movement was started with a view to encouraging youth to travel in order to learn and know more about the country and also to socialize, it had an educational value. As such, no service was provided in the inn. The persons staying in the inn were themselves required to look after the inn. Subsequently, exclusive youth hostel buildings were constructed to accommodate young trayellers.

Youth hostel can be defined as a building which offers clean, moderate and inexpensive shelter to young people exploring their own country or other countries and travelling independently or in groups on holiday or for educational purpose. It is a place where young people of different social backgrounds and nationalities meet together and come to know each other. The objective of youth hostel is therefore not merely to provide accommodation and board, but also to serve as centres which offer opportunity to young people coming from different parts of the country as also young travellers from abroad to know and understand each other. It is a place of friendship, recreation and out-of school and college education.

The youth hostels are equipped to accommodate young men and women who travel on foot, by bicycle or other means of locomotion and who, at very little cost, are provided with place to sleep, cat or to make their own meal. The services provided include accommodation, meals and also recreation. The charges for these services are very modest. The hostels are also equipped to enable the users to prepare their own meals if they so desire. The accommodation provided in the hostels is for a limited number of days.

In most of the countries, youth hostels are developed and managed by non-commercial organisation whose main aim is the development of youth tourism. Since World War II, the number of such hostels has increased greatly. These hostels are now planned to provide comfortable accommodation as also, such other services and facilities which are required by youth. Also the number of those using these hostels has grown tremendously. Many hostels receive increasing number of groups and organise stays for winter sports or sailing.

The construction of youth hostels is baged on certain norms laid down from time to time all over the world. International requirements for these include provision of separate dormitories for men and women, appropriate and clean toilets, wash rooms for both men and women, a kitchen where hosteliers can prepare their own meals, common rooms, living accommodation for warden and a left luggage room. There is also a provision of a kitchen where warden and staff can prepare meals for supply to hosteliers, separate small room for instructors, a dining room and classroom for school parties and a warden's office. Some youth hostels have playgrounds attached for the use of hosteliers.

(3) Caravan and Camping Sites. Caravan and camping sites constitute a significant accommodation category in many holiday areas. These are very popular in some European countries as also in the United States of America. These are also known as open-air hostels, tourist camps or camping grounds. Camping, originally practiced by hikers on foot is increasingly giving way to car camping. The sites are usually located within the large cities in open spaces. Equipped to receive mobile accommodation in the form of caravans, the camping sites provide facilities for parking, tentpitching, water, electricity, toilet, etc. Though the services provided generally include restaurants, recreational rooms, toilets and at certain places a grocer's shop, the type of services often vary from place to place. Some countries have enacted legislation establishing the minimum facilities that must be provided which include health and sanitation standards and prices to be charged for parking and use of various services and facilities.,

(4) Pension. This type of accommodation is very popular in certain European countries. Particularly in Italy, Austria, Germany and Switzerland these establishments are used extensively by the tourists. Pension is also described as a private hotel, a guest house or a boarding house. Catering facilities are optional and are usually restricted to the residents. Many of them stay fora longer and such definite periods as a week or a fortnight. The reservation of accommodation is made in advance. Mostly managed by a family, pension accommodation is much cheaper than hotel accommodation.

(5) Bed and Breakfast Establishments. Also known in some countries as apartment hotels and hotel garnis, they represent a growing form of accommodation units catering for holiday as well as business travellers. These establishments provide only accommodation and breakfast and not the principal meals. These are usually located in large towns and cities along commercial and holiday routes and also resort areas and are used by en route travellers. Some of these establishments are very popular with holiday-makers.

(6) Tourist Holiday Villages. Tourist villages were established in some European countries after World War II. These villages are situated at warm sea sides and in the regions which offer certain facilities for the tourists. In certain countries like Italy and Spain, tourist villages are located in the regions which are economically not developed thereby helping the region economically. The villages are mostly promoted by important clubs, social organisations and also by tourist organisations.

The village complex is a centre of accommodation providing extensive sports and recreation facilities, riding, swimming, tennis, volleyball, football, sauna, mini-golf, badminton, table tennis and yoga. These provide both board and lodging. The atmosphere in these villages is kept as informal as possible. Telephones, radios, newspapers and TV are banned unless there is an emergency. Wallets and other valuables are locked away at the beginning of one's stay. Instead of money one uses colourful beads which can be worn anywhere as bracelets, necklaces, etc. The staff are chiefly educated young people who live on an equal basis with the holiday makers. The accommodation provided is usually in multiple 'units and may provide for self-catering. The furnishing provided in the rooms is minimal. The easy mixing 01 guests is encouraged by the banning of advance booking of tables in the village restaurants so one rarely finds oneself sitting with the same group twice.

The holiday villages are usually based on family units, each providing a convertible living room, bath/shower and sometimes a kitchen. The villages are self-sufficient providing almost all necessities required by the residents. There is also a small shopping complex where one can buy articles of daily need. The services of a doctor are also available in the village. The accommodation is sold for a week or a fortnight at an all inclusive price. In Spain and Italy, these are classified into three categories according to the services and amenities provided.

Classification, Registration and Gradation

Tourist accommodation is one of the important components of the total tourist product. It is thus an individual component. As an individual product it is intangible, often bought in advance of its use. The tourist at the time of making purchase thus cannot inspect or accept or reject. Accommodation as such, raises some issues in its development and in its marketing, both as an individual product and as a part of a package. It creates a need for reliable and accurate information for both the tourists and the travel agents and therefore may require supervision and control. An individual operator needs to bring information about his accommodation to the tourist before he sets off on his journey and also when he reaches his destination. Similarly the tourist on the other hand, needs to know in detail what accommodation is available at what price in particular destination from which he can make a choice about what and where to stay. Schemes of classification, registration and grading of the tourist accommodation are intended to meet these requirements.

The United Nations Conference on International Travel and Tourism held in Rome in the year 1963 also emphasised the need for some sort of regulation of the accommodation with a view to safeguard interests of the users. Considering that special attention should be given to relations between the public authorities and the operators of tourist accommodation facilities, the conference advocated that adoption of a hotel trade charter codifying the regulations applicable to the hotel industry and, in particular, giving official tourist organisations powers enabling them to perform the activities devolving on the state in that field.

The conference observed that many states classify tourist hotels or are considering doing so. Acting upon the recommendations put forward by IUOTO and the International Chamber of Commerce, the conference advocated the standardization of methods of classification and in particular the sub-division of hotels into five categories each identified by a conventional sign (stars) in conformity with sets of standards appropriate to different climatic conditions. The conference also considered the question of classifying supplementary means of accommodation such as tourist bungalows and camps.

Classification

Classification separates accommodation into different classes or categories on the basis of certain criteria, for examaple, by type of accommodation such as hotels, holiday camps and caravan sites. A scheme of classification seeks to present information about tourist accommodation in a form which will enable the user to find information he requires easily and quickly and to be able to compare it with similar types, Apart from having the information classified by location, a tourist needs to know the availability of accommodation which meets his requirements as to type, price and other criteria.

Registration

The aim of registration on the other hand is to provide a complete list of register of tourist accommodation within a particular definition. A registration scheme results in an inventory of accommodation which can be kept up-to-date. In order to be comprehensive, it normally has to have statutory legal authority and is administered by a government authority or a statutory body. Because of the wide range of accommodation used by the tourists, a scheme of registration should normally cover all forms of accommodation used by them.

Gradation

Grading separates accommodation into different categories or grades on the basis of judgements such as standards of amenities and service. A grading scheme provides qualitative judgements on the amenities and facilities of a particular accommodation unit in a form which enables the user to choose the quality of accommodation he requires. This may refer to the physical facilities, food and other services of the establishment, various amenities provided etc. The establishments are graded individually or collectively by way of giving them numbers, letters or symbols.

The schemes of classification, registration and grading in operation in various countries differs. Some countries incorporate only registration, others classification and some grading. The standards adopted also differ from country to country.

Chaning Pattern Accommodation Sector

The accommodation sector has undergone substantial changes in recent years. New developments in tourism and transportation, changes in the organisation of travel and technological innovations are some of the factors which are responsible for these changes. In addition, increasing consumer demand among tourists due in turn to the improvement in living standards and economic conditions has also changed the profile of the accommodation sector. All the above factors seem to have influenced the structure of the hotel industry as a whole. The tendency among middle income groups to take holiday at any time of the year has encouraged accommodation operators to offer novel kinds of arrangements which are now available in addition to traditional hotel accommodation.

New types of accommodation, particularly holiday villages suitable for family type tourists, condominiums and apartment houses, private villas and camping facilities have proved very successful and to a certain degree are replacing traditional hotels and boarding houses. These changes reflect changes in demand with new, often younger groups entering the international travel market and also new approaches to the problem of providing facilities in a very competitive industry with a highly seasonal demand.

The probable future developments in the accommodation sector were the subject of study undertaken in WTO's 1978 1979 research programme. Some conclusions which emerge from the study are as follows:

(a) a significant growth in accommodation supply will continue to be contributed by chain operators, including airlines. This expansion will result mainly from the further development of management contracts and franchise agreements;

(b) there will be a continuing move towards the further diversification of accommodation. The development of budget accommodation, covering budget hotels, and also supplementary means of accommodation is likely to continue as mass tourism stimulates new demands for competitively-priced accommodation;

(c) the standard of accommodation will continue to rise. Demand for recreational and sporting facilities will increase in both business and leisure accommodation;

(d) rising building and operating costs, growing environment and conservation pressures, as well as the need to deep staffing levels at a minimum, will influence design and construction of accommodation units;

(e) advances in technology will both influence the traditional construction methods, for example, more frequent use of pre-fabricated building techniques, as well as traditional methods of hotel operations.

❑

2

Objectives and Policies

In seeking to explain why thousands earn their living by owning and operating hotels, it is tempting to say that they do it to earn a profit. But this is an over-simplification. From the point of view of the community and of hotel customers, the purpose of an hotel is to provide certain facilities and services to its users. From the point of view of its employees an hotel is a source of employment. From the point of view of its owners an hotel provides a return on their investment. These are very disparate purposes, and viewing them in this way recognizes that there is not one but at least three main parties to the hotel business, each with one or more primary objectives. Expressed in purely financial terms, customers may have a particular interest in low prices, employees in high wages, owners in high profits. But each party has a wider concern in its participation in the hotel business. Hotel customers, for example, are also concerned with the quality of facilities and services, hotel employees with working conditions, hotel owners with the security of their investment and with other satisfactions they may derive from their role.

Some of these interests may be in conflict. It is the task of hotel management to reconcile the competing and conflicting objectives of the parties, first in the formulation of the objectives of the business, and then in its subsequent operation. The maximization of one party's objectives, be it the customers', the employees' or the owners', to the neglect of the others', is not a formula for a sustained prosperity of an hotel, or for that matter of any other business, nor can it be the sole purpose for its existence.

General and Sectional Policies

On defining the objectives of an hotel, its management has a focus for its actions and decisions. It is also a start in the formulation of its policies, which may be described as a set of guidelines for management. By stating the ends to be pursued and the means by which they are to be pursued, the business defines formally its attitude and approach in its dealing with customers, employees, shareholders, and also with such other parties as, for example, its suppliers. In so far as this definition postulates general guidelines for the hotel as a whole, it is a general policy, formulated and promulgated by top management—the owner/manager in a smaller business, the board of directors in a company.

In order to provide adequate guidance for management decisions and actions, there is a need for more detailed guidelines in particular aspects of the business and in particular activities. These are developed as sectional policies, which flow from the general policy and extend it from broad policy indications into operational terms.

As the customers, employees, shareholders and suppliers are the main groups of people with whom an hotel deals, the main sectional policies are commonly formulated in relation to them to embody the principles to be observed in these relationships:

(i) Thus a customer policy normally says what the hotel is aiming to do in terms of its markets and quality standards of what it provides, includes its concept of good value and its approach to price, discounts and credit; it states its attitude to complaints and refunds.

(ii) An employment or personnel policy covers such matters. as recruitment, selection and training; remuneration, conditions of employment, welfare; promotion, retirement, termination; consultation, negotiation and the handling of disputes.

(iii) A policy towards suppliers postulates what is expected from them regarding the quality of supplies, delivery and terms, and how each can expect to be treated by the hotel.

(iv) A shareholder policy defines what the owners are entitled to expect in terms of their rewards, information and participation in the business, and what is expected from them.

Sectional policies defined by reference to the main parties in the internal and external relationships of the hotel are a logical and most helpful basis of providing guidelines. However, for many situations guidelines are required also in the discharge of functional responsibilities of the hotel, for example in such specialist areas as financial management, marketing and purchasing. Financial management may enter into all the four relationships described above and elements of financial guidelines may be incorporated into each. A marketing policy may be viewed as an extension of a customer policy and a purchasing policy as an extension of a policy to suppliers. But it is often helpful in practice to subject these functional areas to policy guidelines of their own. A third dimension in sectional policies arises in the existence of guidelines relating to each main hotel product-accommodation, food and drink, and functions. These may be viewed again as an extension of the hotel's customer policy, but it is often helpful in practice to state the principles on which these individual activities are to operate for the guidance of those concerned separately and in some detail.

Policy Formulation, Communication and Review

The approach described so far to defining the objectives of the hotel and the principles by which it is to be operated as its policies, implies that there are statements expressed in writing, which are laid down from the top, passed down the organization and at least in part also to the outside world, and that these are laid down for all times. It is, indeed, very desirable that policies should be committed to paper and many hotels do, in fact express them to a greater or lesser extent in writing and distribute them to those concerned. Leading hotel companies have found that to tell their customers about their policies can be a powerful marketing tool, that personnel policies communicated to staff can have a favourable impact on their image as employers and on personnel relations, that to provide clear policy guidelines for all functional areas and departments to those operating in them is highly conductive to smooth and efficient hotel operation. The need to communicate formally in writing is to some extent a function of size. It is difficult to do otherwise in a large organization, particularly in one with a number of hotels, which may be dispersed over a wide area. In a smaller organization where there is a high degree of personal contact between the owners, management and employees, and between them and their customers and other parties, and a conscious endeavour in this direction, what the hotel is aiming to achieve and how, can be often passed on informally by word of mouth. But the need to be clear about one's objectives, the need for guidelines, and the need to communicate them, remains and is not a function of size.

To define the objectives and the policies is the responsipility of hotel management, but this extends from the directors through managers to heads of departments and supervisors. In all but the smallest hotels and companies there are at least these three levels, all of which are to a varying extent required to contribute to the attainment of the objectives and to the implementation of policies. All three levels can to a varying extent also contribute to their formulation. How much they do so in practice, depends on the style of management. In a strongly authoritarian environment most policy making emanates from the top, with little or no contribution to it from below. In a more participative environment at least those in any position of responsibility can contribute to it. This is not to deny that management is allowed to manage, but a recognition of the fact that there is more than one level of management, that each has a contribution to make according to their respective involvement in the hotel, and that most people carry out policies in whose formulation they participated with greater commitment than those which are just laid down for them.

Objectives and policies change. At any time they should express the best current view of the business and the rules to be adhered to. But as markets, environments in which hotels operate, and most external and internal factors which affect the hotel business change, hotel management has to keep their objectives and policies under review, to meet changing circumstances. New trends in leisure and recreation may provide new opportunities and call for changes in products; new consumer or employment legislation may require changes in the policies of the hotel towards its customers and employees; new sources of supply may suggest changes in purchasing policies and in departmental operational policies.

Hotel Philosophies

A clear view of the objectives forms a focus for the management of an hotel or a group of hotels; a clear expression of policies establishes a more or less formal frame of reference for decisions in various situations. But in most hotel operations there are also many rules, beliefs and conventions, which are not formulated as policies, and yet they influence how people act, and are accepted by them as part of their everyday conduct of the hotel. They make up what is sometimes referred to as the common doctrine or the philosophy of the business. Some of the philosophies have to do with ethical standards, which guide management and staff in their dealings with guests, suppliers and others. So for example, we may believe in being as helpful as possible to those whose bookings we cannot accept when we are full and suggest alternatives; in admitting to our suppliers that we gave a wrong specification when we ordered by telephone; in treating with courtesy the local authority inspector and making his job easier by our co-operation. By contrast we do not discuss disparagingly our competitors with our guests, we do not recruit staff and withhold from them a fact which we know would materially affect their decision to join us or not, and we do not accept gifts from our suppliers. Our philosophies may be concerned in concrete terms with our operational standards. If we develop a particular concern with and pride in hygiene, impeccable standards of cleanliness in our hotels may become part of everybody's approach to their jobs, and as such part of our philosophy in the conduct of our business, accepted and observed by all our employees.

A philosophy may also express a more general attitude of management. If management has a genuine belief in the contribution employees can make to the conduct of the hotel and in the right to be consulted in matters which affect them, participation in decision-making may become part of our philosophy, adopted more or less automatically in its management and operation. The philosophy of a business has been well described as 'the way we do things around here'. Some of what comprises the philosophy of an hotel may be regulated by law; philosophy is not made up of legal rules, although to do what is lawful and to avoid what is illegal, may be one of its tenets. There is no sharp dividing line between policies and philosophies. Both are codes dealing with the outlook and approach guiding the hotel in its dealings with others. The former may be more formal and more general, the latter less formal and more specific.

Hotel Plans and Strategies

In pursuing the objectives of the business, hotel management is guided by the policies and philosophies. In order to attain the objectives it is possible just to do one's best, let things happen, and see how it all turns out. A more effective alternative and one more reliably conducive to the attainment of objectives is to plan what is to happen. Planning is developing a constructive concern with tomorrow, deciding what can happen, what should happen, and how the desirable is to be accomplished.

Plans are, therefore, instruments, which extend the attainable objectives of the hotel in concrete actionable terms, for a few months or a year ahead (short-term), for several years (medium-term), for periods longer than a few years (long-term). As such plans are normally more numerate instruments than, for example, policies, in that they postulate targets to be achieved, and that they do so, as far as possible in measurable terms for given periods of time. Return on invested capital, volume of sales, and rates of growth of each, are examples of financial targets; hotel occupancies and. rates of labour turnover are examples of physical measurement of attainments in particular areas of the hotel operation. Plans may be viewed as an expression of the strategies of the hotel. In order to meet the needs of particular markets, people and money are the main resources it employs in pursuing its objectives. Decisions have to be made on how to compete in the chosen markets and this extends to the whole of advertising, promotion and public relations (market strategy). In deciding how many people to employ, in what positions, and with what skills, decisions have to be made on how to compete in the labour market (labour strategy). When we determine what sources of capital to use in financing the hotel, how to ensure that the cash flow is adequate, and how to contain costs, financial decisions are made regarding profitability (profit strategy). Hotel strategies are, therefore, links between objectives and plans and a means to action-orientated planning in the hotel business. Hotel entrepreneurs and managers have been often successful in their strategies based on intuitive inspiration rather than systematic exploration, and without systematic planning.

In the long-term an hotel can survive, prosper and meet the aspirations of its owners and employees only through sustained profitability. Its performance cannot be left to chance. Hotel sales, costs and profits have to be charted in advance. Objectives, plans and strategies have to be translated into budgets and budgetary control becomes the process to keep the hotel on its course. Operating budgets concerned with income and expenditure are prepared for individual departments and activities and consolidated into a budgeted profit and loss account. Capital budgets concerned with the hotel assets and liabilities are incorporated into a budgeted balance sheet. Continuous comparison of actual and budgeted results showing departures from what was planned enables corrective action to be taken or provides a basis for a revision of what is to be achieved.

In practice the planned performance is not confined to financial targets and even these are not necessarily related to individual performance. It is, therefore, necessary to identify those who make key contributions to the performance of the hotel, to evaluate what these contributions are, and to relate targets, both financial and others, closely to individual responsibilities. This approach finds an expression in what is known as management by objectives and enables members of the management team to adjust their performance because what is I expected of them is based on what they can control and influence, within the totality of the whole hotel. In practice budgetary control and management by objectives are two distinct but interlocking systems.

The Framework of Hotel Management

An existing city hotel with its established ways of doing things may have a somewhat different approach from a new resort hotel seeking to establish itself in its market. But both need to be clear about what they are trying to achieve and how to go about it. There are the objectives—what the hotel is in business to attain. Policies are the rules, on which management bases its decisions in the conduct of the business, and these are supported by the philosophies of the hotel—the less formal rules and conventions. Plans and strategies are the instruments, which direct management towards the attainment of the objectives, with the use of such techniques as budgetary control and management by objectives.

❑

3

Introduction to Hotel Groups

The increase in the size of hotel firms has come about by firms building or acquiring hotels in different locations and placing them under central management. The hotels may be grouped within a restricted geographical area or distributed widely within the country or even internationally. Of Iilte, the traditional pattern of an hotel industry made up of individually-owned hotels has been changing in many countries and has come to resemble more closely that of other industries, with a small number of companies increasing their share of the market, the remainder being shared by a large number of smaller firms, most of them operating single hotels. The independently-owned hotel may be still the typical firm in the industry, but the growth of the industry has been increasingly associated with hotel groups. By late 1988 there were more than 30 hotel groups in U.K. with more than 1000 rooms. The largest, Trusthouse Forte, accounted for more than 26000 rooms in over 200 hotels throughout the country and represented about 5 per cent of the total UK market, in addition to its interests overseas. Several dozen other groups owned and operated more than one hotel. There were at the time many more hotel groups with more than 1000 rooms in the United States, and a number of them exceeded the capacity of Trusthouse Forte in Britain, *e.g.* Holiday Inns, Sheraton and Howard Johnson. Similarly in India Taj Group and Welcome Group of Hotels are most noteworthy.

The hotel groups normally operate hotels owned by them or leased by them from their owners to whom they pay a rental.

Sometimes they manage hotels as agents for the owners under management contracts, which provide for the payment of expenses, management fees and/or the sharing of profits. The groups may also operate under franchise agreements, which allow one party (the franchisee) to sell a product designed, supplied and controlled by the other party (the franchisor), tn return for a fee or a share of profits; in this arrangement an hotel group may be in the role of a franchisor or in the role of a multiple franchisee.

The first part of present chapter is intended to describe the advantages and the problems of hotel groups, the main issues facing them, and their approach to group operation. Hotel group operations under management contracts and under franchise agreements have much in common with any group operation, but both are based on particular agreements between the parties and introduce elements specific to the relationship between them, which are quite distinctive.

Advantages of Groups

The nature of the hotel business and the limits of many hotel markets provide the main explanations for the growth of hotel companies through groups. The advantages, which may accrue to hotel groups are the resulting advantages of size, known as the economies of scale. Some of these, *e.g.* the technical economies may apply also to individual hotels, if they are large enough, but their full realization is open particularly to groups of hotels. Groups extend the size to which an hotel firm may grow, economies of scale tend to accompany groups for a long time before pronounced managerial disadvantages set in, and some of the economies, such as those of risk-spreading, are open only to groups. Because economies of scale are available to groups rather than to single hotels, generally a higher profitability is attainable by a group than could be generated by the sum total of its hotels operated independently. The advantages of hotel groups may be summarized as follows.

One of the main financial economies is the ability of the group to marshal capital resources from its own cash flow and from external sources. A group may be able to borrow from lending institutions and to do so on favourable terms because it is big and because its hotels provide a good security to its lenders. This is of particular value in financing growth by adding further hotels to the group, in modernizing hotels, and in covering the initial period of operation of new hotels before they become profitable. A group can also deploy its financial resources to advantage by balancing the working capital requirements of its hotels over a period of time and thereby alleviating the strain on individual units caused by seasonality and other fluctuations in revenue and in expenditure. Because of its size a group can enjoy marketing economies. It can create a group image in the market, which may extend to a common name, facilities and standards throughout the group, and it can engage in promoting its hotels together. Individual hotels may to a greater or lesser extent specialize and provide facilities and services complementary to the other hotels, such as conferences. Public relations, advertising, and sales promotion can be undertaken with an impact for the whole group. Each hotel within the group can promote other hotels and generate business by onward reservations. An hotel group has open to it economies of buying because it can buy in bulk and negotiate advantageous prices and terms with its suppliers of a wide range of goods and services on behalf of the whole group.

Management costs need not keep pace with an increase in the volume of business and an hotel group can enjoy managerial economies. It can attract high-quality staff through the prospects it can offer within the group and the availability of training schemes, and benefit from an interchange of staff between its hotels. It can also provide centralized services to its hotels and in these it can employ specialists with the time and skills to exploit the advantages of group operation in such areas as finance, personnel, purchasing, and marketing.

Various technical economies may arise with size in individual large hotels but also in groups, particularly when the hotels are concentrated geographically within a limited area. The volume of business may then make it possible to concentrate such operating facilities as central food production, maintenance, and laundry, when reductions in unit costs may be achieved as compared with providing the facilities in individual hotels or buying the services from outside firms.

Last but not least, there may be economies of risk-spreading which enable groups to reduce risk by product and geographical diversification. Hotels that cater primarily for business and for holiday markets tend to have different seasons; some may specialize in functions and others in conferences. A decline in demand for a particular hotel may be offset by a high volume of business in another hotel and thus even out the fluctuations for the group as a whole, as we have seen above when considering the financial advantages of groups.

It can be seen that the advantages of scale that may accrue to hotel groups arise from several sources: from the weight the group has in markets (whether it is in its markets with customers or suppliers, or in the markets for productive resources, in particular capital and labor); from providing certain services to its hotels; and from operating them as a group. These sources of economies are complementary.

Contrainsts Faced by Hotel Groups

The hotel group shares several main problems with any large organization, especially problems of communications, control and costs. In order to operate as a group, the centre has to communicate policies, procedures and other matters to individual hotels, which in turn have to communicate information, requests and other matters to the centre. In a closely integrated group individual hotels also have to keep in contact with each other.

Unless smooth lines of communication are established and maintained, this can mitigate against the effectiveness of group operation and the attainment of the advantages. Action may be delayed and result in a loss of revenue or additional costs, in time and effort wasted in clearing up misunderstandings, and in antagonism that may be generated. Whatever the degree of central direction and monitoring of individual, units, there is a need for some control to be exercised over the conduct of the hotels, to ensure group decisions being carried out and the accountability of individual hotels for their performance.

Unless a clear and effective control mechanism exists, hotels may act against the interests of the group and affect its performance as a whole. However, a complex control mechanism may generate disproportionate costs and affect the initiative and performance of the hotels as well as of the whole group. A group operation gives rise to its own costs, through the need for communication and control, and through the provision of central services to hotels. If the advantages of group operation are to be-realized, it is clear that these additional costs have lo be outweighed by the benefits which they bring about, if the group is to produce-higher profitability than the individual hotels would if operated independently. In addition to the quality of group management, the extent of the above problems depends on three main factors: the number of the hotels in the group, the geographical dispersal of the hotels, and the extent to which the various aspects of the group operation are centralized. The less of each, the less likelihood of these problems being serious. But the smaller the group and the less centralization, the less is also the prospect of the advantages of group operation being realized.

Scope for Centralization

A group management may adopt a mainly passive ownership role. At its extreme this means the appointment of local managers who are expected to achieve results by their own initiative, with a minimum of central direction, support and supervision. In these circumstances the performance of the group is made up of the more or less independent actions of individual hotels, with a loose monitoring by the owners directly or through a group manager, a managing director, or even a company secretary, with little or no staff of their own. Outside specialists, such as professional stock-takers, may be employed, and the company auditors may perform two roles—that of accountants preparing the accounts of the group and that of auditors verifying the view of the business presented by the accounts; their work may include, in greater or lesser depth, an operational audit. However, in order to obtain the advantages of group operation, a more positive group management approach is necessary. The group management has to formulate the objectives, policy and operational guidelines, evolve strategies and plan on behalf of the group; it has to direct and co-ordinate the separate units, and it has to control them financially and in other way's.

The economies of scale do not accrue to the group automatically. Common ownership may bring about certain financial advantages, but to realize most or all the advantages, decisions have to be taken on which functions of the group to centralize and on the extent of centralization of each. The major issue for an hotel group is, therefore, how much to centralize, and the principal functions which offer scope for centralization are:

(i) personnel services

(ii) sales and marketing

(iii) purchasing

(iv) accounting and finance

(v) technical services.

As we have seen, these are the areas in which the main economies of scale lie, and the main influencing factors are the number of hotels and their geographical distribution. Different degrees of centralization are possible in each function: even when centralization is affected, each function has to be divided between the centre and the hotels; how much each does and the relationship between the two are of crucial importance.

At a modest level a centralized personnel function is concerned with staffing levels, salary and wage structure, and with employee records. It normally deals with recruitment, selection and placement, sometimes for all employees, sometimes only with particular grades and categories and others are recruited and engaged locally. When the personnel function is more extensive and highly developed, it may cover all conditions of employment, training and welfare, and also employee consultation, negotiation, and industrial relations generally. As substantial economies may be achieved by centralized purchasing, few group hotels buy all or most of their supplies directly from any supplier they choose. The centralized purchasing function may be concerned with varying range of supplies and essentially take one of three basic forms or a combination of the three. In some instan es, when the hotels are located in a limited area, supplies are bought for central stores, from which they are distributed to hotels. In the absence of central stores, orders may be placed centrally against requisitions by hotels and delivered directly to hotels. The third form is the placing of orders by individual hotels against centrally negotiated contracts, with nominated suppliers who deliver directly to the hotels.

However dccentralized the group approach may be to accounting and control, such aspects as the preparation of the final accounts for the group (even if only as a consolidation of the accounts of individual hotels), capital accounts, cash management, and detailed analysis of the financial performance of each hotel, are normally central functions. Beyond these more obvious areas, the main possibilities for centralization arise, depending on circumstances, in accounting for purchases (particularly where purchasing is centralized), payroll (for some or all employees), and credit sales accounts (particularly with such large hotel users as business firms, tour operators and travel agents), stocktaking, and internal audit.

There are several other operations, which may be carried out by individual hotels, or obtained from specialist suppliers, or provided to hotels in a group as a central facility, if their volume is large enough and if the hotels are close enough to be served centrally. These were earlier referred to as offering scope for technical economies and can be located in one hotel serving others or separately *e.g.* various technical services.

Concentrated Hotel Group

The aspects discussed in this chapter are illustrated first with an example of an hotel group, which operates 18 London hotels with a total of 3,500 rooms, 26 restaurants, 28 bars and almost 100 function rooms in these hotels, and which has some 3,500 employees. The largest hotels have several hundred rooms and employ several hundred people, the smallest hotels have less than 100 rooms and less than 100 employees. In this example the central functions of the group below board level and above the level of an individual hotel comprise 165 employees; more than 100 of them are accounted for by a large Estates Department, which employs directly a wide range of maintenance staff. Each general manager is concerned with central functions as well as with individual hotel operations through an assistant general manager. Each hotel has a manager and, according to size, between one and three assistant managers. All central functions are linked with the responsibilities of particular managers and assistant managers in the hotels.

The arrangements vary as between individual hotels. Normally the manager himself retains responsibility for public relations and for estate functions, in liaison with the corresponding central departments, and in all but the largest hotels also for one or more other functions, in addition to the general management of the hotel. Each assistant manager has also one or more functional responsibilities in addition to assisting the hotel manager generally in the large hotels with more than one assistant manager, one may be responsible for sales, one for personnel, and one for accounts and purchasing; in the smaller hotels with one assistant manager, all the specialist functions are divided between the manager and his assistant. The personnel function is normally the main or the only responsibility of an assistant manager. This arrangement provides for a direct relationship between each central department and a designated individual in each hotel.

SMALL HOTEL

Hotel ownership offers considerable attractions to people willing to invest money, time and effort in building up a business. It offers economic indepe dence in a business, which provides a means of livelihood in an activity full of human interest, and it offers scope for individual flair. As with other small-unit industries, such as agricul-ture, building, and retail distribution, there are good chances of setting up one's own business in the hotel industry. Since many individuals enter the industry with modest capital and to a great extent use their own financial resources, they tend to do so on a small scale and their hotels remain small.

The nature of the hotel business also helps explain the importance of the small hotel, because it is concerned with providing personal services. Its size is limited by the size of the market and by the extent of competition. Many markets for hotel services are small and many small markets are served by more than one hotel. Moreover, size is not a requirement of a viable hotel operation, as it is in some other industries.

Most hotels provide more than one product-rooms, meals and refreshments, and sometimes also other services and they do so in various combinations. It is, therefore, less than satisfactory to define a small hotel for our purposes in terms of a particular room or bed capacity. Such other criteria, as a given level of investment or sales, mean different things in relation to hotels of different standards and price levels, and their values change with time. In this chapter the small hotel is, therefore, seen as an establishment, which is owner-managed through the personal involvement of the proprietor in the day-to-day conduct of the business.

A small hotel defined in this way often has more than minimal capital invested in it, employs non-family labour, and is perceived as a business by its owners. This distinguishes the small hotel discussed here from, for example, a private household providing some holiday accommodation, or a bed and breakfast establishment letting a few bedrooms, without differentiating too sharply between the small hotel and the larger guest house.

Ownership and Finance

Traditionally the small hotel has been owned by an individual or a family, and the common legal form of ownership has been an unincorporated firm, a sole trader or sometimes a partnership, but increasingly it is a private company in order to obtain the advantages of limited liability. Although some small hotels are owned by those with other business interests, more often than not the establishment as a place of business, and the firm as a unit of ownership and ultimate control, which raises capital and employs and organizes productive resources, coincide. Hotels require short-term, medium-term, and long-term finance for particular purposes. The dependence of the small hotel on one individual, the owner/ manager, and the type of security available for a loan, are among the factors that have tended to mitigate against the availability of external finance from lending institutions. It is common for small hotels to provide most of the finance of all three types from retained profits and from personal savings, sometimes drawn from the realization of other assets, and the main external sources are bank overdrafts and loans; this applies not only to short-term requirements, but also to much fixed capital expenditure. Much longer-term finance is drawn from private sources and from the financial involvement in the business of private individuals who are prepared to lend. Some may become 'sleeping' partners oreven directors of private companies, usually confining their participation to their financial stake, and leaving the day-to-day conduct of the business to the owner/manager, who is often the principal owner of the business. Small hotels, therefore, tend to have a high proportion of 'equity' capital, contributed by one or more individuals, and a low proportion of loan capital, contributed by a limited number of sources open to them.

Income to owners of small hotels, unlike those of large ones, accrues in four different ways. In addition to the appreciation of land and buildings and annual profits, the two sources common to both, many owner/managers and their families derive a significant income in kind, because they live on the premises, as well as any salaries they may pay themselves. It is often difficult to differentiate clearly between profit as return on investment and the emoluments of the owners in the form of cash and non-cash benefits, which they derive as a reward for managing the hotel. However, there is much to be said for attempting this at least annually, in order to assess the profitability of the business meaningfully.

Products and Markets

Independent owner-managed hotels have commonly up to twenty or thirty rooms and less than twice that number of beds, a restaurant or a dining room, and a bar, and sometimes also offer a few other guest facilities and services. Their main distinguishing features are the range and scale of the facilities and services.

Rooms may, but need not necessarily, represent the largest single source of hotel revenue. Some small hotels have relatively extensive restaurant and bar facilities in relation to their room capacity, when they serve local residents and others as well as hotel residents. But in many small hotels these facilities are often used primarily by hotel residents, with restricted meal times and fixed meal charges; hotel residents' bars then usually take the form of lounge bars. Telephone, newspapers and guest laundry are the main and often the only services provided by small hotels, in addition to sleeping accommodation, food and drink. If the hotel caters at all for functions, they are likely to be small meetings, parties, and such family occasions as wedding receptions.

The products of the small hotel relate to its markets, which are likely to be more specialized in a large city with a variety of hotels than in a small town where the hotel may be one of only a few small hotels or the only hotel serving the town. Because of its size, the users of small hotels are individuals and families rather than groups, and few small hotels can accommodate such organized groups as coach tours, which require a minimum room capacity, although some may cater for their meals and refreshments. Like all hotels, if it is open to non-residents, in its catering markets the small hotel is usually in competition not only with other hotels, but also with restaurants, pubs and clubs, and other types of outlet for meals and refreshments.

There is an important difference in the way large and small hotels seek to match their markets and products. Large hotel operators increasingly assess their markets, formulate operations to meet apparent market needs, and set out to sell their hotel products to identified market segments by employing promotion on a large scale. Small hotels tend to approach their markets less formally and more intuitively from their detailed knowledge of their guests' requirements, based on their close contact with them. They tend to adjust their services more readily to the known preferences of their guests and to rely for selling their products more on personal recommendation and repeat visits than on systematic promotion.

Organization and Staffing

In large hotels ownership and management are normally separate functions, both conceptually and in practice. The business is owned by shareholders. The top management is entrusted by them to directors who in turn delegate the day-to-day conduct of the business to operational management. A managing director may provide a link between the top and operational management, and according to the size, of the business there may be several levels of operational management. The operation is divided into departments, in which employees perform more or less distinct tasks, and there may be line managers as well as specialists.

In the small hotel the owner/manager is an entrepreneur who normally combines not only ownership and management but often also the functions of top and operational management in one person. Whatever the legal form of ownership, it is he who undertakes the investment and the financing of the hotel, decides the objectives and the policies, and is responsible for planning, direction, organization, staffing, and control.

He may turn for outside advice and help and usually does-on accounts and finance, architecture and design, business promotion, law, maintenance of equipment and services, and on other matters. But the owner/manager tends to be to a great extent his own marketeer, buyer, personnel officer, as well as the man who organizes and coordinates the hotel facilities and services generally, and who represents the hotel to the outside world.

The scale of operation has two main implications for its organization and staffing limited departmentalization and the likelihood that it can be supervised without, or with no more than one, intervening level. This may be illustrated with an organization chart of a small hotel with some twenty employees shown in Chart-1.

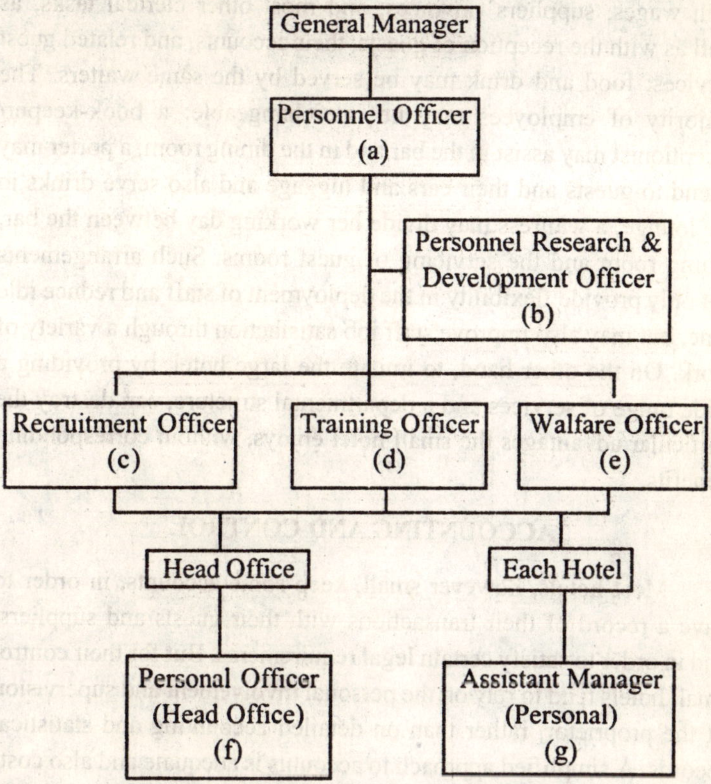

Chart 1. Organisation Chart of Small Hotel

In this hotel two people assist the owner in his office and the other eighteen have specific but quite wide 'departmental' responsibilities. The office is the nerve centre of the hotel, in which are brought together all the central functions of the hotel, including accounts, purchasing, sales promotion, and general administration. The general assistant has a part in all these directions, as well as in assisting the owner with the overall co-ordination of the business, but does not have a direct authority over those involved in the six main operational areas.

It is possible to see in this illustration how the division of work may be reduced still further in a small hotel, so that the owner may actually supervise all employees directly himself. One office may deal with wages, suppliers' invoices, and most other clerical tasks, as well as with the reception of guests, their accounts, and related guest services; food and drink may be served by the same waiters. The majority of employees may be interchangeable: a book-keeper/ receptionist may assist in the bar and in the dining room; a porter may attend to guests and their cars and luggage and also serve drinks in the lounge; a waitress may divide her working day between the bar, dining room and the servicing of guest rooms. Such arrangements not only provide flexibility in the deployment of staff and reduce idle time, but may also improve staff job satisfaction through a variety of work. On the other hand, to imitate the large hotel, by providing a wide range of services and a departmental structure, can destroy the particular advantages the small hotel enjoys, without corresponding benefits.

ACCOUNTING AND CONTROL

Most hotels, however small, keep some accounts, in order to have a record of their transactions with their guests and suppliers, and in order to satisfy certain legal requirements. But for their control small hotels tend to rely on the personal involvement and supervision of the proprietor, rather than on detailed accounting and statistical records. A simplified approach to accounts is adequate and also cost-effective.

Three main basic accounting records satisfy most requirements of most small hotels:

(i) A visitor's tabular ledger with individual accounts for all resident guests may be extended to include separate accounts for functions, as well as for total cash and credit sales in the restaurant and bar to customers using these facilities without taking up sleeping accommodation. In this way the tabular ledger represents an analyzed daily summary of all business done.

(ii) A receipts and payments book records all cash transactions. In the course of business sales accounts and invoices are filed separately and only recorded in the book after payment has been received or made. At the end of the period unrecorded transactions such as outstanding sales accounts, unpaid invoices, prepayments and accruals are taken into account in preparing final accounts.

(iii) A wages book, which includes all employee and related payments, provides a comprehensive record of all payroll transactions.

The proprietors of a small hotel tend to view each hotel product or department as an integral part of the whole and are more concerned with the overall profitability of the hotel than with the relative profitability of its parts. However, different hotel services generate different profit margins, and even a simple breakdown of revenue and expenditure can provide a helpful analysis of performance:

(i) to establish a basis for monitoring and comparison;

(ii) to indicate the relative profitability of the different parts;

(iii) to enable an assessment to be made of the effect of any changes introduced in operation.

If the basic records are kept in an analyzed form, the input data for a meaningful analysis of results are available without much additional effort. It is, therefore, quite easy even for small hotels to produce informative accounts, and to do so more than once a year, from the basic records outlined above. They are helped in this by the relatively small total volume of transactions, many of which are on a cash basis. What is realistic in most small hotels, may be summarized as follows:

(i) It is normally adequate to analyze income and certain expenses under no more than four headings: rooms, food, liquor, and miscellaneous. The last category is residuary and covers what may be analyzed into several separate minor operated departments in a large hotel, but is unlikely to be very significant in a small hotel.

(ii) Cost of sales data for food and beverages can be derived from an analyzed receipts and payments book and adjusted for changes in stock levels, to give the gross profit. (Because room sales do not involve the sale of goods, there is no cost of sales for rooms, and miscellaneous sales are not likely to be significant.)

(iii) An extended visitors' ledger can provide analyzed details of all revenue.

(iv) Each employee is allocated to the department in which he is primarily employed, or an employee's payroll cost may be divided between the departments to which he contributes. The balance of profit after the deduction of cost of sales and payroll costs from sales is the net margin.

Although in a large hotel the analysis is taken further by deducting from the net margin those other expenses that can be allocated to a department, in order to arrive at the departmental operating profit, it is not necessary to proceed beyond the net margin in a small hotel, because this stage tends to account for between a half and two-thirds of the total costs of most hotels and gives a good indication of the profitability of individual hotel facilities and services. The analyzed results produced in this way can then be compared periodically with the budget, with figures for the previous year, or with figures for the previous period, prepared on the same basis to monitor the performance of the hotel.

❒

4

History of Hotel Management

Within the last few years Hotel Industry in world has also achieved a remarkable progress. Many hotels have been also built during last few years in India. The new hotel era was first dominated in India by the Oberoi group, ITC, ITDC, Hotel Corporation of India and other large luxurious group of hotel & quickly followed. Keeping with this trend the hotel business proliferated throughout India and State Tourism Corporations also many establishments for providing food and accommodation the growing tourists and business traffic. Today, while, the building costs in the hotel sector are certainly substantial, the industry has gradually become more attractive to private investors with assurance of financial incentives from government. Thus, hotel industry in India is fulfilling its meaning 'Hospitum' that means a hall in a medieval monastery where guests were given hospitality.

Hotel Business Organization Categories

1. Sole Proprietorship. Sole-Proprietorship or Individual Ownership means one man ownership of a business etc. especially of a hotel. In connection with hotel industry, sole-proprietorship hotels can be defined as such type of hotels, where all required capital is provided by one person and he takes all the risk, manages the hotel and is single authority to receive the total profit after providing for the expenses of operation and the cost of borrowings needed for the running of hotel business. 'One-man-business' is very common because of the nature of hotel business. In this type of business the owner enjoy all the profits in case of business prospers but in the case of failure he goes alone to the bankruptcy court. He has to pay for the debts and losses incurred by the operation. The main problem of individual type hotel is the lack of capital. The hotel owner has only his own resources so has to face the problem in the expansion and development of business.

2. Partnership. Partnership is the relation between persons who agreed to share the profits of a business carried on by all or any of them acting for all. In this type of hotel business the business is started with atleast two persons and capital is provided by them to own the hotel on agreement basis. This type of agreement is known as partnership agreement, partnership deed or articles of partnership. The agreement points out the aims, objects, rights and duties, authorities and responsibilities of each partner. It also includes a clause for setting differences between partners and the circumstances and the manner in which the contract can be terminated. This type of hotel is generally bigger than individual type of hotel and smaller than joint stock company basis. On of the feature of partnership hotel is that all the partners are liable for debts of the partnership. The firm's creditors have the right to sue all or any of the partners to the limit of their personal and business resources. It is notable that a relieved partner is also liable for debts incurred during the period in which he was a partner unless the other partners release him, but incoming partner will be free from liability for existing partnership debts.

3. Co-owner Chain. In this type of hotel an agreement is made between the parent company and the local investor. In this category of partnership 50% of the stock of the hotel is owned by the local investor and 50% by the parent organization. The parent company is responsible of selection of site, designing, financing building and furnishing and the supervision of the hotel management.

4. Heritage Hotels. Heritage Hotel is a new category of hotel introduced by the Indian Hotel Industry for its quick and efficient development. Heritage hotels can be defined as hotel running in palaces, castles, forts, and residence of any size which were built prior to 1950. As it was not possible for the Indian princes in independent India to maintain their large and stylish palaces so they have changed their palaces into luxury hotels to make ends meet. It is essential for a Heritage Hotel that the outward appearance, architectural features and general construction of the building will have the distinctive qualities, ambience and decor in keeping with the traditional way of the place. Parking space for cars is also an essential feature for this type of hotel. It is required that all public rooms and areas will be well maintained and well equipped with carpets, furniture, fittings etc. Reception cash and information counter are attended by trained personnel which provide money changing facilities and many other facilities. A well equipped, well furnished and well maintained dining room and a well equipped bar is essentiai for a Heritage Hotel. Apart from these facilities a well maintained ground and garden is a symbol of Heritage Hotel.

5. Chain Type Hotels. A group of three or more hotels, or resorts operated under a common name are known as chain type of hotels. During last few years chain type of hotels have become very common and are very popular due to its efficiency. Statler, Hilton and Sheraton groups of hotels got a remarkable momentum and began to grow rapidly. Chain type of hotels have so many advantages for capitalising group as a means of increasing business and reducing duplication, inefficiency and waste. Chain hotels saves money in purchasing anything from food stuffs to furniture. It can be in a position to get the services of top specialists in every phase of hotel operation-engineers, food controllers, decorators, architectural planners, its large income sources. The chain hotels can easily advertise itself through magazines and newspapers than single hotels because the expense is divided among numerous hotel and thus they receive full benefit of national coverage at the fraction of total cost. Reservation system is very easy for chain hotels as about the fourth of all room reservations are made through free teletype reservation services which permits a chain access to the various hotels in the group while it is out of reach of independent hotels. In India Taj, Oberoi, ITC groups and in foreign Holiday Inn, Hilton, Sheraton and Intercontinental are the dominant international groups which have changed the organizational structure and management of hotel enterprises.

6. Multinational Hotels. Multinational hotels earn revenues from accommodation—the suites, flat lets and studio rooms and from catering services. Their restaurants provide entertainment also to the customers alongwith good food service. Multinational hotels have limited capability. There is a need for limited hotels in a particular region. These hotels are openable in the largest of communities where there are prosperous businessmen.

7. Time Sharing Resorts. With the changing need of tourists and travellers Time Sharing Resorts' or Resort hotels have acquired valuable place in the field of hotel industry. For the purpose of suitable climate the rich go out in summer as well as in winter. Apart from this group a number of families travel during vacations and so a place is needed to stay and relax during holidays. Although travelling is sometimes limited to a particular season of the year, most of the hill and beach resorts are getting vacation spots for summer as well as winter. So there are year-round resorts also existence alongwith time-sharing resorts. Resort hotels are generally located in tourist resort areas. A resort hotel have rooms less than fifty and it is classed as luxury type hotel due to size of guest rooms and provision of facilities such as dining, restaurants, bar, recreation, etc. Resort hotels are mainly of three types:

(a) ***Natural Recreational Resort Hotels.*** Some hotels are located near natural recreational areas such as sea shore, large lakes, national shrines, parks, ski slopes, hill resorts, legalized gambling areas etc. These hotels are known as Natural Recreational Resort Hotels. These hotels are based on either European plan or modified American plan.

(b) ***Summer Resorts.*** Summer resorts in India are operated during May, June, July. As this season is very short so the operation depends upon the elements like rain etc. Shimla, Srinagar; Mussoorie, Nainital, Darjeeling hill stations are best example of summer resorts.

(c) ***Self-Contained Resort Hotels.*** These resorts are American plan based resorts and provide all the recreational facilities

for its guests such as: Indoor and outdoor pools, Horse back riding, Tennis courts, entertainment, Golf courses, etc.

(d) ***Ski Resort Hotels.*** The third type of resort hotel is ski-resort hotels. These hotels are located far away from the cities where the areas for the various functions depend upon the anticipated number of hotel guests plus the amount of a patronage expected from the community.

(e) ***Cold Winter Resorts:*** These are places mainly having facilities for winter sports like skating. Gulmarg is the best example of such resorts.

(f) ***Warm Winter Resorts.*** Warm Winter Resorts means a resort where the traveller can enjoy the hot sun, the golden beaches etc.

(g) ***The Year Round Resorts.*** These resorts are located at those places where the climate at those places is pleasant during the whole year. So the travellers of can enjoy here a twelve month season.

Most resorts, hotels are seasonable establishments who may be closed in the off season. The hotel industry aims building up a regular holiday trade because it is more valuable to sell the house in advance year by year. These resorts are no being made to open during summer or winter by capitalising skiing and other seasonal sports. Off season prices are lower and are often sold in combination with special rate, combination of transportation entertainment etc. These hotels frequent encourage business by cooperation with airlines and of carriers to offer a single price covering travel, lodging, meals a often entertainment.

8. Franchise. *(i) Organization.* Franchise is a technical word that means to name from a reputed firm or organization in return of a agreement. In regard with hotel business; Franchise agreement between a hotel company and an independent owner whereby for a fee the owner is allowed to use the is trade marks and various services offered by the chain, continuing relationship in which a franchiser provides a privilege to do business plus assistance in organizing, merchandising and operation management, in return consideration from the franchisee. Franchise system provides a large scale of opportunity to go into business as the parent organization assist the newcomer at any and all times. They provide the advantage of brand name or trade mark in advertising, sales promotion and advance registration. On the other hand the parent organization is also benefited by Franchise system. At first, franchising provides an opportunity for an organization to spread its name rapidly and widely throughout the country at a minimum amount of expenses. Secondly, franchise operations act booking agents for the hotels of the organization and thus the referral business proves a two-way street and excellent sources of rooms and food and beverage business for the metropolitan hotels. Apart from these two benefits the hotel companies receive a great deal of money through this system. As every franchisee pays a franchise fee and a daily charge to the organization, there is plenty of money to be made in franchising. Holiday Inn, Hyatt, House Sheraton Inn, Hilton, Congress Inn, Howard Jonshon's, Quality courts, Albert pick, Down towner, Marriott, Ramada Inns are some of the well-known franchise chains.

(ii) Services. There are many services offered by a franchiser to a franchisee such as:

(a) *Technical Assistance.* Technical assistance are provided by the franchiser in return of payment of additional services provided. Assistance during the development of potential sites, assistance in obtaining finance, preparation of cost budgets and feasibility studies are various forms of technical assistance. Besides this architectural services, interior design services, purchasing services, project management and construction supervision can also be obtained from franchiser as technical assistance.

(b) *Marketing.* Marketing is one of the important service, provided by the franchiser. It is an important ingredient in a agreement. Advertising, sales and reservation are the three sources of providing marketing services.

(c) *Methods.* At first, operating procedures established by the franchiser are used by the franchisee to run the business successfully. Training programme, deputation of regional manager are the forms of operating procedures provided by the franchiser to a franchisee.

Lease Operation

Lease operation is one of the most popular trend in the of hotel industry. There are many hotel companies which are field operated under lease agreements. Lease agreements are of many types, such as:

1. Profit Sharing Lease Agreement. When the hotel is leased in legal terms to an operator, but the owner by an agreement participates in its profit then it is known as profit sharing lease agreement. Under such type of agreement, provisions are made for payment of the property taxes and fire insurance by the landlord out of the rent he reserves and that is his participation in the profits. The legal status of operator is the same as that of an operator with a straight lease.

2. Sale and Lease Back Agreement. Sale and lease back agreement is basically a financing arrangement designed to afford certain advantages in cash flow to a hotel operator and provides certain income tax advantages to the buyer of the property.

3. Straight Lease Agreement. Under this type of agreement a tenant pays a fixed monthly amount to the land lord Iot the complete use of a specific hotel or hotels. Generally, a lease agreement cover only the land and building not the furniture and equipment in it except a few hotels. The lease agreements cover and clearly specify the responsibility for the payment of certain fixed charges like property taxes, fire-insurance, sewer-rent, water, garbage disposal, etc. Procedure for prompt payment of these items is also included in the agreement. A lease agreement is done for a maximum period of twenty years for the successful operation of a hotel.

Hotel Manager: Role and Functions

Management is an integral part of the hotel industry. It is such an important part of the hotel industry that can make or spoil the industry. Management is both science and art. It can be defined as a technique of getting things done through the efforts of others. Although this is not a right and complete definition because people cannot achieve the ends of the organization. In fact, management is a technique for the attainment of some objective or objectives.

It is not possible for an organization to run successfully unless there is someone to manage its affairs. Management is also defined as an agency to guide and control the activity or activities of the people in the organization, so an organization cannot survive without management. New ideas and vision to the work group is provided by the management and it also integrates the efforts in such a manner as to account for better results. Smooth flow of work is ensured in the organization by strengthening weak links, overcoming difficulties and establishing team spirit amongst the personnel, through management. In regard with importance of management it can be said that an organization cannot be successful without the utilization of effective and efficient management. It is the management which determines the goals of group activity and then puts them into action by organizing the human and non-human resources. It plays a key role in the field of national development. Neither capital investment nor technical know how can be succeeded if these are not managed properly. Thus, management has no substitute.

Manager's Role

A "Manager" is that person who works in an organization so that human and material resources may be effectively used to achieve the desired objectives. He is like an athletic coach who tries to help each member of his team to strengthen his good points and to improve upon the weak points. A good manager possesses a systematized body of knowledge which provides fundamental truths which he can utilise in his job. It is essential for a good manager to possess following qualities for handling his role efficiently.

(1) The manager requires an ability to think clearly in regard with deciding management policies.

(2) To be able to devise workable plans and have a capacity for dealing with new problems with energy, initiative and imagination.

(3) The manager must have proper understanding of human behaviour, because he has to win their confidence including ability to convince and persuade.

(4) The manager must be expert in communication.

(5) The manager must have a ambivalent personality with freedom from a strong extrovertism so as to develop effective planning, accuracy in details and sensitivity to the feelings of others.

(6) He must be emotionally matured.

(7) When anything goes wrong he should keep patience together with ability to preserve and overcome discouragement.

(8) Capacity to appraise organizational performance against objectives, policies and goals of the organization and also to assist in appraisal of employees performance related to organizational goals is essential for a manager.

(9) For confidence and good-will establishment between management and working people he should possess the strength of character, integrity, reliability and a sense of justice.

(10) He must have the ability to identify with a person or object.

(11) The manager must be highly educated because good education increases the ability to make systematic research and investigation.

In regard with above said qualities the manager has to fulfill the duty of understanding of dynamic process in which free men pool their efforts and abilities. He holds his organization, discovers and adopts sound, up-to-date policies on employee relationships and, on occasions review them. He formulates appropriate actions to implement and carry out these policies in actual programmes and practice.

The role of a Hotel manager, can be summarized as follows:

(1) He establishes and maintains an adequate organizational Structure and a desirable working relationship among all the members of the hotel by dividing the tasks into functions, positions, jobs and by defining the responsibility in the organization.

(2) He tries to achieve an effective utilization of human resources for the achievement of organization goals.

(3) He secures the integration of the individuals and groups by reconciling group or individual goals with those of an organization in such a manner that the employees feel a sense of involvement, commitment and loyalty towards it.

(4) He recognizes and satisfies individual needs and group goals by offering an adequate and equitable remuneration, economic and social security in the form of monetary comensuration, and protection against such hazards of life.

(5) He generates maximum development of individuals within an organization by providing job opportunities through training and job advance education or by offering transfers or by providing retraining facilities.

(6) He maintains high morale and better human relations inside an organization by sustaining and improving the conditions so that employees may stick to their job for a longer period.

Functions of Management

In an organization, management is related with the functions of planning, organizing, delegating, actuating, forecasting and controlling.

Planning. Planning is the basic function of management because all others result from it. It is a continuing process and the means by which the manager decides in what direction he wants his group to move. Planning is that mental process which requires use of intelligency, imagination, foresight and sound judgement. In fact, planning is the determination of a course of action to achieve the desired results. Planning may be defined as a process of thinking before doing. The aim of planning is to think ahead, determine clearly objectives and policies, and select a course of action towards the accomplishment of the goals. As planning is a thinking process so the planner must be an experienced man. He should be thoroughly conversant with the present situation and should have a clear cut vision for future. Before planning, the planner has to take into consideration the main difficulties and hazards that he has to face to reach the goal. He should also take into consideration the different states of operation and he should check the earlier calculations and guidelines to see whether they are going well or not. If anything goes wrong then the whole plan should be revised because rethinking is the main feature of planning.

Organizing. Organizing is the second step of management. The management combines the human and material resources through organizing. The organizing function identifies activities and tasks, divides tasks into positions and puts like tasks together in order to take advantage of special abilities and skills of the worker and use his talents effectively. But the main function of the organizing process is the establishment of relationship among all other functions of management.

Actuating. Actuating means "getting work done with people." It is concerned with employees as human beings. The manager should be alert to increase worker's productivity through careful, intelligent guidance and counselling and by effective supervision.

Forecasting. Forecasting is an important factor in effective planning for the future operating programme of any company. Forecasting is based on objective study of past and present situations. Social, economic, political and other environmental conditions are external factors involved in forecasting while size of plant and productivity of the personnel are some internal factors, involved in forecasting. Although it is not possible to get a high degree of accuracy in forecasting because of the uncertainties of the future, it has the merit to provide some helpful information and to call attention to current problem areas within the organization.

Delegating. Delegation of authority is essential to distribute work loads to qualified individuals at various levels. According to A "Carnegie" Delegating marks a big step in man's development when he realizes that other men can help him do a better job than he can do alone".

Staffing. Staffing comes as the fifth step of management. To fulfill the requirements of the enterprise the management, after determining the number and staff of personnel, starts with recruiting, screening and selecting the people. Staffing is concerned with those activities which are essential to manage and keen the positions created by the organizations structure. It includes the task of determining the requirements with regard to number and type of people for the jobs to be done, laying down qualifications for various jobs to be done and recruiting, selecting and training people to perform those jobs effectively and efficiently.

Controlling. Controlling is a necessary function of all areas of food service because thorough control standards of acceptability and accountability are art for performance. A good control system prevents present and future deviation from plans and does much to stimulate an employee to maintain the standards of the food service director. The control function should be one of guidance rather than command. It should be concerned with employees as human beings with interests to be stimulated, attitudes and abilities to be directed and developed and comprehension and understanding of their responsibilities to be increased.

Finance. Finance or Financial management is the hub of all management function. It is the chief function of every catering manager to make good and proper financial management to achieve the goals of his organization.

The function of financial management involves:

1. The financing decision which means the decision as to how the total funds required by the hotel will be made available through issue of shares or raising of loans or keeping back the profit etc.
2. The investment decision which is concerned with the utilization of funds in one activity or the other.
3. The dividend decision. It means the decision in respect of the part of profits which will be given to the shareholders in the form of cash dividend and the amount which will be kept back for utilization by the hotel.

To make proper financial management, it is essential to make a financial policy. To formulate the policies is one of the important function of finance manager. It helps the manager in their decision-making. Following are some of the policies required to be framed for effective financial management:

1. Policies regarding control of the business.
2. Policies in the matter of estimation of capital requirement.
3. Policies that guide a management in the selection of the sources of finance.
4. Policies regarding use of borrowings and the extent.
5. Policies governing the servicing of the capital.
6. Policies regarding investment in fixed capital and working capital.

A hotel manager should take the decisions within the framework of above mentioned financial policies.

After formulating the policies the hotel manager has to perform certain routine functions for effective financial management. These are as follows:

1. Management of cash centrally and supplying the needs of various divisions and departments without unduly keeping idle cash at any point.
2. To keep track of actual and projected cash inflows and cash outflows.
3. Negotiations and relations with banks and other financial institutions.
4. Investment of funds that may be available and free for a short period.
5. Maintaining a constant and close relationship with debenture holders and shareholders so that the hotel is not faced with any sudden development from these quarters.
6. Preparation and issue of the prospectus for raising funds through issue of shares and debentures.
7. Maintenance of liaison with production and sales departments for seeing that the working capital position is not upset because of inventories, book debts, etc.
8. Keeping management informed of the financial implications of the various developments in and around the hotel.

As we know that financial management requires a good deal of expertise so this function should be performed by a qualified and experienced person. In fact, a finance manager should have following qualities:

1. Knowledge of investment market and the stock exchange operations.
2. Expertise with money matters and money market.
3. To be honest.
4. Expert in the art of communication.
5. Ability to establish close relationship with all other functionaries in the business and win their confidence.

At last, it can be said that financial management is the control point of all management function. It plays a vital role in proper motivation of the people working in the hotel or catering organization, Financial management establishes total amount of funds that are required by a hotel or the achievement of its objective and determines th optimum method of obtaining these funds, The manager ensures that the funds available to the hotel are used in the most profitable manner and the earned profit are disposed of to the best advantage of the shareholders. Thus, the manager plays a role of philosopher and a specialized practitioner.

ESTABLISHMENT AND DECISION MAKING REGARDING COMPANY POLICIES AND PROCEDURES

Establishment of a hotel is a majortask which requires three things—Desire, Resources and Activities. This is a very complex task that calls for expert service in many fields like—Finance, Architecture, Engineering, Interior Designing, Food and Beverage facilities, Planning and so on. These fields are of complex nature and play a great role towards the success or failure of a hotel. So, before establishing a hotel following factors must be kept in mind. This is the key to success.

Entertainment. Entertainment is a chief factor in selection of the site. The necessity of space and resorts for treatment and recreation brought into existence distinct type of establishments. Concentration of entertainment is another factor which helps in the choice of location of a hotel. Creation of attractions, swimming pool, golf course, tennis courts, riding tracks, sailing and boating, lakes among landscape appreciate the value of the location.

Site or Location. According to Mr. Neil Staler—"The three scales of success are location, location, location." This is the first step in establishing a hotel. The selection of sity should be based on the following factors: Transport: The location of a hotel should be determined on the basis of transport routes and facilities, as they exercised a distinct influence on the location of the hotel.

Industry and Trade. Industry and Trade have a great influence over the establishment of a hotel because they often create transit and terminal accommodation in and between population centres.

There are also many other factors which should be kept in mind while selecting the site or location. These factors are:

— The central business activity,

— Shopping centres,

— Concentration of catering establishments,

— Location of major tourists, cultural and ethical facilities.

— Facilities of travel agency and tour operation.

— Availabilities of necessary utilities like water and electricity,

— Anticipated future trends,

— Climate,

— Local political scene,

— A vailability of all materials—prospective hoteliers should consider the availability of all materials for starting and carrying on the hotel business.

Market Analysis. Market analysis is very important for the need to analyze in depth the potential markets at home and abroad to ascertain their requirements to the project. In order to make a thorough analysis the following information needs to be collected:

1. Information about local hotel market like the number of rooms, published rates, situation of hotels, quality and extent of facilities, overall hotel occupancy, should be collected.

2. The principal competitive. hotels should also be studied and information regarding location; number of rooms, average room rate, occupancy, quality and facilities of services offered should be collected.

3. As demand is the main basis on which the hotel business is to run efficiently and profitably so is a need to analyze the principal sources demand which is based on business trave growth in air traffic, growth in employment conventions and business meetings, number conventions, type and size of conventions etc.

Micro Supply. The principle of supply and demand plays an important role in the establishment of a hotel. Supply refers to the number and type of competitive accommodations located within a defined market area. The main objective of micro supply is to evaluate local supply and demand relationship to determine how a hotel will fit into the market. The micro supply trends often show a significant effect on local hotel particularly with respect to size, layout, and decision for chain affiliation, financial structure and type management.

Economic Analysis. Economic analysis is an important stage of hotel establishment. It is based on the data provided by the market surveys and takes into account both the current and projected costs of building and operation. Economic analysis is the key part of hotel establishment.

Staffing. Staffing is necessary for hotel establishments. It is a major headache of the prospective hotelier because of the dearth of trained personnel especially of craftsmen like cooks, waiters, barmen, housekeepers, bakers, receptionists etc. Apprenticeship scheme, catering institutes and food craft centre are helpful in this respect.

Investment and Appraisal. This is the final stage in hotel establishment. It determines whether the proposed operation will provide a sufficient return on investment. The first thing is to calculate the percentage net profit return on total capital cost. The result should be compared to the interest rates that could be secured in government securities.

Import Licence. To maintain international standard, licence is required for the import of equipments.

Name and Symbol. Name and symbol is an important factor, for the establishment of all hotel projects. Name and symbol play a very important part for all the hotels. According to Campbell Smith "The name must be easy to remember, readily associated with the product and easily pronounced. It must be free from unpleasant association and, preferably suggest pleasant one as it must be consistent with the image of the product. Finally it must be legally permissible and if possible registerable". Thus, it is clear that hotel business is of a specialized nature and requires a complete and detailed analysis before any decision is taken to start it.

Decision-making. Decision-making is an indispensable tool of management. No work at any level can be performed without making decisions. At kitchen, decisions are taken regarding materials, methods of work, quantities, quality and so on. At management level, decisions are taken regarding staffing, sorting out grievances, taking joint decision with trade unions, etc. Further decisions regarding policies of the establishment, changes in response to factors in the environment, setting goals, competing with others in the trade as well as investment decisions are required to be taken. The process of decision-making involves three basic steps:

(a) Making a mental effort,

(b) Listing out alternative courses of action within the structure of a situation, and

(c) Choosing from among many alternatives, a single course of action.

There are two main type of decisions taken in catering establishments. Some are routine and repetitive which do not require fresh thinking each time the need arises. For example, the decision to place a pan on the cooking range when any food is to be cooked, or switching on the oven when a cake mixture is being prepared. The second type of decisions are unprogrammed decisions. For example, such decisions which are required to be taken if an accident takes place in the kitchen or when some incident of misbehaviour has to be tackled, or a piece of equipment breaks down in the middle of food being cooked in it. This type of decisions require the use of judgement creativity, presence of mind and initiative. The routine type of decisions act as a tool for managing time well because the become quite automatic and require practically no mental effort on the other hand, unprogrammed decisions are important for managing emergency or pressure situations.

HRM IN HOTEL AND CATERING INDUSTRY

Human Resource Management in hotel and catering industry is concerned with utilizing the manpower resources most productively. According to the Institute of Personnel Management Human Resource Management is a responsibility of all those who manage people as well as being a description of the work of those who are employed as specialists. It is that part of management which is concerned with people at work and with their relationships within an enterprise. Human Resource Management aims to achieve both efficiency and justice, neither of which can be pursued successfully without the other. It seeks to bring together and develop into an effective organization the men and women who make up an enterprise, enabling each to make his own best contribution to its success both as an individual and as a member of a working group of team. It seeks to provide fair terms and conditions of employment and satisfying work for those employed'.

Manpower Management Cycle

Human resource management is basically concerned with having the right type of people available as and when required and improving the performance of the existing people to make them more effective on their jobs. It starts with 'Manpower Planning'. Job analysis, job specification, recruitment, selection and promotion, performance appraisal training are the other steps of such management.

Manpower Planning

"Manpower planning is the process by which management determines how the organization should move from its current manpower position to its desired manpower position. Through planning, management strives to have the right number and right kind of people at the right place, at the right time, doing things which result in both the organization and the individual receiving maximum long run benefit".

According to Garden Macbeth 'Manpower planning' involves two stages. The first stage is concerned with the detailed planning of manpower requirements for all types and levels of employees throughout the period of the plan and the second stage is concerned with planping of manpower supplies to provide the organization with the right type of people from all sources to meet the planned requirements.

In hotels, manpower planning has become valuable due to the considerable costs of labor and the growing staff shortages during recent years. 'The shortage of staff and growth in labor costs led in particular to' accurate manpower planning so that an employer has the right resources; available' when required and also so that labour costs are not necessarily high.

Manpower planning can be divided into two separate and distinct parts: operational and strategic. Operational is concerned with the day-to-day: The strategic part of manpower is concerned with ensuring that the right manpower will be available in the long term. Those hotels that are not even built doing manpower planning are the best example of strategic manpower planning.

For operational level manpower planning knowledge of manning ratios are necessary. Each hotel has its own manning ratio, such as two waiter for ten covers and one chambermaid for fourteen rooms. For strategic level management needs accurate manpower statistics are required in order to, develop the undertaking's long term plans.

Manpower planning is difficult to implement effectively without adequate records and statistics. These are required for several reasons.

(a) To provide information for re-employment and reference purposes.

(b) To provide detailed operational information such as monthly strength returns and payroll analysis.

(c) To provide ratios or data such as wastage rates, age analysis and service analysis for planning purposes.

(d) To provide information for statutory purposes such as National Insurance, Redundancy payment or registered disabled person Act.

(e) To provide information on individuals for administration purposes such as salaries and pensions and to provide information for career development purposes.

For manpower planning and management development purposes in a hotel following are the basic tools.

1. Personal Dossier. This contain all documents relating to an individual employee such as:

(a) Copies of letters of offer and acceptance

(b) Application form

(c) Copy of engagement form

(d) Various reports and correspondence

(e) Performance appraisal

(f) Changes of conditions *e.g.* salary increases

(g) Records of company property issued to the employee.

The dossier is generally kept for one or two years in case of queries after an employee has left.

2. Personal Record. Personal record card is the backbone of a good record system which provides valuable information quickly and easily. The card contains concise infofmation common to most employees such as age, education, qualifications, training, marital status. It is used mainly for statistical exercise or for the speedy retrieval of information.

3. Engagement form. This form is prepared for a new employee to inform all the relevant departments so that appropriate action is initiated. This will vary according to the system being used. It is a form of prime importance to ensure that the employee is paid and insured.

4. Employment Requisition. This document is presented by the head of departments to their authority for the purpose of an addition to staff. This form will vary and depend on the degree of authority of individual heads of department. For example, some head of departments will need no special authority so long as the person to be recruited will be within the laid down staff establishment or within authorized budget levels. On the other hand, some large hotels executives insist on personally authorizing the recruitment of all new staff whether they are replacing Ie avers or exceeding the staff establishment.

5. Strength Returns. This statistical information shows the numbers of employee of each department and also change in numbers. It may also incorporate 'establishment' numbers, that is the agreed number to be employed in each department.

6. Staff or Labour Turnover Analysis. This information can assist considerably in staff recruitment and retention by identifying the problem areas.

7. Termination Form. Termination form is used to initiate documentation and auministration procedures. It provides statistical information regarding labour turnover and re-employment purposes.

8. Payroll Analysis. Payroll analysis is presented by a variety of departments and includes a breakdown of labour costs. It should be produced on a regular periodic basis.

9. Manpower Audit. Some large hotels conduct detailed studies. periodically which provide a complete breakdown of the labour force divided into various sections including job grades, age and service. They may also report on the quality of staff, their qualifications, performance and potential. Manpower plan is a part of this audit.

10. Age & Service Analysis. It is necessary for a medium and large sized hotel to look at the make up of the labour force and particularly the age profile of the management team. In case it is not done an unanticipated spate of retirements and resignations can leave an undertaking without the necessary trained personnel. So age and service analysis must be done to produce an annual age profile of management and to link with service in special conditions.

To sum up, it can be said than manpower planning has become much more apparent in the hotel and catering industry. There are many ways being used for effective pianning and control to ensure that the future of the organization remains brighte despite change. It is dear that manpower planning is; concemed with anticipating future manpower needs at different levels in the organization, visualizing the future and determining how the needed manpower can, be recruited. Systematic manpower planning is thus a must for every dynamic hotel.

Job Specification

Job specification is a broad statement of the scope, purpose, duties and responsibilities involved in a job. It is one of the main document that helps to perform the job more efficiently. A job specification contains more details than job description although its content will depend on its purpose. If the purpose is to specify the qualities required of an employee with regard to a certain post or to expand on the duties performed by an employee for training purposes then this must be considered when preparing the specification. In case of joint consultation job, specification is prepared by the personnel department if it is for recruitment purposes or by a training officer if it is for a training purpose. Job specification is an essential part of hotel management as in some cases brief descriptions only may be sufficient whereas in others quite detailed and complete documents are called for to perform the job satisfactorily. Job analysis or a detailed statement of the job is also needed to specify the precise skills and knowledge to carry out the various component tasks, of a job. Thus a job specification is necessary to expand on details regarding duties. The preparation of job specifications normally requires a more skilled approach than that needed for the preparation of job description. The uses to which such documents are to be put should determine who prepares them. For example; if job specification are to be used for training purposes they should, be prepared by training specialists, on the other hand, if they are to be used as a basis for work measurement, work study specialist should work with line management. Job specifications are used in recruitment, selection, training, and job evaluation as needed by, the personnel function and as set by the standards required by a hotel.

(a) Housekeeping Department

The housekeeping department in a hotel is concerned with duties which covers the residential accommodation facilities, also includes the activities of the area known as the linen room where linen towels are stored, processed and accounted for. There are many staff in a hotel housekeeping department.

The house keeping department has separate specific to which are: *1.* Cleaning; *2.* Polishing; *3.* Preparing bedroom; *4.* Dealing with guests' laundry; *5.* Dealing with guest's special request; *6.* Dealing with lost and found property; *7.* Employing personal grooming and hygiene techniques; *8.* Using the telephone; *9.* Preparing public rooms; *10.* Dealing with pests; *11.* Receiving and issuing linen; *12.* Dealing with complaints; *13.* Transferring guests; *14.* Giving first aid; *15.* Taking fire prevention and safety action; *16.* Serving beverage or food in bedrooms; *17.* Dealing with repairs and maintenance; *18.* Creating floral and decorative arrangements; *19.* Repairing fabrics; *20.* Marketing fabrics; *21.* Removing stains; *22.* Taking action in emergencies;. *23.* Seasonal opening; *24.* Co-ordinating work with front office; *25.* Seasonal closing down; *26.* Planning and controlling the work of the department; *27.* Speaking foreign languages appropriate to the task; *28.* Inspecting; *29.* Record keeping; *30.* Giving on the job training; *31.* Taking inventory; *32.* Drawing up duty rosters.

(b) Front Office

The term 'front office' refers to that area of activity of a hotel which has administrative responsibility for guests and potential guests from before their arrival and on their arrival, to their departure and after departure. This department is also concerned with day-to-day administration and accounting, enquires, communications, reservations and liaisons.

The front office department has its own specific tasks which are: *1.* Preparing for guest arrivals; *2.* Dealing with arrivals; *3.* Receiving guests; *4.* Installing guests; *5.* Checking out guests; *6.* Dealing with departure; *7.* Dealing with enquiries; *8.* Dealing with complaints; *9.* Dealing with messages; *10.* Paging; *11.* Dealing with mail; *12.* Using the telephone; *13.* Keeping relevant guest records; *14.* Dealing with business correspondence; *15.* Using public address system; *16.* Disseminating information; *17.* Dealing with deposits for safe custody; *18.* Selling; *19.* Compiling guest bills; *20.* Keeping visitors' tabular ledger; *21.* Operating front office billing machines; *22.* Keeping debtors' ledger; *23.* Producing reports and statistics; *24.* Receiving cash; *25.* Paying cash; *26.* Operating cash register; *27.* Banking; *28.* Operating telephone switchboard; *29.* Night auditing; *30.* Operating telex machines; *31.* Taking action in emergencies; *32.* Employing personal grooming and hygiene techniques; *33.* Dealing with room reservations; *34.* Giving on the job training; *35.* Supervising; *36.* Operating sundry office machinery; *37.* Giving first aid; *38.* Speaking foreign language appropriate to the task *39.* Taking fire prevention and safety action; *40.* Providing security; *41.* Dealing with room service order; *42.* Controlling room keys; *43.* Drawing up duty rosters; and operating lift.

Bar

There are so many tasks related to the Bar in a hotel. These tasks are: Preparing the bar service area; Cleaning bar and equipment; Using telephone; Cleaning; Preparing bar for operation; Speaking foreign language appropriate to the task; Employing personal grooming and hygiene techniques; Serve drinks; serve snacks; Dealing with complaints; Operating cash register; billing manual and computerised; Preparing mixed drinks; Planning and inspecting the preparation of bar; Drawing up duty rosters; Taking inventory of equipment; Supervising; Giving on the job training; Using public address system;

Taking fire prevention and safety action; and Taking action in emergencies .

The Kitchen

The kitchen department is concerned with following main task: Cleaning fixed equipment; Cleaning portable items; Operating dish washing machine; Starting the work shift; Cleaning kitchen and stores; Finishing the work shift; Preparing vegetables, poultry and game birds, fish, dairy products, beverages; Preparing and cooking cereals and farinaceous dishes, stocks, sauces, soups and broths, vegetables, eggs, fish, shellfish, meat and furred game, poultry and game birds, fruits and berries, desserts, salads; Preparing and baking dough and pastries; Preparing and serving cold buffets; Carving meat, poultry, fish in the restaurant; Dealing with food orders in kitchen; Dealing with complaints in the kitchen; Planning and writing menus; Using the telephone; Drawing up duty rosters; Planning and inspecting work in the kitchen; Buying commodities; Receiving goods; Storekeeping; Stock taking and controlling; Taking action in emergencies; Taking fine safety action; Taking inventory; 'Supervising; Giving first aid; Planning and operation of portion control; Giving on-the-job training; and Operating cash register.

The Restaurant

The restaurant is that department of hotel which has the maim areas of activity. These areas of function are:

(a) Manipulative Area. This area involves the preparation, carrying and handling of equipment both in and outside the restaurant area.

(b) Selling Area. This area involves communication with guests and general behaviour with management and colleagues.

(c) Service Area. This area involves serving of food items.

(d) Billing Area. This includes all administrative activity in connection with accountancy at whatever level is required of the restaurant staff.

(e) Supervisising Area. This area involves certain tasks which are performed only by tthose in supervisory jobs.

The above said restaurant areas are concerned with following main tasks: Cleaning; Cleaning restaurant equipment; Preparing service table and sideboards; Preparing room service pantry; Employing personal grooming and hygiene techniques; Closing down the restaurant; Ordering and carrying food from the kitchen; Ordering and carrying beverages; Speaking foreign language appropriate to the task; Cleaning table in self service; Serving cigars and cigarettes; Serving non-alcoholic beverages; Serving food; Serving wines; Serving alcoholic beverages; Preparing and serving buffets; Taking food orders; Compiling food and beverage orders manually; Taking alcoholic beverage orders; Compiling food and beverage orders mechanically; Carving meat, poultry and fish in the restaurant; Flaming dishes; Dealing with complaints; Billing manually; Billing computerised; Billing self service; Operating cash register; Planning menus for special occasions; Arranging special occasions; Making table reservations; Planning and inspecting the preparation of the restaurant; Making daily cash reports; Giving fire prevention and safety action; Receiving restaurant guests; Operating dispense bar; Drawing up duty registers; Taking inventory of equipment; Supervising; Giving on the job training; Using public address system; Taking action in emergencies; and Giving first aid.

Recruitment

Recruitment is the art of attracting suitable applicants from whom the most suitable person may be selected. It depends upon adequate information being available including full details regardingt be conditions of employment and the job to be performed preferably in the form of a job description.

It is one of the main functions of the personnel department to place the right person in the right job and in order to do this the personnel department uses various methods to attract applicants for different vacancies. The large hotelsuses recruitment methods according to the status, skill and type of employee required. These methods take into consideration company policy and finance available for recruitment. 'Recruitment method is also influenced by the urgency of the need to fill the vacant post.

Recruitment methods is divided into two categories—internal methods and external methods.

Internal Methods. Internal method means that method of recruitment in which the employees are selected within the organization itself. Internal recruitment is done in liaison with heads of departments. It is conducted democratically, making staff ;aware of the vacancies by internal advertising so as to avoid accusations of favouritism and resentment. Many hotel organization in India are using this recruitment method. In doing so the employee's seniority, merit initiative, accuracy of work job knowledge and personnel record are taken nto consideration and thus selection is done on the basis of merit. Internal recruitment is done through bulletin board, employee newspaper of special cyclostyled announcements circulated in department. Some hotels even maintain a file for recording voluntary applications which can be referred to in the future. In this method of recruitment the applicants are informed immediately about their success and failure and they are informed tactfully why they could not be selected.

Advantages of Internal Recruiting Method. The internal recruiting method enhance the general morals of the staff. In short this method has following advantages:

(a) The valuable contacts with major suppliers are kept.

(b) It builds loyalty among the employees.

(c) It creates a sense of security among the employees.

(d) It ensures stability from continuity of employment.

(e) It encourages other executives and employees in the lower ranks to look forward to rigging to higher levels.

(f) The persons are already familiar with the organizations' activities and requirements.

External Methods. When there are no suitable existing staff available, then a hotel uses external method of recruitment. In other words, external methods of recruitment are used to encourage application from employees outside the working environment. This method of recruitment is probably more suitable for junior members of staff and for unskilled and semi-skilled jobs like chambermaids, catering assistants, porters etc. The external sources of recruitment include the following:

Advertising through:

(a) Newspaper, National, local and trade

(b) Agencies

(c) Executive selection and management consultants

(d) Posters

(e) Colleges of further education

(f) Armed forces

Advertising Through Newspaper. Advertisement through newspapers is the most effective source of recruitment of all. It is not costly and depending on the size of the locality and the newspapers circulation, an advertisement can reach a great number of people. There are three main ways of advertising through newspapers which are known as display, semi-display and classified. Among these three ways Display is the most expensive way as it takes up the most space and involve the most work. The second method 'semi-display' gives the advertiser some prominence, in the classified section. 'Classified advertising' is the least expensive and usually the least effective.

Advantages of External Method. Like internal method of recruitments, external method has also some advantage, which are as follows:

(a) Fresh view points are attracted.

(b) The employees possess varied and broader experience.

(c) The employees develop the ability to change old habits.

Common Recruitment Sources for Indian Hotels

In Indian hotels, several sources of recruitment are used for selecting employees. In a public sector hotel staff are recruited through:

(a) Employment exchange

(b) External advertisement

(c) Internal advertisement

(d) Training Institute

(e) Deputation personnel

(f) Transfer from other public undertakings.

The private sector hotels commonly uses following sources of recruitment:

(a) Casual callers or employment seekers

(b) Newspaper advertisements

(c) Schedule tribes and scheduled castes

(d) Employment exchange

(e) Internal advertisement

(f) Displaced persons

(g) Relatives and friends

(h) Employee recommendation, and

(i) Training schools.

These are several sources of recruitment commonly used in Indian hotels. But the *(1)* Newspaper advertisement and *(2)* Relatives and friends are the two most renowned sources of recruitment among all these sources.

❐

5

Organization of Hotel

Till recently—about the middle of the last century and even later than that—the typical hotel of almost any size was characterised by a large number of individuals and departments directly responsible to the hotel manager who was closely concerned with his guests and with all or most aspects of the hotel operation. There might have been one or more assistant managers who had little or no authority over such key individuals as the chef, the head waiter or the housekeeper. The hotel manager usually combined the 'mine host' concept of hotel keeping with a close involvement in the operation. He normally had all or most of the technical skills that enter into the business of accommodating and catering for guests. Although he might have given more attention to departments, in which he felt confident about his expertise, and less to those in which his knowledge and skills might have been lacking, his approach was essentially that of a technician rather than the manager of a business. Hotels served those who chose to use them. The financial control was exercised by. the owners or by accountants on their behalf. Personnel management rarely extended beyond the 'hiring and firing' of staff. Hotel buildings and interiors were not often viewed as business assets required to produce a return comparable to other commercial investments; maintenance and energy were cheap.

Several influences have tended to change this profile generally and the approach to hotel organization in particular in the second half of the twentieth century. The market for hotels, the number of hotels, and the size of individual operations have grown, against the background of economic and social conditions in most parts of the world. Business and management thought and practice have found their way into hotels, with the entry into the hotel business of firms engaged in other industries, development of hotel education and training, and higher quality of management. Innovation in hotel organization, at first largely confined to a few firms in North America, has spread to others in other countries. These and other influences have brought about changes in the ways in which hotels organize their activities today.

Three particular developments illustrate the changes in hotel organization in post-war Britain. One relates to the grouping of functions. In the early 1950s hotel reception, uniformed services and housekeeping were invariably regarded as separate departments, each reporting directly to the hotel manager; twenty years later many large hotels had front hall managers, rooms managers, or assistant managers with specific responsibilities in this area. Similarly, over the same period in most large hotels food and beverage managers came to be appointed, responsible for all the hotel activities previously organized in restaurants, bars, and kitchens under the direct control of the hotel manager. Secondly, there has been a growth in specialists. In the early 1950s only a few large hotels had a staff manager, a public relations officer or a buyer; by the early 1970s personnel, sales and marketing, and purchasing departments were common features of the large hotels and of hotel groups. Thirdly, where each hotel used to be more or less self-sufficient in the provision of its various guest services and supporting requirements, many of these are now provided through internal rentals and concessions and through specialist suppliers and operators such as outside bakeries, butcheries and laundries.

Organization is a function of purpose and the complexity of the hotel business arises because it is concerned with several distinct products, services and facilities, which are offered in various combinations, as we saw in this textbook. It is helpful to arrange these, and the hotel activities described in this textbook, into a simple framework along the lines of those six chapters, and the classification of activities outlined below follows the common pattern of uniform and standard systems of accounts in use in a number of countries:

Operated departments (revenue earning)	Major (primary)	Rooms Food
	Minor (ancillary)	Beverages Guest telephones Guest laundry and valeting Other guest services
Support service departments (undistributed overhead)		Administration and general Marketing Property operation, maintenance and energy

In this schedule a distinction is drawn first between revenue-earning services operated by the hotel and activities that service the hotel. The revenue-earning services are divided further into primary and ancillary. It has been found in practice that the most effective hotel organization structures follow this classification and provide for clear profit and cost centre responsibilities.

Rooms

The accommodation function of the hotel can be described in terms of reception, uniformed services, and housekeeping. Several typical organizational approaches may be identified in respect of these activities in practice:

(i) all three activities operate as separate departments with their own heads of department;

(ii) reception and uniformed services are grouped together as the front hall or front house of the hotel under an assistant manager for whom it is his sole or main responsibility;

(iii) reception and uniformed services are grouped together as a front hall or front house department with its own head of department;

(iv) all three activities are grouped together as the rooms department under an assistant manager for whom it is his sole or main responsibility;

(v) all three activities are grouped together as the rooms department with its own head of department.

The first approach provides for a direct line of responsibility and authority between each separate head of department and the hotel manager and hence for a close contact between the two levels of management; however, it extends the hotel manager's span of control and he is required to co-ordinate the separate departments. The other four approaches are designed to reduce the hotel manager's span of control and provide for a co-ordination of related activities at an intermediate level, but increase the number of levels through which management has to operate, and reduce the amount of direct contact between the hotel manager and the departments concerned.

Several activities were described in connection with rooms, which may be arranged differently in large hotels:

(i) In smaller hotels guest accounts are normally handled by bookkeeper/receptionists, but strictly speaking guest accounts represent an extension of the accounting function of the hotel. Therefore, where guest accounting is handled by bill office clerks and cashiers, they normally form a part of the accounts department.

(ii) In most hotels advance reservations form an integral part of hotel reception and the same employees deal with them and with other reception tasks. But advance reservations may be dealt with in a separate section of the reception office or in a separate department, to enable employees to concentrate on the respective tasks without conflicting demands on their time and attention. Sometimes all advance reservations are concentrated in the sales department, which has a responsibility for maximising hotel occupancy.

(iii) In some hotels room service is provided by housekeeping staff, but room service is clearly part of the food and beverage function of the hotel.

Food and Beverages

The food and beverage function of the hotel is described in terms of the food and beverage cycle, the main sales outlets, and the related support services. Several typical organizational approaches may be identified in respect of this function in practice:

(i) each sales outlet and supporting service operates as a separate department with its own head of department;

(ii) several of these departments are grouped together as one department under its own head of department;

(iii) several departments are grouped together under an assistant manager for whom they represent his sole or main responsibility, *e.g.* purchasing and storage, bars and cellars, the 'back-of-the house' activities including the kitchen, and so on;

(iv) all food and beverage activities are grouped together as a food and beverage department with its own head of department.

(v) all food and beverage activities are grouped together under an assistant manager for whom they represent his sole or main responsibility;

The same observations apply to these approaches as are made above in relation to rooms, regarding lines of responsibility and authority, span of control and levels of management; the size of the span of control and the number of management levels are conflicting considerations.

Many aspects of the food and beverage function are closely related to each other but also to other parts of the hotel operation:

(i) Most hotels have facilities serving both food and beverages, although in some of them food or beverages may predominate. Whilst it is usually relatively easy to separate the revenue from each, it is often impractical to separate accurately all the costs of operation other than the cost of sales, because the same employees may handle both products, and because other goods and services provided in the same outlet may not be readily identifiable as either food or beverages. In these circumstances food and beverages are treated together, analysed by sales outlet, and the related responsibilities are reflected in the organization structure.

(ii) Food and beverage control based on the food and beverage cycles described in this textbook may be appropriately seen as part of the total accounting function of the hotel. In these circumstances such employees as restaurant cashiers and cost control clerks are included on the staff of the hotel accountant.

(iii) Where there is a separate sales department, food and beverage sales are usually closely monitored by that department, and such arrangements as reservations for functions may form part of the responsibilities of the sales department.

Miscellaneous Guest Services

Miscellaneous guest services can be illustrated in terms of such activities as telephones and laundry and the typical organizational approaches for most of them are shown to be of twn main kinds:

— the services are operated under direct management of the hotel as minor operated departments;

— the services are operated under rental and concession arrangements with the hotel by another firm.

The alternative arrangements may apply in the provision of the following main services to guests:

(a) beauty shop and hairdressing

(b) florist

(c) garage

(d) laundry and dry cleaning

(e) squash courts and tennis courts

(f) gifts and souvenirs

(g) newspapers and magazines

(h) secretarial services

(i) swimming pool

(j) tobacconist.

Direct management of these services normally provides for a closer direct control and supervision by the hotel and for greater flexibility in operation. In many hotels the services are merely grouped as residuary hotel activities for accounting and control purposes and are in practice provided as part of the services of other hotel departments, *e.g.* reception, uniformed services, housekeeping or general administration, and are not separate departments in the organizational sense. Only when the volume of a particular service is sufficiently Jarge, it may be organized as a separate department. And it is only then that the option arises for the service to be provided for the guests by another operator, because it warrants his involvement, under a rental or concession arrangement. Such arrangement then relieves the hotel from operating what is often to the hotel operator an unfamiliar service and allows it to concentrate on its primary activities.

Hotel Support Services

Earlier in this chapter hotel activities were classified into revenue earning and support service departments. The first of the support service departments—administration and general—relates to functions of general management (some of which are considered in this chapter), purchasing, personnel, and accounting and control. The remaining support services are covered in this book.

In practice the non-revenue service activities are organized in one of three main ways:

(i) retained among the hotel manager's own responsibilities;

(ii) assigned to an assistant manager as one of his responsibilities;

(iii) assigned to a separate department with its own head of department.

To a greater or lesser extent each of these activities may also draw for its performance on external specialist advice and assistance.

The main specialist activities, which may be organized in one of these ways, and examples of the external sources of advice and assistance available to the hotel in respect of each can be summarised as follows:

Accounting and finance	Hotel accountants and consultants Public accountants and auditors Professional stock-takers
Personnel services	Personnel recruitment and selection specialists Work study, personnel and industrial relations advisers Training boards and other agencies
Purchasing	Hotel accountants and consultants Furniture and equipment specialists Various suppliers
Sales and marketing	Market research agencies Advertising agencies Public relations consultants
Property operation, maintenance, energy	Architects, builders, designers Consulting engineers Utility undertakings

Advisory services are also sometimes provided by professional bodies, trade associations for their members, the technical press and other agencies.

Apart from any operational philosophies, the adoption of the organizational approaches, in respect of a particular activity, is largely determined by the size of operation: the first is normally associated with a small hotel; the second with medium size; and the third with large operations, but no hard and fast rules apply. Each of these activities comprise specialist knowledge and skills, as distinct from normal operational know-how inherent in the primary operating activities.

Structure of Management

Following the discussion of the division and grouping of operated and service activities into departments, it is next necessary to consider the total management structure of the hotel; this comprises all positions of responsibility and authority below top management, which is represented in an hotel company by the board of directors. The management team consists of the hotel manager, one or more deputy or assistant managers, and the heads of departments. A discussion of the management structure is concerned with these posts and with the relationships between them. According to the size of the hotel and the particular arrangement in operation, the hotel chief executive may be variously designated as managing director, general manager or simply hotel manager. He may to a greater or lesser extent participate in the formulation of the hotel policies and strategies, and he is invariably responsible for their implementation and for the hotel performance. In larger hotels this level may be sub-divided between a managing director or general manager and the hotel manager or a resident manager. The former then reports to the board and normally co-ordinates the work of the specialist departments and of the hotel or resident manager, who is in turn responsible for the day-to-day management of the hotel activities.

The complexity and continuity of the hotel activities normally give rise to the need for one or more deputy or assistant managers.

A deputy hotel manager normally has authority over the heads of departments. But there is much variation in the role, authority and responsibilities of hotel assistant managers. In some instances they are the hotel manager's deputies in all but name, in respect of the whole operation or some parts of it, *e.g.* food and beverages, front hall, 'back of the house', and so on; in other cases they have these specific responsibilities in addition to their general role as the manager's deputies.

All the roles described above may be appropriate in particular circumstances, but effective hotel management calls for a clear definition of responsibility and authority. The relationships with heads of departments are especially important in this context. Titles, which describe the particular roles, can be helpful in this direction. In order to provide clear-cut lines of responsibility and authority and an effective co-ordination of related activities, some hotels function without assistant managers as such: those who would normally be in such positions are allocated specific responsibilities and appropriate titles to describe them.

Those in positions of heads of departments fall into two distinct categories. Heads of operated departments are known as line managers, with direct lines of responsibility and authority to their superiors and to their subordinates in respect of each operated department. Heads of service departments are specialists who provide advice and service to line management, and relieve them of such specialist tasks as are considered to be more effectively discharged through the appointment of specialists; they have no direct authority over employees other than those of their own departments. Line management includes *e.g.* head receptionists, head housekeepers, head chefs, and restaurant managers.

It is also relevant to refer in this context to a confusion, which often arises with various trainee positions. It is difficult to justify such titles as 'trainee manager' unless its holder has been designated to fill a specific post, for which he is training. A person who is undergoing training with a view to an ultimate unspecified position of responsibility is more appropriately described as a management trainee.

Organization Structure of a Large Hotel

Some of the concepts discussed in this chapter are illustrated in the organization chart of a large London hotel with several hundred rooms, extensive food and beverage facilities, and several hundred employees (Chart 1). In this instance a conscious attempt has been made to introduce a management structure designed to reduce the span of control of those concerned with the co-ordination of related activities and to provide a high degree of delegation.

Each position in the chart carries specific responsibilities and also overall responsibilities common to all management positions, such as the implementation of policy in relation to sectional requirements, employee motivation, training, safety, adherence to budgets and accountability for the performance and results of the department(s), for which a particular individual is responsible. However, each individual is responsible only for those results, which he can control.

The organization chart is supported by schedules of management responsibilities, which state for each position the title, the responsibilities of the post, the immediate superior, the relationships with other management positions within the organization, as well as the requirements of the post in terms of age, education, training, experience, and any special requirements.

A 'principle of three' has been introduced in this hotel in decision making. For example, menu planning for each outlet is undertaken by the food and beverage manager, the chef, and the appropriate departmental head; full-time members of staff are engaged by the personnel officer, the immediate, and the next but one 'superior of the employee.

Chart 1. Organization Chart of a Large Hotel

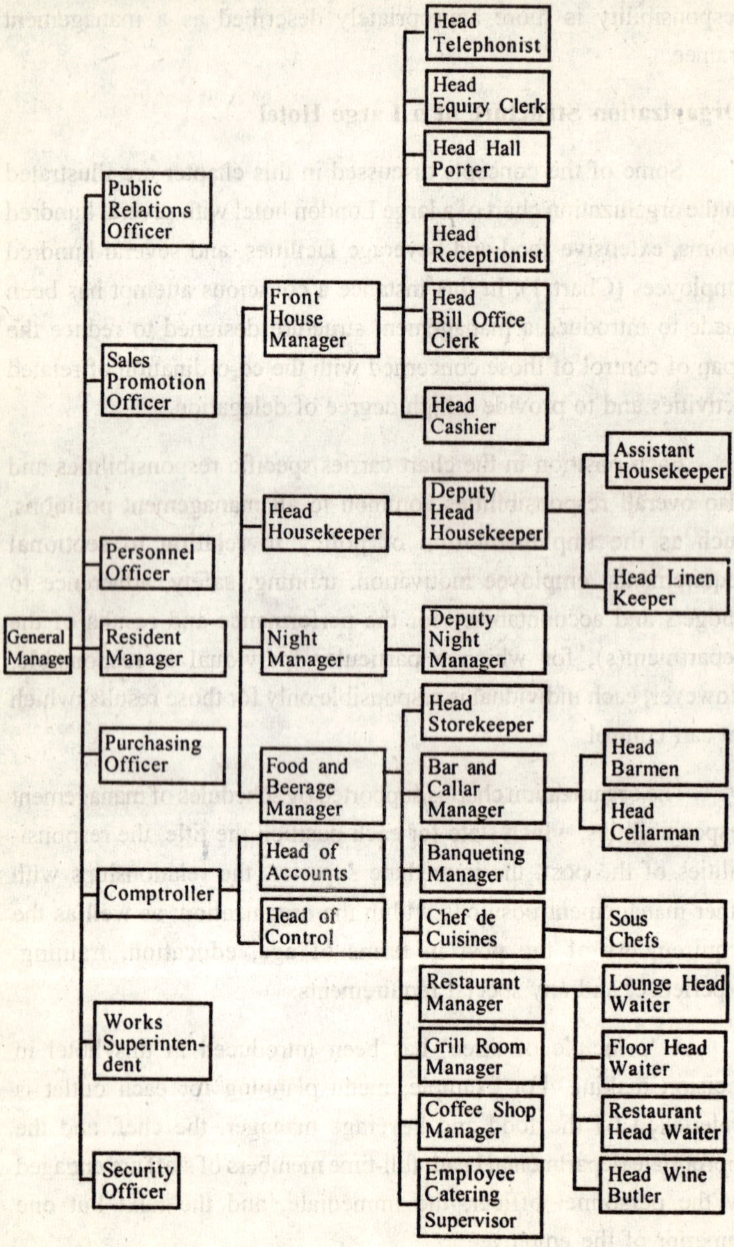

In relation to menu planning this approach is considered helpful in securing maximum utilization of kitchen facilities and in giving full recognition to the position of each departmental manager. In relation to staff engagement the principle is considered to be conductive to good selection, to creating a favourable impression on future employees, to securing the acceptance of new employees by their superiors, and to establishing a close knowledge of employees by management.

Accounting and Control

In hotel uniform and standard systems of accounts operational expenses relating to the whole hotel, as distinct from those relating to particular operated departments, are treated as undistributed operating expenses. They are commonly classified in four main groups: administrative and general; marketing; energy; property operation and maintenance. The first category, administrative and general expenses, covers in broad terms payroll and other expenses of general management, personnel management, accounting and control.

❑

6

Housekeeping, Safety and Sanitation

Housekeeping, which is one of the most labour-intensive functions and largest cost-centers in the hotel, is very important. However, it is neither universally understood nor respected by the bulk of the hotel's department managers, employees, and to a large extent, guests and clients. There are some encouraging signs, however, that this situation is swiftly changing.

Some hotel companies are experimenting with taking housekeeping out or the rooms division and making it a staff function, with the director of housekeeping reporting directly to the general manager. Others are combining housekeeping and other property management functions such as maintenance and engineering. One study found over 60 percent of the housekeeping managers responding were college graduates and over 40 percent were male. This tends to refute the traditional stereotype of the director of housekeeping as a female who has worked her way up through the ranks of the housekeeping hierarchy.

Information on hotel housekeeping administration has traditionally been organized around models as set forth in textbooks that date back to the 1951 treatment of hospital housekeeping by LaBelle and Barton. Brigham focused her analysis of the structure of the housekeeping functions and responsibilities on the small hotel. Tucker and Schneider, Schneider and Tucker, and Martin have provided a comprehensive inventory of the theoretical constructs, responsibilities, relationships, and techniques important to the modern housekeeper in a range of operational situations.

These works present information in a structure similar to that used in Holiday Inn University's housekeeping curriculum, which says the housekeeper administers "four major areas of responsibility."

1. Management of people, equipment, and supplies.
2. Preservation of building finishes, fabrics, and furnishings.
3. Controlling costs.
4. Keeping records.

In analysing the differences between the "folklore and fact" of the manager's job, Mintzberg concluded that there were substantial differences between what the popular or academic notion of managers' jobs entailed and what managers actually did.

The research mentioned above grew out of similar curiosities: what is the relationship between all that has been written about housekeeping and what housekeeping directors themselves deem important.

A survey was sent to a national sample of house keeping executives asking them to rate, on a scale of 1 to 5, the importance of 100 thepretical constructs common to the housekeeping literature. Statistical procedures grouped the housekeepers' responses into eight groupings. While the traditional responsibilities of records, costs, supplies, and furnishings were still important, the issues central to the management of people were of overwhelming importance. Specifically highlighted were the following:

— Leadership

— Communication

— Strategic planning

— Hotel organizational interactions

— Departmental management

— Training

The authors concluded that new arrangements of traditional knowledge, constructs, and tactics such as those explored in their model may present future managers with windows of operational, educational, or marketing opportunity to improve competitive position or streamline the transfer of knowledge. The dissemination of this knowledge in the most efficient and effective manner is also important, for, as Mintzberg points out, "the manager is challenged to find systematic ways to share his privileged knowledge." Since 1985 there has still been very little if any analytic empirical research done on operational aspects of housekeeping and other labour-intensive hotel departments. Until such a time as there is, there will be little forward movement in the "theory" of housekeeping. There is, though, no lack of inspirational practical experimentation on the part of housekeeping managers.

Housekeeping Organizations

Hospitality is the cordial and generous reception and entertainment of guests or strangers, either socially or commercially. From this definition we get the feeling of the open house and the host with open arms; of a place in which people can be cared for. Regardless of the reasons people go to a home away from home, there is the presumption that they will need to be cared for. They will need a clean and comfortable place to rest or sleep, food service, an area for socializing and meeting other people, access to stores and shops, and secure surroundings. Americans have often been described as a people on the move, a mobile society. Even as our country expanded we required bed and board, Travellers in. the early 1700s found a hospitality similar to that in countries of their origin, even though these new accommodations might have been in roadhouses, missions, or private homes, and the housekeeping might have included no more than a bed of straw that was changed weekly.

Facilities in all parts of young America were commensurate with the demands of the travelling public, and early records indicate that a choice was usually available, based on where you might find the best food, overnight protection, and dean facilities. Even though the inns were crude, they were gathering places where you could gather the news of the day, socialize, learn the business of the area, and rest. The business of innkeeping has graduated to become the hotel industry of today, but the main components remain: a clean, comfortable room, access to food and entertainment facilities, and a courteous and concerned staff who mean it when they say, "may we be of service."

Housekeeping departments play a vital role in today's lodging industry. People involved in housekeeping operations service guest rooms, maintain and service public and special areas, and in many instances, operate laundry, recreational, and health facilities.

In addition, the people of housekeeping are a part of the overall team of hosts and hostesses who add their own welcome to hotel guests. They show concern and care when something goes wrong with the guest's visit, and they are quick to initiate action that will make things right again. Major hotel companies have been quick to recognize the value of housekeeping and other service industry workers. Good hotel maaagement does not see housekeeping work as demeaning or menial. To the contrary, all operational management personnel in quality hotels have at one time or another performed housekeeping functions and, as a result, understand the worth and value of those people who perform such functions regularly.

The Rooms Department

Front Desk and Housekeeping

The rooms department of a lodging establishment is the department that is directly and solely involved with all aspects of the sale, occupancy, and servicing of guest rooms. It is managed by a person usually called the resident manager. Although the title is somewhat misleading in that it presupposes that the resident manager lives on the premise, most do not. Other titles synonymous with resident management are rooms manager, rooms director, director of rooms operations, or, simply, hotel manager. The rooms department is usually thought of as a combination of two principal operating departments—the front office and the housekeeping department. The manager in charge of the front office oversees several sub-departments: reservations, front desk, bell staff, PBX, transportation, possibly concierge, and any other form of guest reception function.

The manager in charge of all housekeeping functions is most commonly known as the executive housekeeper. Depending on the size of the hotel, other subdepartments may come within the housekeeping sphere of operations, such as an in-house laundry or recreation department and, in some cases, corporate policy. The person in charge of housekeeping may have anyone of a number of different titles, all considered synonymous with executive housekeeper. A few such titles are:

(a) Housekeeper

(b) Housekeeping manager

(c) Director of services

(d) Director of internal services

(e) Director of housekeeping operations

For the purposes of this chapter, all such responsibilities will be considered functions of the manager known as the executive housekeeper. At one time most executive housekeepers worked under the direction of the front office manager. They were, in fact, not executives but people who had worked their way up from a maid's position and had little or no training as a manager. Today, however, the size, cost, and complexity of housekeeping operations have put the executive housekeeper on an equal footing with other department managers. As a result, they now have equal responsibility under the resident manager for the operation of rooms departments.

The hotel industry is a highly labour intensive business. There may be more total employees involved in food and beverage operations than in any other area. Also, because of the diversity of such operations (restaurants, lounges, banquet services, and kitchen), there are usually more managers to control the total operation. In housekeeping, however, there is one department head (the executive housekeeper) who is responsible for the largest staff, operating cost-center, and physical area of the property.

Today's modem executive housekeeper must be a trained manager skilled in planning, organizing, staffing, directing, and controlling operations. He or she must also be skilled in employee and human relations, have a superior knowledge in cost controls, and have a strong technical background in purshasing, decorating, and renovation. Last but not least, the executive housekeeper must be an able delegator. Without a strong expertise and inclination to delegate tasks to others, convey the necessary power to act, and, finally, hold others accountable for their actions, the executive housekeeper must personally perform all working functions. And this writer has never found the person yet who could make 3,000 beds in one day.

Housekeeping organizations are as varied as there are types and sizes of hotels. Except for the very small bed and breakfast operations, the trend today is away from the 80-room mcm-and-pop hotel. For the purposes of discussing housekeeping organizations, it is appropriate to have as a model a hotel whose size would allow for the greatest variation.

The organization to be discussed would fit any hotel of 200 or more rooms. In most hotels greater or smaller than that number, there would be identical functions, but size would dictate that one person might perform several such functions in the smaller hotel. Obviously, the larger the facility, the greater the need for a big staff, with more individuals to fill each unique function. Consider then, the following hotel:

(a) Modern suburban corporate transient hotel

(b) Three hundred fifty rooms

(c) Two restaurants (one 24 hours and one dinner-hours only)

(d) Banquet area with 15,000 square feet of meeting space

(e) Room service

(f) Kitchen to support all food services.

(g) Main lounge with nightly entertainment

(h) Banquet beverage service, and service bar outlets for both restaurants and room service

(i) Outdoor pool, and winter indoor pool with health club facilities, sauna, and steamroom

(j) Game room (video games, pool, and table tennis)

(k) In-house laundry for rooms department and banquet linen

(l) Two company-owned gift shops

(m) Fully computerized front desk with a property-management system

Hotel Organization

Prior to investigating the housekeeping department organization, it is helpful to visualize the organization for the entire hotel.

Executive housekeepers may occupy greater or lesser positions in any organization. Some executive housekeepers might report directly to the general manager; others might hold corporate executive positions; and still others might report to the chief of maintenance. In this case, however, our executive housekeeper occupies the position of a middle manager, a full department head equal to the front office manager and the other principal department heads within the staff. There are two junior managers who will report to the executive housekeeper, the housekeeping manager and the laundry manager. Both the executive housekeeper and front office manager report to the resident manager, who is a member of the property's executive committee. This committee is the top policy-making body for the property under the general manager.

The Housekeeping Organization

The housekeeping manager is the first assistant to the executive housekeeper and has been placed in direct charge of all guest rooms in the hotel. This emphasizes the delegation that has taken place, the housekeeping manager is not just an assistant to the executive housekeeper but a Junior manager with a functional responsibility. There are several ways in which this part of the organization can be managed. The individual room attendants can be scheduled independently or they may be grouped into work teams. In this illustration, team staffing and scheduling provide for a more efficient technique of daily scheduling.

The laundry offers another utilization of a junior manager. In this case, the technical expertise required is more specific. Such expertise would inclutie knowledge of commercial laundry machinery and equipment, knowledge of piecework production, the utilization of chemicals, and their resultant effects on an expensive inventory of linen. Both junior managers and the executive housekeeper have line supervisors who report directly to them. Each supervisor in turn would have one or more hourly workers who report to them. Below the management level, employees are paid by the hour at a given wage as opposed to being on salary.

The organization under the housekeeping manager is incomplete. The number of floor supervisors, (or team leaders) needed, along with room attendants and other team members, depends upon the number of rooms each room attendant might be expected to clean in a given eight-hour period. The national standard for rooms cleaned by one room attendant in one eight-hour period varies from 13 to 20 rooms, depending on the market mix of the hotel occupancy. Hotels occupied primarily by travelling or group business transient guests are more efficient to clean since single occupancy prevails and such guests depart their rooms early each day. Also, they tend to leave their rooms in a lesser state of disarray. In such cases, room attendants can clean from 18 to 20 rooms per day.

When there is more double occupancy, such as with families on vacation, access to rooms for cleaning is more difficult and will cut into the efficiency of staffing. In such cases, room attendants will not be able to clean as many rooms in the same eight-hour period.

Staffing and Scheduling Concerns

In the case of our model hotel of 350 rooms, assume an 18-room workload per day. On any 100 percent occupancy day we would need approximately 20 room attendants to clean all guest rooms. Placing these room attendants in teams of five under one floor supervisor creates a need for four such supervisors. Also, assume that one section housekeeping aide will be assigned to each team to handle corridor cleaning, provide certain services to room attendants during the day, and care for other public areas within the guest room portion of the hotel. Finally, assume that five laundry workers will be needed in the laundry regularly, and that persons hired to relieve room attendants on days off can also fill in for the laundry workers.

The complete organization should now come into focus, except for one remaining concern. Hourly personnel cannot work seven days a week but are usually confined to a five-day work schedule. The following formula can serve to fulfil. the entire room-cleaning, laundry, and relief staff requirement. It increases the staff to allow for days off for regular room attendants, laundry workers; floor supervisors, and section housekeeping aides. At 100 percent occupancy on a continuous basis:

Regular staff × seven days =

Total staff × five-day maximum

$$S_1 \times 7 = S_2 \times 5$$

$$S_2 = S_1 \times 7 + 5$$

For our model hotel, $S_2 = 25 \times 7 \div 5 = 35$ total working staff, all limited to a five-day workweek. The additional ten employees can be organized into two special teams identical in composition to the regular teams and the laundry workforce.

These two teams would be "swing teams," relieving all regular and laundry personnel teams two days a week and having two days off them selves. This portion of the organization can now be scheduled to work by team units rather than as individual workers, which greatly simplifies personnel scheduling.

The functions to be performed by the balance of the housekeeping organization are noted. For purposes of illustration, these functions must be scheduled individually.

Specifically, personnel required for the second shift, persons required to staff the linen room housekeeping communications central, and personnel organized under the senior housekeeping aide for public area cleaning and maintenance round out the total department staff.

The entire housekeeping department staff might then resemble the organization provided in the Staffing Guide, which is a document created to accurately list the need for total personnel. Every position within the department is listed and can be used as a guide to fill vacancies when they occur.

This identification system shows which are regular teams, laundry teams, and swing teams. This particular staffing guide presumes that a 100 percent staff has been hired to support an occupancy averaging 85 percent or more for an extended period of time. Should occupancies be forecast as a lesser amount, a 100 percent staff need not be hired, and staff vacancies can be distributed over the entire team network. Fluctuations in daily occupancy should be dealt with by scheduling down within each team on a fair and equitable basis. Nsneed to schedule down because of daily occupancy can be delegated to the floor supervisor, but controls must be in place to guarantee fairness to all who will lose work due to low occupancy.

Personnel and Jobs in the Housekeeping Department

The basic function and scope of responsibility will be indicated for managers' positions and for hourly jobs; titles and responsibilities will be listed. Where several different names or titles apply to the same function in the hourly structure, each name will be noted.

The Executive Housekeeper

The executive housekeeper usually assumes complete direction, operational control, and supervision of the housekeeping, laundry, and recreation departments. The scope of responsibility is normally broad to ensure that the incumbent is given the freedom necessary to do the job. This position is now recognized as a step enhancing future career growth. The executive housekeeper is to operate the departments under his or her control in the most efficient manner possible through effective application and enforcement of company policies, the use of methods described in standard operating procedures, and the use of sound management principles. The incumbent is primarily responsible for the cleanliness of guest rooms and public areas assigned to the housekeeping department. The incumbent will accomplish tasks through proper training, motivation, and supervision of all personnel assigned to the housekeeping, laundry, and recreation departments.

The Housekeeping Manager

In the model organization the housekeeping manager assumes primary responsibility for guest room cleaning and servicing and acts as the primary assistant to the executive housekeeper. Under the direction of the executive housekeeper, the incumbent is responsible for the efficient and orderly management of guest room cleaning, servicing, and the reporting of room status. He or she represents those employees directly involved in room cleaning, and should be directly involved in their work schedules. In doing scheduling, he or she must take into account occupancy in order that costs be kept under control.

The Laundry Manager

The laundry manager normally assumes primary responsibility for operation of the hotel's in-house commercial laundry. He or she will also act as second assistant to the executive housekeeper. Under direction of the executive housekeeper, the incumbent is responsible for the efficient and orderly management and operation of the hotel laundry. Through the proper use of personnel assigned, the laundry manager will provide clean linen to the house and to the banquet department according to plans and budgets.

Hourly Employees

The Guest Room Attendant

The guest room attendant is also known as the GRA, maid, or section housekeeper. The incumbent to this position is primarily responsible for guest room cleaning and servicing. He or she is usually assigned a workload of a designated number of rooms to be cleaned each day. In general, the room attendant performs the same functions in each room assigned. The room attendant will also conduct certain room checks at set times to assist in determining the condition of the house. These conditions include rooms occupied, rooms ready (vacant and ready to rent), and rooms on-change (vacant but not yet serviced, also known as checkouts).

The room attendant will also participate in "general" cleaning (in-depth cleaning) one or more room each day as it is serviced in order to keep quality standards high. Most room attendants work in compliance with standard operating procedures (SOPs), which may specify as many as 60 items that must meet a given standard in each guest room. This is not as foreboding as it may sound, but the SOP system guarantees coverage where necessary. Finally, the room attendant should reload his or her own linen cart at the end of each workday. If the hotel is so organized, the room attendant will be one of several members of a housekeeping team under a floor supervisor.

The Section Housekeeping Aide

The section housekeeping aide was previously called the section houseman. The incumbent to this position works in the guest room portion of the hotel, attending to the regular and daily cleaning of corridors, elevator cabs and landings, stairwells, service areas, floor linen rooms, vending areas, and other special or unique public spaces in the vicinity of the guest rooms.

The section housekeeping aide also provides help to room attendants when associated with a general cleaning, if necessary. He or she will also remove soiled linen and rubbish from room attendant's carts on a regular schedule and will bring supplies from storerooms to floor linen rooms when needed. The section housekeeping aide works at the direction of the floor supervisor, and, when the hotel is so organized, also works as a member of a housekeeping team.

The Floor Supervisor

The floor supervisor as also sometimes known as the senior housekeeper or inspectress. Floor supervisors are team leaders, having several room attendants and a section housekeeping aide reporting to them. They are assigned to specific divisions of the room section of a property and are responsible for the quality of work performed in the several room sections to which their room attendants are assigned. They also are responsible for the public sectors assigned to their section housekeeping aides. They make inspections and reports and are in all respects supervisors of the persons assigned to their teams. They also assist in the personnel administration of the people assigned to them. The alternative title of inspectress may be a misnomer. Many floor supervisors are inspectresses by virtue of the fact that they also inspect rooms. Other inspectresses do nothing but inspect rooms, reporting directly to the manager on what they observe, but they have no responsibility to correct discrepancies where found because no staff is assigned to them for work purposes.

The Senior Housekeeping Aide

The senior housekeeping aide is a major supervisor in the housekeeping department. He or she is usually placed in charge of all public areas not directly associated with guest rooms. Lobbies, major public corridors, public restrooms, offices, and other areas specifically negotiated as part of the overall housekeeping responsibility are the domain of the senior housekeeping aide. He or she is usually responsible for basic training of section housekeeping aides and for supervision of utility housekeeping aides who might perform specific tasks such as shampooing carpets, washing windows, or project work.

The senior housekeeping aide often assumes responsibility for the storage and accountability of cleaning and guest supply inventories. He or she normally works as a supervisory assistant to the executive housekeeper and performs such other tasks as that person might direct.

The Night Supervisor

The night supervisor presumes a second shift that has no management regularly assigned to it. This can vary depending on the size and complexity of night operations.

Other than intermittent visits by housekeeping management, the night supervisor assumes total control of the department after the major room and hotel cleaning for each day have been concluded.

The night supervisor works closely with the hotel night manager, is usually on a beeper, and makes routine inspections throughout the hotel until the department is secured each evening at the designated time. The night supervisor, like the senior housekeeping aide, is a major supervisor within the department.

The Laundry Supervisor

Working as a principal assistant to the laundry manager, the laundry supervisor oversees the activities of the laundry attendants. Normally the laundry supervisor is the head washperson and is in charge of all major wash equipment and chemicals.

The incumbent to this position would also supervise the workload process and production. In our model hotel, when the laundry supervisor and team of laundry attendants are scheduled off, a swing team supervisor would assume the responsibilities of the laundry supervisor and world bring his or her swing team into the laundry. Since there are two swing teams, with each swing team working in the laundry one day each week, this provides the entire department with maximum flexibility and training.

The Linen Room Supervisor

The main linen room is actually the hub of housekeeping communication and activity of the hotel. As a result, this physical service area might be better described as "housekeeping central" The linen room supervisor under the executive housekeeper is in charge of main linen room operations.

Maintaining and operating the communication link to the front desk, engineering, and to each guest in need of housekeeping attention are the prime responsibilities associated with the job of the linen room supervisor. In addition, the linen room supervisor is sometimes referred to as the chief status operator for housekeeping.

The Recreation Supervisor

In our model hotel, the recreation supervisor under the direct supervision of the executive housekeeper would assume responsibility for all recreation areas of the hotel. All swimming pool attendants would work for the recreation supervisor and would be fully Red Cross water-safety-instructor-qualified. Pool attendants under the direction of the recreation supervisor would also service the health club, sauna, and game room to provide service to guests, cleanliness, and maintenance of order.

Other Employees

Other employees might be found in the housekeeping department, and their title indicates their activity and who they might work for. Almost all positions have titles appropriate to either a male or female employee and are therefore nonsexist. Such positions are as follows:

— Utility housekeeping aide

— Linen room attendant

— Lobby housekeeping aide

— Seamstress

— Laundry attentlant

— Housekeeping trainer.

New Horizons in Housekeeping

The National Executive Housekeeper's Association (NEHA) has long recognized that persons performing housekeeping functions in hospitals, hotels, and nursing homes have similar responsibilities. NEHA draws its membership not only from hotels, retirement centers, and contract cleaning establishments but also from hospitals and nursing homes. Also, the movement of management personnel between these fields is well documented.

When asked how difficult it is for a manger to make the transition from one field to another, a member in hospital service once remarked, "The main function of housekeeping in both areas is to clean rooms and public areas, and to dispose of trash and rubbish. There is only one major difference, however, and that is in hospitals, we know exactly what we are walking into, and in hotels, you don't know what you may be dealing with." That was true—until the advent of the AIDS crisis.

On December 2, 1991, new federal rules issued by OSHA made it mandatory that employers provide to all employees who might come in contact with human blood or other bodily fluids as a result of their job classification with information and training. Employers must comply with federal precautions designed to maintain a safe workplace with regard to bloodborne pathogens.

Specifically, department managers must establish control plans to combat the threat and to provide access for employees to read and understand the OSHA compliance standard. Employees such as housekeeping and laundry personnel, who as a part of their regular duties, may come in contact with bodily fluids such as blood, semen, sputum, vomit, or spent needles that have been discarded in the trash by diabetics or drug users, must be advised of the potential dangers.

Furthermore, they must be trained and tested in how to handle such risks when they occur, and they must be offered the opportunity to be inoculated against the HBV (Hepatitis B) virus at company expense. Records must be kept of all training conducted and of all exposures that occur.

A Cost-saving Approach to Housekeeping

Like many hotel operators, Country Hospitality has had to deal with labour shortages in certain markets. We have dealt successfully with this shortage in our housekeeping department by developing an innovative compensation plan similar to one that the manufacturing industry has relied upon for years. By paying housekeepers by the room cleaned, instead of by the hour, our properties have recorded increased productivity, cost control, and staff retention.

The Plan

Most lodging properties pay housekeepers by the hour, but hourly rates do not give employees a strong incentive to achieve maximum productivity. Because the employees are being paid for their time, managers often spend their time monitoring the length of employees' breaks and the time employees spend stocking carts and cleaning rooms. Time that could be spent on training is used to babysit employees. Instead of concentrating on effectiveness (clean rooms), managers must concentrate on employees' activity levels.

Boosting Productivity

Productivity improves immediately when housekeepers are paid by the room. The employees quickly recognize that more efficient work means higher wages. With the opportunity to make more money by working more efficiently, many room cleaners increase their productivity.

In our Burnsville Country Inn, housekeepers regularly clean 2.5 to 3 rooms per hour. That figure represents a productivity increase of 25 to 50 percent over our old hourly system. Needless to say, the increased productivity reduced the housekeeping payroll. When the programme started, we expected that each housekeeper would clean one room each half hour. To determine the wage per room, we divided our existing hourly wage by two. So, housekeepers who were paid $5.00 per hour were to be paid $2.50 per room.

After observing the actual productivity of 2.5 to 3 rooms per hour, we increased our benchmark productivity level to 2.25 rooms per hour and reduced our per-room payment to $2.22, a cost reduction of 11 percent (but still $5.00 per hour). The housekeepers did not oppose that change because they knew there would be plenty of days when they could beat the productivity benchmark. On weekdays, for instance, the Burnsville property attracts a large number of single business travellers whose rooms are relatively quick to clean.

By paying housekeepers by the room, our managers instantly gained a grip on costs. The system ensures that the hotel achieves its budget targets for the cost per room cleaned, since that amount has been established from the outset. In contrast, the hourly payment system required managers to ensure that housekeepers meet their expected productivity levels so that the hotel could meet its budgeted cost per room cleaned.

Seasonal Factors

Paying by the room is particularly effective at hotels with a strong seasonal business. During slow times, managers struggle to. give all their housekeepers a full work week. Housekeepers are torn between their responsibility to meet expected productivity guidelines and their desire to generate as many hours and dollars as they can. Rather than try to maximize the number of hours worked, housekeepers under the pay-per-room system will be anxious to get to work, get their rooms cleaned, and go home.

The pay-per-room system also allows managers to reduce the number of full-time housekeepers needed. Since most properties have occupancy peaks and valleys, they often swing from being overstaffed to understaffed, depending on the time of year.

Nothing is more frustrating to managers than recruiting, hiring, and training new employees, only to lay them off or have them quit when there isn't enough work. The employee, too, is frustrated by the lack of hours. Since housekeepers are paid by the room cleaned, managers can challenge and encourage them to clean additional rooms during the high season, thus enabling the property to get by with a smaller staff. The housekeepers make more money during the busy time and do not face the prospect of being laid off.

Beating Turnover

This system also reduces turnover and hiring costs. Because they have partial control over how much they earn by working more effectively, our housekeepers are enjoying their work more than before. Turnover at the Burnsville property has declined considerably, and it is attracting better applicants because current employees recommend the hotel to their friends.

SAFFTY

Sense of safety is the foremost prerequisite in hotel industry. Safety consideration is very vital not only for the guests but for the welfare of the hotel staff also. The safe atmosphere free from possible accidental hazards not only provides peace of mind but also assures the operators not to worry about possible claims and compensations in lieu of damages to lives and properties of the guests. Some major safety precautions applicable to hotel business in particular are discussed on the following heads:

Safe clothing

Safe storing

Safe floors

Safe doors and drawers

Safety with containers

Fire safety

Safe handling of food preparation equipment

Safe handling of machines

Safe handling of dishes

Safe handling of knives

Safe handing of Insecticides of pesticides.

There is a popular saying "Prevention is better than cure" and the person in charge of a kitchen should foresee the possible causes of accident and eliminate them.

Safety-instructions should be displayed properly and the attention of the kitchen staff directed to them.

One major cause of accidents lack of knowledge of the right way to do things, or by deliberately or thoughtlessly doing things the wrong way. Most accidents are caused because of excessive haste: WalkDon't Ever Run or Slide!

The Work environment conditions affect the safety of staff. A smooth working environment which creates among staff an interest, satisfaction and contentment with work contributes much, not only to improved job performance, but also to a reduced accident rate.

Work performance is greatly affected by external environmental influences. Illness at home, financial problems etc. can cause a worker's concentration to wander, and a chef can quite absentmindedly fail to use a kitchen cloth when picking up a hot cooking pot.

Negligence of similar nature can occur as a result of poor health.

Alcohol and drugs abuse have fatal effect upon the safety of the worker.

A strict vigil and watch must be kept on misbehaving and absent minded staff or who arc involved in general horseplay, within the kitchen such action may lead to serious accidents.

Guidelincs for Safety. We have categorised various safety measure systematic way which will help over the accidents.

Safety Precautions. Safety rules should cover personnel, equipment and premises from the following aspects:

Safe Clothing. Ensure that protective clothing is worn;

Safe shoes with closed toes.

Sensible heels provide balance

Do not wear loose clothing, you may easily get caught,

Safe Storing. When opening boxes, remove nails. Don't bend them down.

Store heavy materials on bottom shelves, medium weight next above, light weight on top.

Food containers should always be covered provided when in actual use.

When opening anything keep away from food containers, they might catch splinters, bits of paper wrapping etc.

Get rid of dirt, trash and grease to reduce fire hazard.

Use ladders, not boxes and chairs to get things from high shelves. A void loosing your balance.

Store full containers below eye level.

Don't overload trolleys.

Don't carry bulky objects too big for you to see over or around.

Safe Floors. Keep floors in good repair, dry and clean.

Clean up spillage promptly.

Tile floors may be slippery when weather is humid, be careful to avoid falls.

Never leave utensils on the floor, someone might trip over them. Walk-don't run or slide.

Safe Doors and Drawers. Be careful in closing drawers, they might pinch fingers and hand. Open and close doors by handles.

Safety with Containers. Don't overflow containers.

Place food scraps in protected sanitary containers.

Keep hands out of mechanized garbage disposal machines.

Fire Safety. Smoke only in designated areas. Report any fire immediately.

Know where the fire extinguishers are located and how each should be used.

Know the fire exits.

Follow the fire instructions.

Have fire doors, exits, staircases clear of equipment.

Don't let grease accumulate on grill canopies and filters.

Point out the location of switches to shut off electricity supply.

Safe Handling of Food Preparation Equipment. Use only dry cloth, towels, to handle hot cooking utensils.

Lift edge over cover on side of pot away from you first, so that steam does not blast into your face.

Don't peak into open steam kettles.

Keep handles of pans away from the stove and out of the size so that they won't be brushed off.

Get help in moving hot, heavy containers.

Keep oven doors closed and out of aisle, when not in use.

Ventilate a gas oven several minutes before lighting. Strike matches away from clothing. Open gas gradually.

Don't clean ovens and stoves before they are cool.

Protect food from foreign substances.

Avoid overfilling containers with hot liquids or foods.

Warn service people of hot dishes.

Safe Handling of Machines. Ensure that machines are kept in good working order and are operated correctly.

Never use any machines you have not been trained to use.

Be sure that all safety devices are in place before use.

Put plug into "off" position before cleaning or adjusting the machine.

Check all switches.

Don't start a mixing machine until the bowl or the kettle is locked.

Always use the proper tool for pushing food into the grinder.

Particular care must be exercised in cleaning the slicing machine.

Pull the plug-turn the gauge to zero-don't touch the edge of the cutting blade-clean the blade from the center out-while cleaning hold a protective cloth in the other hand to use in rotating the blade.

Safe Handling of Dishes. Take care in handling dishes and glasses. Sweep up large pieces of broken glass with broom; use dampened paper towel to pick up silvers.

Put broken glass or china in a special container. Chipped or cracked glassware should be discarded. If you suspect broken glass in soapy water, drain water first. Don't use cups to hold disinfectants and solvents.

Safe Handling of Knives. Use knives correctly and store them correctly.

Cut away from you body, and away from fellow workers:

When drying a knife, keep sharp edge away from your body.

Use cutting boards-never a knife edge against metal.

Keep all knives in proper storage place when not in use.

Don't leave knives anywhere where they can't be seen (sink)

A sharp knife is safer than a dull one.

Sharpen knives properly, Remove any additional steel burns. Never reach for a falling knife.

Use the knife for the operation for which it is intended.

Be careful when handling knives, pick them up by handles, not by blades.

Knives should be carried with the blade point downwards.

Never bone frozen meat, because knife would slip too easily.

Safe Handling and use of Insecticides & Pesticides. Because of the dangers involved, safety precautions for the use, storage, and disposal of pesticides and other hazardous materials are listed below. One should carefully observe the following:

1. Use a selective chemical that has the least effect on non-target species.
2. Treat only the area affected.
3. Take care to avoid the contamination of food and drinking water (for animals as well as man), streams and lakes and inhabited areas.
4. Time the treatments to coincide with the presence of the pests.
5. Use the most suitable chemicals and the minimum amounts needed to achieve the desired result.
6. Store chemicals in properly labelled containers out of reach of children and animals and away from food. Supplies should be kept in a separate locked building away from housing areas, food, animal feed, water supplies, children, and irresponsible persons and above the highest possible flood level. Do not transport chemicals in vehicles used for carrying people, food, animals or animal feed.
7. Follow the directions on the label exactly in preparing chemicals, and use the proper equipment when applying them.

8. A void inhalation of dusts and fumes and contacts with the skin, personnel should wear protective clothing and headgear, and change their clothing and wash thoroughly with soap and water after applying pesticides.
9. Do not spray on a windy day. Protect guests from accidental poisoning by pesticides.
10. Dispose of used or leaking pesticide containers immediately by burial to a depth of at least 45 cm (18 in) in an isolated marked area, downhill and at least 60 m (200 ft) from any water source and 1-2 m above the highest groundwater level. Do not bury containers in sandy soil.
11. Work in well ventilated areas. In confined areas wear an approved type of respirator. Wear a respirator for outdoor spraying or dusting organic phosphorus compounds.
12. Never transfer pesticides to unlabelled or mislabelled containers. Keep in clearly labelled containers.
13. Pesticides are toxic and hazardous; use with extreme caution. Security in hotel business covers many things and depending upon the social, political and other consideration the mode of security in hotels has to adopt appropriate metholls. There are two major aspects of security. One for the protection of the guest. Second is to protect the hotel premises and its properties and records.

For guest protection following major points should be taken care of:

1. Responsibility begins at the time of registration. Once the guest is registered, the hotel necessarily is concerned with the protection. The hotel's staff simultaneously needs to realize that it also must be concerned with protection.
2. The issue of guest security, including the guest's property, is one of the most difficult and delicate problem confronting hoteliers throughout the world. The difficulty largely is due

to the fact that most incidents would have been avoided, if the guests themselves were not so careless. The delicacy of the matter revolves around the question of how one educates guests on the subject of self protection without frightening them to the point where they avoid a particular property altogether.

Tent cards mention the availability of safe deposit boxes. Most guests ignore them. The answer to the question of guest education seems to lie with a combination of both verbal and written suggestions. For example, at registration time front desk personnel should ask specifically if guests would like to avail themselves of the safe-deposit-boxes. A written message would urge them (tent card in the guest room) not to leave valuables lying in drawers or on table tops, but rather to secure them.

3. A far more subtle, but not less important consideration involves control over information regarding the rooms to which guests have been assigned. The ease with which room assignment data can be obtained frequently has been used to advantage by persons intent upon every form of mischief ranging from bombings, robberies and assaults to celebrities. Concerned hoteliers should instruct both, switch board and front desk personnel that room assignments are not given out upon inquiry. All telephone calls for guests simply need to be put through to them, and messages can be taken in their absence. Such steps are designed to help protect guests and their property. However, for optimum effect other security factors such as patrols, employees training must be considered.

4. An overwhelming majority of front desk personnels will make keys available upon request, and without question. In most cases one need merely to walk to the desk to ask, may I have the key 926? Rarely will that person be asked

for a name to check against the information rack and to verify registration before the key is handed over.

Security of guest's automobiles must also be considered, (including contents). Two important deterrents to garage and lot of problems are adequate lighting, and a patrol force that makes regular, (unregular) frequent area inspections.

(1) Perimeter Security

(a) ***Entrances.*** The best way to provide this type of perimeter protection is to lock the door. Either using a kev also involving a person, or an electro-mechanical lock, controlled and activated at the front desk. The outside should be well illuminated.

This would be for the main door. One of the first things to be considered by management is the period, if any, during which the main entrance can be secured.

Two or possibly three other entrances still require attention in so far as perimeter protection is concerned. The Receiving Entrance Employees' Entrance Entrances from an outdoor swimming pool or car park.

(b) ***The Receiving Door.*** Should be heavy duty steel or aluminium, overhead or side coiling type, approved as a fire door. A window-type vision panel and pass door may be included.

The Receiving door should be opened only when necessary, preferably during predeterminated hours.

(c) ***The Employees' Entrance.*** If it is possible to secure the main entrance during certain prescribed hours, it is equally possible to close the employees' entrance. The periods will be determined by the time of shift changes. This should also be a fire door with steel frame, easily observed by the time-keeper/security guard.

(d) ***Other Doors.*** If there is a door the sole purpose of which is to provide direct access between a swimming pool and/ or a parking lot and the building, it would be closed and located at all times if activity is minimal. The hardware should be the same as that used on the emergency exits.

(e) ***Light.*** Is one of the least expensive but most effective deterrents to the commission of a wide variety of crimes.

(2) Internal Design, Sites of

(a) ***Securitytime-keepers Office.*** Should enable them to see clearly and easily every person entering and leaving *via* employees'/receiving entrance. If the time clock and time card racks are not located in his office, they should be in a place where he can easily see them. The office itself should be large enough to accommodate facilities for the safe storage of parcels brought to work by employees. This room should also be assigned as the Hotel Security Office.

(b) ***Receiving Clerk-Cost Controller.*** Their offices should be adjacent to the receiving platform. The Receiving Clerk should be located as close as possible to the receiving platform.

(c) ***Store Rooms.*** Should be placed near the receiving area, foodstuff-dry store, general store.

Storage areas for silver, linen, furnitures need not be.

Laundry, Uniform Issue and Housekeeping Operations should be in adjacent space.

(d) ***Personnel Office.*** Should have easy access to the employees entrance, for applicants employees as well as those already employed. The corridor leading from the entrance to the office should be easily observable by the time-keeper/Entrance Security Guard.

(e) ***Lobby.*** In planning lobby designs, every possible effort should be made to avoid having the front desk cashier near an exterior door or near a stair well. By the same token, the front desk should be so situated that duty personnels have a good view of the lobby generally, and an unobstructed view of both, the hotel main entrance and the passenger elevator bays. The space allocated for safe deposit boxes whether for guest or hotel use, may be incorporated with the front desk-cashier station, or it should be adjacent to and observable from that position.

(f) **The Hotels Telephone Operating Room.** Should not be near the stair well. From an operational point of view, it is a sensitive activity requiring some degree of protection.

(g) ***The Executive Offices.*** Should be accessible, but not to the extent that needless traffic or disruption is encouraged.

(h) ***Elevators.*** In designing new facilities, it is best to avoid combining pool and service lifts. Otherwise there will be virtually uncontrolled access to the entire house, especially between the hours of 11.00 p.m. to 7.00 a.m. when service is minimal if not non existent.

(3) Doors and Locks

Wood doors – generally offices rooms

Steel doors – store-rooms, F&B lockers, walk in refrigerators Doors leading to Head Cashier's office to Telephone operation Room.

Fire doors – must satisfy local requirements and acts if any.

Electro-mechanical locks for these and for the main door. Pad locks for refrigerated units.

Time recording locks on store rooms if available.

All types of stores, linen closets, house keeping supply rooms, general stores etc. should be locked at all times, except when appropriate staff are physically present.

(4) Storage and Protection of Valuables

(a) Safe deposit boxes are useful for the storage of guests' valuables. They also can be used by the hotel staff for the safe keeping of cashier's boxes and of certain select keys.

(b) Cash, other negotiables, and important records should be stored in secured facility.

(c) Other important records, such as personal files the same degree of protection as corporate records, insurance policies accounts receivable and payable, or contracts should be given. They should not be available for unauthorized persons. Standard metal like cabinets secured at the end of the working day are adequate.

There are other fields such as administrative, store, purchase and engineering and transport departments, where adequate security measures are to be taken to protect the loss and pilferage of properties in particular and to guard things from possible sabotage during the course of strike etc. Hotels having out door gardens, garden chairs, decorative light fittings etc. should accordingly arrange adequate security measures outside the buildings as well.

System of Key Control in Hotels

In hotels, guests rooms, entrances, doors to the various other rooms need locking system for security purposes. Age old process is to lock the rooms with good quality locks, latches and by similar other arrangements. In very sophisticated hotels, electronic door locks are now being used in many countries. The system is a development based on electronically linked computer located in a central place usually in the reception department. An electronic key looks like a piece of plastic coated card. Imprinted on the key are a number of notches making it useful for number of terms with different combinations. Electronic keys are lighter and easy to store and handle. Housekeeping staff are usually responsible for key control. Otherwise the job is looked after by security department staff or by staff deputed for the purpose by the management according to the hotel policy.

In Western type hotels, the following key systems are in use:

Grand Master Key. Usually kept by the duty officer or by the housekeeping manager. It works on every lock in the building—internal as well as external.

Master Key. This key works on any internal door

Sub Master Key. This is for a particular floor or for a section. It is kept by the floor housekeeper or by person responsible for the cleaning etc. of the floor.

Room Key. This is given to the guest when he checks in and is taken back when he checks out. It is usually attached to a long tag on which the room number is engraved. Sometimes hotel's name, address or logo are also engraved or written. The purpose is for easy location and prevent it from easily lost during use. All keys should be stored out of general view of the public. A record should be maintained each time after issue and return from the authorized staff for security purposes. It is also advisable to limit the number of unlocked entrances and exits. Never lend out room keys—or master keys.

SANITATION

Food Establishments

The main factors of health protection in food establishments are as follows:

1. cooking to proper internal temperature of pork (67°C), poultry, and all stuffed meats (74°C); holding of hot foods at 60°C, and thorough reheating (71°c) of refrigerated cooked food before service;
2. adequate refrigeration equipment and prompt and proper refrigeration (at 70°C) of perishable and prepared foods;

3. use of wholesome food and food ingredients;
4. cleanliness and good habits of personal hygiene in employees, who should be free from any communicable disease or infection transmissible through food or food service; a minimum handling of food;
5. clean surfaces for food preparation and adequate properly constructed equipment that is easily washed and sanitized;
6. structurally sound, dean facilities in good repair and adequately lighted and ventilated premises that can be properly cleaned;
7. an adequate supply of potable water (hot and cold), detergents and equipment for the cleaning and sanitization of dishes and utensils; elimination of connections or conditions that may permit backflow or backsiphonage of polluted or suspect water into the water supply piping or into equipment;
8. control of rodents, flies, cockroaches, and other vermin and proper use and storage of pesticides; and
9. proper storage of refuse and disposal of all liquid and solid wastes.

Personal Hygiene

All employees should wear clean outer garments, preferably uniforms supplied and cleaned daily by the management. The employees should maintain a high degree of personal cleanliness and observe hygienic practices while at work. Hands should be thoroughly washed after every break in food service operations, particularly after use of the toilet and after the handling of raw foods such as poultry and meat. A conveniently located wash hand basin with warm water, soap, and clean towels (in addition to those placed in the toilets) is necessary to facilitate personal hygiene and cleanliness.

Architectural Features

The structural soundness of the building housing the food establishment, the facilities provided, and the layout of equipment are also important for food hygiene. All outside openings should be screened during the fly season with 1.5 mm (l6-mesh) screens. The building should be of rodent-proof construction. Walls, floors and ceilings should be easy to clean. Adequate lighting and ventilation are needed in all working areas, storage rooms, passages and toilet rooms. Toilet and hand-washing facilities must be provided for the use of employees. Potable hot and cold water under pressure and proper sewage or other waste-water disposal system are essential requirements. Advice on the layout and design of new food establishments and the placement of equipment should be obtained from professional designers and health authorities.

Equipment Layouts

These should be planned efficiently as well as for easy cleaning and appropriate servicing. Temperature regulated equipments should properly confirm the temperature standards and in general, equipments should be corrosion resistant and non-toxic.

Main Plumbing Principles

While certain details of plumbing installations vary with location, the basic sanitary and safety principles are the same. The essential criteria are as follows:

1. **Adequate Water Requirements.** Plumbing fixtures, devices, and accessories shall be supplied with water in sufficient volume and at pressures adequate to enable them to function properly and without undue noise under normal conditions of use.

2. **Potable Water Supply.** All permanent premises intended for human habitation shall be provided with a supply of potable water. Such a water supply shall not be connected to unsafe water sources nor shall it be subject to the

hazards of backflow or backsiphonage. Faucets should not be provided on non-potable water lines in areas accessible to the public but if this is unavoidable the outlet must be labelled as urisafe and should preferably be operable only by means of a special key.

3. **Water Conservation.** Plumbing shall be designed and adjusted to use the minimum quantity of water consistent with its proper performance and cleaning requirements.

4. **Dangers of Explosion or Overheating.** Devices for heating and storing water shall be so designed and installed as to guard against dangers from explosion or overheating as well as risks of carbon monoxide poisoning and asphyxiation.

5. **Disposal of Wastes.** Every building with installed plumbing fixtures shall be served by an adequate sewerage system.

6. **Plumbing Fixture.** Plumbing fixtures shall be made of durable, smooth non-absorbent and corrosion-resistant materials and shall be free from concealed fouling surfaces. All such fixtures shall be protected by an air gap between the water outlet and fixture overflow rim, or by other approved means, from the possibility of backflow or backsiphonage.

7. **Drainage System of Adequate Size.** The drainage system shall bc designed, constructed and maintained to prevent undue noise and vibration fouling, deposit of solids, and clogging; it should be so arranged that pipes may readily be cleaned.

8. **Durable Materials.** The piping of the plumbing system shall be of durable material free from defective workmanship and be designed and constructed to give satisfactory service for a reasonable life span.

9. **Liquid Sealed Traps.** Each fixture directly connected to the drainage system shall be equipped with a liquid-seal

(non-siphoning) trap to prevent the entry of sewer gas into the building.

10. **Lighting and Ventilation.** No water closet or similar fixture shall be located in a room or compartment that is not properly lighted and ventilated.

11. **Prevention of Sewage Overflow.** Where a plumbing drainage system is subject to backflow of sewage from the sewer, suitable provision shall be made to prevent sewage overflow in the building.

12. **Proper Maintenance.** Plumbing systems shall be maintained in a safe and serviceable condition in relation to both mechanical functioning and health.

Storage and Protection of Cold Foods

Refrigeration equipment should be capable of maintaining perishable foods at a temperature of 7°C or below. Frozen foods are generally kept at or below-18°. The refrigerator capacity should be adequate for the needs of the establishment so that all perishable foods can be kept under refrigeration at all times. Cooling of cooked foods to room temperature prior to refrigeration permits the growth and multiplication of bacteria and the production of toxins that can cause foodborne illnesses. Prepared perishable food should be sliced or cut into small portions if necessary placed in shallow pans to a depth of 5-8 cm (2-3 in) and refrigerated within half an hour.

Storage and Protection of Hot Foods

Equipment used for keeping or serving hot food should be capable of maintaining the food at a temperature of atleast 60°C. At this temperature the growth of pathogenic organism is inhibited and destroyed in many cases.

Catering

Where food is prepared for off-the-premises service or consumption special additional measures are necessary to prevent food contamination and to inhibit the growth of micro-organisms. This applies to catering operations for airlines, railways, and bus companies, to group catering as well as to restaurants that use ready prepared foods. The food should at all times be protected from contamination by airborne contaminants, insects, rodents, and from handling during storage, transportation and service.

Facilities for maintaining proper refrigeration temperatures and for heating foods should be available at the place of service. Special precaution should be taken to keep hot food hot, and cold foods cold until they are served. If it is impracticable or undesirable to keep prepared foods at or above 60°C they should be chilled promptly and refrigerated at 7°C or below. Refrigerated foods as well as other unserved foods should be reheated, as previously noted to an internal temperature of 71°C just prior to service.

Cleaning and Sanitization of Eating and Drinking Equipments

All crockery, glassware, cutlery, and kitchen utensils should be cleaned and sanitized after use. Food preparation and serving equipment should be cleaned and sanitized as needed during the day. Separate arrangements are usually provided for washing and sanitizing glassware and cooking pots.

The use of approved types of automatic machines is recommended wherever possible for washing crockery, glassware, and cutlery. After washing the items should be rinsed in hot water at 82°C. Handwashing of eating and drinking equipments is acceptable if all items are thoroughly cleaned with hot water and an effective detergent and then rinsed in hot water at 82°C for at least 30 second (2 minutes is recommended). A booster heater in the form of an electric immersion heater or an under-sink gas heater is generally used to keep the water hot, and long handled baskets are essential for submerging washed dishes and utensils in a separate hot water sink, Immersion in a chlorine solution (or other disinfectant) providing at least 50 mg/litre of available chlorine for at least 2 minutes may also be acceptable to the health authorities in place of hot water disinfection.

However, chlorine or other chemical disinfection should not be used as a substitute for hot water. Washed and rinsed articles should be left in a rack or on a draining board to drain and air dry. When water at 82°C is used to sanitize equipment after washing, the heat retained is usually enough to produce rapid drying. Dry clothes should not be used because they may cause contamination and are in any case unnecessary if dishes and utensils are properly cleaned and sanitized in ideal situation.

Mosquito Control

Control must include attack of both larvae and adults, preference normally being given to the control of larvae. Larvae can be controlled through the following measures:

1. Empty and remove all water containers—Cans, jars, buckets, discarded tires etc. from the area.
2. Eliminate depressions, mud flats and other water holding areas by draining of filling.
3. Clear of vegetation likely to harbour larvae and if possible allow water levels to fluctuate to reduce the production of larvae.
4. Treat areas of water with light oil or insecticide against larvae.
5. Introduce top-feeding minnows, goldfish, or similar fish into established ornamental pools to consume larvae.
6. Screen or cover cisterns, water tanks, and other permanent water containers.

The residual fumigant dichlorvos is effective against the adult mosquito for periods of 2.5-3.5 months in enclosed spaces. One dichlorvos dispenser per 28 m^3 (1000 $ft.^3$) of space has been recommended but such dispensers should not be permitted in rooms where infants or sick or aged persons are confined or in areas where food is prepared or served.

Rodent and Insect Control

The proper management of hotels, tourist establishments and recreation areas includes effective control of insects and rodents since their presence can reduce the attractiveness of the area. In addition to being a nuisance many are actual vectors of disease while rodents can also cause economic damage and fire hazards. Many insecticides and rodenticides are available for controlling insects, pests and rodents but the use of these chemicals mus't be considered as a supplement to basic sanitation and other physical and biological control measures aimed at the elimination or control of breeding areas.

Some basic sanitation measures that are particularly applicable in hotels, motels, eating places, camping sites, and resort areas are as follows:

1. elimination or reduction of breeding areas by control of water impoundments, clearing of brush and use of rodent-proof construction methods for all buildings and other structures;
2. proper storage, collection, and disposal of refuse, including manure;
3. screening of doors and windows in all places of work and habitation;
4. pest control operations at regular intervals or as needed; and
5. special sanitation precautions for all food storage, preparation and service areas.

The success of insect and rodent control measures depends largely on the existence of a basic sanitation and environmental control programme. For example, the draining or filling of mosquito breeding areas, if feasible, will eliminate mosquito production. Various chemicals can be used as larvicides to destroy the larvae and their breeding habit to control the adult mosquitoes and may be in the form of residual sprays of dusts, fogs, or other aerosols such as those used in ultra-low volume applications. The objective in pest control should be the application of a combination of physical, biological, chemical, and educational measures to produce the best results with the least use of selective chemical poisons and the minimum hazard to man, domestic animals and desirable wild life.

Cockroach Control

Cockroaches live and breed in moist dark places behind baseboards, around plumbing, under refrigerators and in cupboards, pantries and kitchens. Outdoors they are found in piles of debris, rubbish and garbage. Cleanliness is the first objective in the elimination of cockroaches. All food-handling areas should be cleaned frequently. Diazinon, propoxur, dichlorvos, or malathion can be sprayed into places where cockroaches hide or travel. Painting a band of insecticide 10 cm wide around the base of a room has been found to be most effective in eliminating cockroaches. The band must be continuous to assure contact with the cockroaches as they enter or leave the room. To obtain a quick kill in heavy infestations the use of aerosol formulations of pyrethrum or dichlorvos to flush the insects from their hiding places is of value.

Bedbug Control

Bedbug infestations can usually be controlled by the application of an insecticide to baseboards and mouldings, wall crevices, bedsheets, springs and mattresses. Residual sprays containing lindane, fenchlorphos or malathion have been found effective. A pyrethrum spray applied to baseboards and other protected places just before the residual spray will cause the bedbugs to migrate and ensure contact with the residual spray. Pyrethrum can also be added to the residual spray. Mattresses should not be soaked with the spray and infant bedding or cribs should not be treated.

Scorpions, Spiders and Wasps Control

Scorpions, certain spiders such as the black widow and brown spiders, and wasps are dangerous to man. Recognition and avoidance of dangerous species and elimination of their hiding and resting places are the best protective measures. Chemical control of scorpions can be obtained by spraying their hiding or nesting places with carbary (1-2%) chlordane (2%) or dieldrin (0.5%), Malathion (2-3%) are effective against spiders. Nests of wasps yellow-jackets and hornets can be treated with water based sprays containing propoxure (0.5%), carbaryl (2%), diazinon (0.5%) or malathion (2%).

Rat Control

Domestic rats and mice live in close proximity to many, being found in living quarters, kitchens, storerooms, out houses and animal quarters. In addition to their disease transmission potential, rodents can cause substantial structural damage and consume and contaminate large amounts of food-stuffs.

Amazingly, rat consumes about 8 kgs (17 lb) of food (including garbage) yearly and can produce 4 or 5 litters a year. Rat control should start with a survey to determine the source of the rats and the conditions that encourage the infestation. This is followed by a programme to *(1)* kill the rats by poisoning; *(2)* remove their sources of food and water; *(3)* eliminate their harbourages and make them ratproof and *(4)* educate and obtain the cooperation of the people affect. If the food supply is removed first, and if this is done effectively, the rats will migrate to other areas, making their poisoning more difficult. Trapping is of limited value since it eliminates only a small proportion of the rat population. These measures by themselves are usually inadequate unless they are supported at all times by proper food storage and the collection, storage and disposal of refuse. Continual surveillance should be maintained and places where rodents have been gnawing to gain entry to a building should be flashed with metal; doors are particularly vulnerable to rodent attach. Materials stored in the open, in sheds or in buildings should be stacked at least 30 cm (1 ft) above the ground or floor.

The use of poisons for rodents is a secondary control measures. Anticoagulant poisons are preferred because of their low levels of toxicity for man and domestic animals; they include coumafurl, diphacinone, pindone and warfarin. While the relative degree of hazard for man varies according to the poisoning of the poison employed, extreme care should be taken in distributing and placing all poison bait. Every possible precaution should be taken to prevent risks to man and animals, particularly children and domestic pets, and the contamination of food. The rodent proofing of structures, elimination of food, water, and harbourage for rodents, and maintenance of proper sanitation should eliminate rats and there should be no need to use poisons for rodent control. However, these control measures are rarely carried out with complete effectiveness and continual surveillance is necessary .

Extreme care should be taken in the transportation, storage and use of insecticides and rodenticides to prevent health and environmental problems arising from their improper use. New insecticide formulations and rat poisons are continually being developed. The chemical compounds mentioned in this chapter as being suitable for pest control were judged to be the best available when this guide was being prepared. The situation may change but the pesticides mentioned will probably continue to be produced and used for some time to come.

Fly Control

The primary sources of fly production are garbage and manure. The elimination of these sources is an essential step in the control of flies. Under warm weather conditions the reproduction cycle from egg to larva to pupa to adult winged fly requires approximately 1 week. For this reason garbage collection and manure removal should be carried out twice weekly. Doors and windows should be fitted with 1.5 m (16mesh) screens and all screen doors should open outwards. Residual sprays, where permitted, will control most species of flies. Walls and vegetation, especially near refuse containers may be sprayed with diazinon, dimethoate, dichlorvos, naled or malathion to control adult flies and larvae. Diazinon and dichlorvos impregnated baits are effective in the control of adult flies. In addition pyrethrum can be used as an indoor space spray for quick knock-down of flies.

Sanitation in Swimming Pools

Many different types of swimming pools are found in recreational areas. The design and operational requirements vary with the type of pool and are discussed only briefly here. New pools generally incorporate filtration, recirculation and chlorination. Guidance should be obtained on the design and operational requirements of swimming pools and plans should be approved by the health authorities before construction begins and before any equipment is purchased. The following basic criteria should be met in the design and operation of pools for public use.

1. A supply of approved water must be available for filling and regulating the level of the pool. There should be no direct connection between the drinking water system and the pool water system.
2. The pool should have a capacity adequate for the expected use by bathers, swimmers etc.
3. Approved materials should be used in the construction.
4. The design should not include features that could create accident hazards—*e.g.* sloping walls, inadequate depths of water for diving, excessively steep bottom slopes in the bathing area, and inadequate walkways or decks around the pool.
5. Provision should be made for continuous purification of the water in the pool. Where the water is recirculated, purification can be achieved by a turn-over rate of 4 times per 24 hours with filtration and the use of a disinfectant such as chlorine to provide a bactericidal residual at all times.
6. The pool should be properly located to reduce air borne contamination by dust, algal spores, leaves etc. The location should not encourage non-swimmers to congregate near the pool. The area around the pool should be drained and fenced.

7. Surveillance should be maintained to prevent bathers with communicable diseases, open wounds, infected sores, or skin diseases from using the pool.
8. Regular bacteriological and chemical sampling of the pool water should be carried out during periods of heavy use. Daily testing for free available residual chlorine and of the pH is required before and during use of the pool.
9. Rules and regulations governing the use of the pool should be pasted in a conspicuous place for the information of users.
10. There should be continuous supervision of pool used by trained lifeguards and operating personnel, and the pool and its related facilities, particularly the recirculation and disinfection equipment, should be properly maintained. Warm water showers can reduce the amount of pollution introduced by bathers.

Standards for the guidance of swimming pool operators are discussed below. Pool owners and operators should adhere to established criteria and standards of this type as a protection against legal claims that might arise.

❐

7

Front Office Management

All the important activities of the hotels in the different parts of the hotel building are broadly categorised in two areas *i.e.* front office and the back office. In the front office guests are in touch with the hotel staff directly soon after the entry and functions are visible to the outsiders. Undoubtedly, 'Reception department' is the most important in the front office area, and the reception department differs from one hotel to the other. Guests visiting any hotel have to approach first the reception desk for information, assistance and answers to their problems and queries. In a small hotel the reception practically manages the entire hotel activities. Receptionists in small hotels will have to act as secretary to the proprietor as well. There is no exaggeration in saying that 'Reception' is the eye and ear of the hotel establishment.

Front Office Staff

The front office staff are vital in the sense that they are required to handle all the jobs of reservation, registration, departure etc. of the guest right from the time guest steps in the hotel. They are also required to handle the guest complaints, public relation and liason works with other departments of the hotels. In big hotels, the staff distribution for the front office job may be described in the following manners.

Front Officer Manager

↓

Assistant Manager

↓

Stenotypist
Front Office Supervisor

↓

Telephone/Telex Ooerator	Reservation Personnel	Information Personnel	Receptionist	Cashier

Orders come from the top to downwards and the accountability and reporting moves upwards. Front Office manager reports to the general manager or proprietor cum manager of the hotel whichever is applicable.

Where in smaller hotels the above elaborate organization does not exist. The receptionist or the supervisor in the reception counter often performs multiple functions within the counter in his or her specified working hours. A model organization for the front office may be chalked out as under:

Receptionist or Reception Supervisor

Porter (Coolie) | Watchman | Registration-cum-reservation-cum-cashier-cum-telephone operator

Receptionist-cum-Telephone | Attendent-cum-cashier

↓ Watchman | ↓ Porter

GENERAL PROCEDURES OF HOTEL RESERVATION

Reservation Through Telephone

One of the popular mode of reservation these days is phone which is instant and quick. It also gives the receptionist the opportunity to clarify any necessary points about payments, arrival time and so on.

Reservation Through Fax

The fax combine the speed of the telephone with the performance of a letter. Most of all big hotels now have Fax facilities in the reservation department. There is less opportunity for misunderstanding because of fax. Another important advantage of the telefax in reservation department is that a message can be transmitted even in absence of anybody at the other end. This is particularly important for hotels with an international clientele. A guest may book from England or France without having to check time to ensure that someone will be available to take, the reservation. Equally the hotel can fax back a confirmation at any time it wishes.

Reservation Through Letter

Hotels at holiday resorts sell much of their rooms by letters. A letter of reservation is also useful because the customer can explain the hotelier when he will be arriving and any special requests he may have. If the guest wishes to charge the account to his company then this can be mentioned in the letter. The hotel in turn can verify if necessary.

Reservation Through Computer (Online Reservation)

With the advent of computers and e-mail this has become a convient mode of hotel reservation, hotels are installing computers in their reservation department. This enable contact to be made very quickly with any other group hotel anywhere in the world. Normally the computer information is updated by each unit, and the programme is set so that if one hotel is full it will automatically offer the closest altetnative. With these systems the updating of reservation is quick, and popular.

Reservation Through Personal Contact

Here, there is direct face to face contact between the customer and the receptionist. Return bookings are frequently made in this way as a guest depart at the end of his stay. The receptionist has the opportunity to find out the maximum information and can answer any queries the guest have. At times the receptionist may also be able to show the guest the room type and utilise some sales techniques to the potential customers.

Recording the Reservation

Record work should be out of the sight of guest and the reception desk should look neat, dean and tidy.

Reservation Form

Telephone and personal bookings are normally noted on a reservation form. The use of a form for this purpose has many benefits: It acts as a check list to ensure that all the relevant information is obtained. It is helpful to tell the guest certain things about price, check in time etc. It can be easily compiled and stored.

Some hotels combine the reservation form with the Registration Card on the other side so that all the relevant information is available together.

RESERVATION FORM

Name......................	No. of persons..............................
Address	Date & time of arrival..................
....	....
....	Days of stay ....
....	Date of departure..........time.........
Mobile No...............	
E-mail....................	Remarks ....
Rate	
	Authorised signatory
	Date..

Confirmation by Letters

As individual letters of confirmation become more expensive, some hotels use a standard letter of confirmation to guest booking accommodation. With the use of window envelopes, these can cut down clerical time considerably.

Confirming Reservations

Usually smaller hotels as per practice confirm the reservation on receipt of advances are taken against booking. Otherwise only big hotels confirm by sending e-mail, fax and phone.

Cancellation Procedure

If a guest wishes to cancel the booking, then the reservation procedure has to be reversed; the booking is crossed through in the diary, the chart entry is erased. The hotel may ask the guest for loss if the guest cancels the booking after contracting but the hotel must make every attempts to sell the room promptly to the wait-listed guests or even to chane guests if available. Besides this hotels formulate some policies to organize the total guest arrivals, last minute cancellations, V.I.P. booking etc. These days many hotels have to handle room reservation for guests from delayed or cancelled flights in odd hours at a very short notice from Airlines Company.

Registration

There is a legal obligation in some countries for a hotel to obtain, and keep for twelve months, certain information about every person who stays there. The basic requirement is full name and nationality. If the guest is from overseas then they have to fill in additional form.

In addition to this legal minimum, hotel requests further information from guests sometimes who stay with them. A home address and signature are asked for in all hotels. Others take the opportunity to find out more about their customers by asking information such as purpose of visit, occupation, proposed method of payment and other details. These requests are for administrative purposes to ensure the smooth efficient running of the operation and marketing-where the hotel takes the opportunity to find out more about customers habits.

HOTEL
xxxxxxxxxxxxxxx
xxxxxxxxxxxxxxx
xxxxxxxxxxxxxxx

Full name	Date Time Arrived from
Home Address (Full)	PASSPORT Date of birth.............................. Number...................................... Date issued................................. Place of issue ....
Nationality	Purpose of Visit No. of Persons
Date of Departure	Probable Destination and address
Date of Arrival in India	Registration Certificate Number .... Date ....
Duration of Stay................... Name &: address of organisation .... Payment will be made by Cash...........Creditcard............. Cheque..................or................	Signature................................. Room... Rate... .... (Signature of authorised staff)

Guest Register

Register is used for checking in guests. Register is a bound book ruled into column which the guest fills out on arrival. It is ideal for smaller hotels where guests arrive individually. A register provides a pennanent record of guests staying in the hotel. Overseas guests are asked to fill out a separate form to provide additional information if required.

Disadvantages of Book Registration

If more than one guest comes to check in there is long waiting. In the case of a group this time could be considerable. Also the receptionist is unable to process registration information whilst a guest is checking in so administrative delays could occur in notifying other departments and opening the bill. In this method the guests find the opportunity to find out information about other people staying at the hotel causing disturbance to the privacy. To overcome this problem, separate registration cards are now widely used all over the world. On recording and kept properly then the card procedure is quick and efficient.

MODEL REGISTRATION CARD FORMAT

Full name:..............................	Other names:..............................
Home address:.......................	Date:..
Phone No:..............................	Nationality::..............................
Arriving from:.........................	Going to::.................................
For overseas visitors only:.......	Place of issue:...........................
Passport No:...........................	
	Signature of the receptionist

Checking of the Recorded Information

The receptionist should always check the registration card or registration book once the guest has checked in to make sure that the card has been completed correctly and if there is a query the receptionist can politely ask the guest for clarification. The receptionist can then inform the guest of the room number and the room rate. However, a receptionist must see the following carefully before allotment of room to the guest.

— that the registration details are correct and legible.

— that guest has no bad records and is not black listed.

— that the room is clean and ready in all aspects.

— that the details of the booking have not changed.

— that the guest knows the room rate and what it includes.

— whether there are any letters or messages for the guest.

It is often noticed that guests are allotted the room on the basis of vacancy information only without ascertaining the actual 'readiness' of the rooms. This happens particularly in hotels where there is little time between guest departures and guest arrivals. In such cases the receptionists must tactfully handle guests without annoyance to them to allow time to the housekeeping department to make room ready. But the guests who have booked their hotels in advance must not be kept waiting for their rooms to become ready under any circumstances. A careful and vigilant receptionist must take suitable decisions. It is also important to tackle things at the reception when a guest desires to overstay and the hotel is otherwise booked.

Room Position

A prime need for every hotel reception is an accurate, upto date knowledge of the state of every room in the hotel. Hotel room may be in one of the stages as under:

(a) Occupied.

(b) Vacant but not ready.

(c) Vacant and ready.

(d) Under renovation/repair (not fit for occupation).

(e) Vacant but needs urgent attention for fault rectification.

(f) Vacant and record but not occupied are to now show.

(g) Occupied but needs attention for some fault.

A room status system must show these positions for handling guest reservation properly and to organize the quantum of saleable rooms.

Arrivals without Prior Reservation

A guest who comes at the hotel without a prior booking is often referred to as a chance guest. Transit' hotels located near by-station, airports, seaports will receive the bulk of their guests as chance arrivals. The receptionist has practically no information about the guests and the backgrounds. In this situation, special procedures are adopted to handle their bookings. Chance arrivals with substantial amounts of luggage are unlikely to be able to leave the hotel without paying. An increasing trend, however, is carrying of small amounts of luggage which means the guest may be able to leave unnoticed. In registering the guest, the receptionist first checks whether they have luggage. If they have, then the registration is processed in the normal way and the registration card is marked 'Chance'. If there is little or no luggage then the receptionist has to ensure that the guest will not leave without first settling his or her bill. This can be done either by taking cash deposit from the guest, or alternatively by taking an imprint of any credit card that the guest may have. It is important that in accepting chance bookings and taking deposits, the receptionist does not suggest to the guest that the hotel thinks he/she may be dishonest, or not willing to pay. Chance guests are often asked to pay cash for all purchases while they are in the hotel, or alternatively a special checks may be kept on the size of their bill so that if the account exceeds some figures, the guest is contacted and asked to pay up to that date. By doing this potential losses from chance guests are minimised.

Room Allocation

When the guest arrives he may desire to use his room as quickly as possible. If he arrives at unscheduled time, it is unlikely

MODEL GUEST MOVEMENT NOTIFICATION FORMAT

Name..................................	Distribution..............................
Old room	Bill office ....
New room.........................	Cashier ....
	Porter......................................
	Signature of the Receptionist
	Date:.....................

that the room will be ready unless it is vacant from the previous night. In smaller hotels allocation of rooms is normally done at the time of booking. Larger hotels with a greater choice of rooms often do not allocate until the guest actually arrives and then place the guest in the room. V.I.P.'s and guests with special requirements may have rooms pre-allocated to them and a note may be placed in the reception area to ensure that they only go to those particular rooms. In allocating rooms the receptionist should satisfy the guests as much as possible. Even in large modern hotels not every room is exactly the same, some may have better views than others and certain rooms may be particularly noisy due to their closeness to the lift or to a service area.

Arrival List

In large hotels this list will be useful to both the hall porter and the telephone operator. The porter or enquiry desk will have to check if there are any messages or letters for guests arriving and the telephone operators answer enquiries from people about the arrival of particular guests. The reception desk will be able to use the alphabetical list to locate guests quickly in the diary.

Departmental Notification

Shifting from one room to another requires an individual notification. Because the records of each department need to be up dated as soon as possible. A format of notification regarding change of rooms is shown in the following:

An alphabetical guest list is usually prepared each evening by the reception department which is known as 'House list'. This is then distributed throughout the hotel, though some departments may only check it occasionally. The telephone department, porter's desk and reception will need to refer to it constantly. A list of guests in room number order is only kept at the reception through the room board, and anyone wishing to know who is in a particular room would have to check with the reception desk.

Morning Call/Bed Tea/Newspapers Etc.

The reception department may keep a sheet at the front desk which records the exact time at which guests wish to be called in the morning, their newspaper order and requests for early morning tea or breakfast. Increasing use is being made of semi or automatic equipment in this area to relieve the pressure on staff during the

RECEPTIONIST'S TASKS PROCEDURE

Receiving guests and checks booking information
↓
Checking registration
↓
Alloting room
↓
Informing other departments
↓
Opening bill
↓
Recording guests expenditures
↓
Hand over mail, messages and morning calls, room service orders
↓
Preparation Bill
↓
Receiving payments
↓
Conveying departure of guests to departments
↓
Takes back vacant and ready room

morning peak hours. Some hotels are installing alarm clocks in guest rooms alongwith tea-making equipment. Breakfast order forms are also placed in the room for the guest to complete and hang outside the door at night for timely service at the morning hours.

Guest History Board

Luxury hotels have already used guest history cards to record details of each individual stay by guests and information on their personal likes and dislikes. This can be simplified by the use of a modified computer system. This allows for more information for better personalised service and attention to guests' needs.

General Information

It is usually the duty of the reception department in most places to pass an information about the place and other details of conferences, meetings etc. which are normally being conducted in hotel conference room or other suitable location.

Information Regarding Medical Attention

At time the hotel reception has to handle the urgent medical attention for the sick guests. This is done through the hotel's registered medical doctor or through hospital or nursing home services.

Departure

As the guest leaves there are a number of tasks that have to be completed by receptionist. Once the bill has been paid, the cashier will pass the registration card back to reception, or send a notification where separate departments exist. The receptionist should then remove the guest name from the room status system and mark the room as vacant but not ready. Notification of the departure should be made to the relevant departments so that they may upto date their house list. The housekeeper attention be able to assign a maid to dean the room. When the room has been cleaned, the housekeeping department will return it to reception and it will then be possible to re-let the room. Early departures and extensions of stay are notified to departments separately to ensure that they are not overlooked.

Mode of Receiving Payment from Hotel Guests

Hotel guests usually settles bills at the time of leaving the hotel and this procedure should require shortest possible time for convenience. Depending upon the types of hotel and depending upon the agreed tenns and conditions with the guests the hoteliers arrange to collect the payment of bills from customers. Universally normal practice is to collect the payments by cash only. However, there are different other ways of collection of bills.

Credit Cards

The use of this system of payment is gradually becoming popular. The credit card issuing companies/banks remain responsible for all bills signed by the customers on the strength of the credit card.

Credit Advice

Many hotels allow their guests to sign the bills at the time of departure and arrange for sending all the bills to the person concerned or to the company at suitable time or at time as previous contract. This facility can be extended to restricted guests having established credibility. On the other hand with desirable customers one can have greater business because it is believed that in view of credit facility guests spend greater amount of money.

Cheques

Care should be taken as to the credibility of the persons tendering the cheque. Signature verifications, outstation clearance charges etc. are to be looked into. There is also possibility of delay because of delayed clearance by banks. Draft is rather safer method than cheque because the clearance is assured regarding the sum for which draft is made.

Traveller's Cheque

This method has been gaining popularity in the country as well as among the travelling public. Because it is always hazardous to carry large sum of money during travelling or in some unknown places away from home. These cheques are issued by Citi Bank other banks on payment of cash to the bank with a commission by the purchasers. Traveller's cheque can verify the signature of the depositors on the spot without difficulty because the signatures of the holders of traveller's cheques already exist over the cheque documents made before the bank. These are available for specific values hence, calculations will be required for setting the bills and handing over the cheques to the bank for deposit in the account of the hotel.

Travel Agent's Voucher

The people who travel with the arrangements of travel agents on agreed terms pay their dues to the travel agents and the travel agents in turn issue coupons or vouchers to the traveller's for use as cash in specified hotels and similar other establishments.

Foreign Currency

Foreigners in India and non-resident Indians are required to use foreign currency for payment in India. Not all the hotels are also allowed by the government to accept foreign currency, only approved hotels by the Governments can receive foreign currency. Hotels permitted to accept foreign exchange must submit the details of foreign exchange received from guests to the authority and should have money changing facilities and proper day to day exchange rate information. The, most popular foreign currency internationally accepted and widely used in the travel market is the American dollar. Hotel cashier must have proper knowledge to identify the foreigners and understand the exchange formalities and foreign currencies.

The hotels need to record properly the various bills from the guests and income received therefrom. For satisfactory service, all guest bills should be kept upto date so that no delay is caused to the customer at the time of payment. This method also ensures that all the dues are recorded properly and on time for recovery.

Tabular Ledger is the most common method of recording all the dues of the guests in hotels. The customer's bill is normally prepared in duplicate. The extra copy is kept for hotel record and accounts. Recently in many hotels machine billing has been introduced and bills are prepared automatically and kept upto date. Electronic machine computers are installed in the front office billing section.

Reference Aids for Reception Department

From extensive survey and research it has been noted that some useful books, printed sources of information connected to the local tourist places etc. are hand tools for receptionist to satisfy the guests queries. These are as follows:

Telephone directory

Local road map

Airlines time table

Location and tariff of important local hotels

Bilingual Dictionary

Lists of local tourist places

Lists of car-rental companies

Lists of travel agents with addresses and telephone numbers etc.

Address of Embassies and consulates.

Lobby Manager Public Relation Officer (PRO)

Lobby manager controls and looks after the team of people for the service of hotel guests at the time of entrance and departure. Guests requirements at the hotel lobby are also looked after by these persons. PRO is another official in big hotels. They are useful for the maintenance of rapport with the regular visitors and with VIPs. The post of PRO is also helpful if competent person mans the post. In general the front office staff particularly the receptionist must rune his or her personality not only to perform the routine tasks of the reception job but to handle people of different mood, culture, civilisation, language and behaviour. Thus, the quality of the receptionist should be such as to handle the guests in happy state of mind as well as in difficult situation. The receptionist's quality lies in the word of 'Personality' itself as drawn by:

P — Pleasantness
E — Eagerness to serve
R — Respect for job and people
S — Sense of responsibility
O — Orderly and methodical work
N — Neatness

A — Accuracy in performance
L — Loyal
I — Intelligence
T — Tactfulness
Y — Yearning for success.

Communication in Hotels

In general, the communication indicates passing of message either oral or written. Messages are also passed through equipments. Here, stress is being on the written communication. These are required for internal staff as well as for clients. Hospitality business faces varied situations and types of people for the sake of communications. For all occasions and whatever may be the reason proper decorum and politeness must be ensured. There should be right choice of words and phrases while drafting written communication. All letters must be addressed properly as accepted rules. Grammar, correctness of words are also to be carefully checked. Reception department usually acts as the hotel's office for the issue of various communications. All inward and outward communications should be properly filed for reference and for prompt reply or other actions in time. A prompt and decent communication creates reputation for hotels and bring business.

Following are some forms of addresses while writing letters:- Letters to men can be addressed as follows: Mr. John, Mr. R. John, or Mr. Robert John. If the courtesy title Esq. is used the surname must be preceded by a first name or initials, and any letter must be put after the Esq. eg Robert John Esq. D.Sc. Young boys can be generally addressed as Master. The plural form Messrs, is only used with the names of business firms which contain a personal name, *e.g.* M/s Chamberlain and Sons.

Unmarried women and young girl can be addressed as Miss. Married women are often identified by their husband's first name or initial.

Professional titles are used instead of Mr. etc., as in Dr. A. Stephen, The Rev. Federick Charles. First names are always used with the titles Sir. Orders, decorations, degrees, qualifications and letters denoting professions appear in that order. Degrees start with the lowest but orders start with the highest *e.g.* Lt. General A. Bagga, PVSM, AVSM, VSM. Orders and decorations are usually included in addresses, but qualifications etc. are only used where appropriate, as when writing to a person in his official capacity. In the 21st century, a great laxity is there everywhere, informal addressing system etc. are more popular.

Postal Address of a Letter

The writer's address should appear in the top right-hand corner with the date underneath. The name and address of the intended recipient should come below the date, on the left hand side of the page.

Postal Beginning and Recapitulation

On the requirement of degree of formality depends this. Some of the most commonly used forms are as follows:

Very formal

Sir,	I am: Sir, or
Mesdames,	Servant
Gentlemen,	I remain, Sir,
Madam,	Your obedient
Formal	
Dear Sir(s)	Yours faithfully
Dear Madam,	
Mesdames,	Yours truly
When correspondent is known	
Dear Mr.	Yours sincerely,
(Mrs.)	Yours truly
between friends	
Dear	Yours ever,
My dear	Yours affectionately.

❑

8

Maintenance of Accounts

PRIMARY BOOKS OF ACCOUNTS IN HOTELS

In an hotel-numerous transactions take place daily. It is not possible for the management or the proprietor to remember all these transactions. Therefore, for the benefit of the management they are recorded immediately at the time of occurrence in the proper books. Primary books are basically those where transactions are immediately recorded after these have taken place. Primary books of hotels are different from those of other commercial undertakings because of the different nature of business. Through this chapter, it is being designed to provide a model of primary books which can be maintained by hotels working in the corporate sector.

The book containing the various accounts is called the ledger. Although it is not a book of original entry, it forms an indispensable

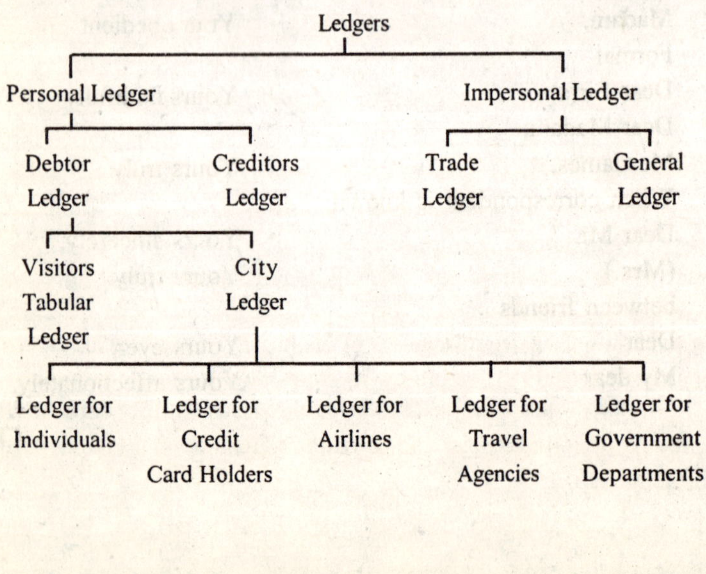

record in accounting as much as it is in this book that the transactions are ultimately posted in their appropriate accounts in an arranged and classified form. Thus, it is the principle book since it, affords information for preparing the Profit and Loss account and balance sheet. The number and types of ledgers depend upon the nature of hotel and the policy of the management. In India so far no standard names have been given to the ledgers which can be acceptable to all hotels therefore the opinion of hoteliers regarding the names of led: gers and the accounts opened therein are in variance. However some types of ledgers that are maintained by large hotels are given above:

Personal Ledger

It is a ledger which is kept in hotels tor maintaining personal accounts of guests or debtors and creditors. For convenience this ledger is further divided in two groups-debtors ledger and the creditors ledger.

Debtors Ledger

It is a ledger in which the accounts of debtors are opened money is to be recovered by the hotel either for services or for supply of meals, beverages and other articles. The debtors ledger is further divided into two groups. One for the debtors who are still continuing their stay in the hotel and the second who are not staying in the hotel. They have either checked out without settling the bill or are responsible for payment on behalf of the guests who availed of the credit facilities of the hotel. For the first group of guests Visitors Tabular Ledger is maintained and for the second City Ledger is maintained.

Visitors Tabular Ledger

In hotel and catering industry, the sales day book is replaced by the visitors tabular ledger, known as the 'Tab', which is a form of analysed or columnar book keeping. It consists of a sheet for each day which has numerous analysis columns—the headings of these vary according to the requirements of the hotel. The entries are made from dockets (checks), or bills sent from the various departments. It is from these entries on the 'Tab' that the personal bill is prepared for presentation to the guest and can be produced upon demand with minimum delay.

On the extreme left of the 'Tab' sheet usually there is a column for entering the numbers of the rooms occupied by guests, followed by a wider column in which are entered the names of guests, the number of occupants of a room (sleepers) and the rate being charged. Next come money columns in which all charges incurred by the guests are entered. The first of these columns (headed Apartments) is for daily room charges. In addition to recording the daily charges of guests, the 'Tab' sheet shows that daily sales of the Hotel, analysed under the respective headings. These headings are normally grouped together in such a way that similar sales and services are side by side. Thus, all sales originating from kitchen are grouped together; the main meals in order of consumption—Breakfast, Luncheons, Afternoon teas. Dinners followed by extra provisions and Beverages (denote to tea, coffee, drinking choclate, etc.) Some hotels like to record early morning teas sales separately from Beverages and consequently have an extra column either immediately preceeding the breakfasts column or adjacent to the Beverage column.

In addition to columns dealing with kitchen sales there are columns for drink sales in the following order—Wines and Liquors, Beers and Ciders and Minerals. Sometimes additional column for cocktails is also made. Generally, many establishments record the sales of spirits, liquor and cocktail under the one heading of spirits.

These columns are followed by a Daily. Total Column in which the total of all the charges recorded in the previous column is entered. The next column is used for entering the totals brought forward from the previous day. These totals, when added to the totals in the Daily Total Column, shows the amount owed by the guests to date. These figures are entered in the following column, which is headed Grand Total. The final four columns are for credit entries and are headed Cash, Allowances, Ledger and Balance carried forward. Throughout the day, as the guests incur charges, the bills from different departments come to Bill Clerk who enters the amount against the room number of the guest concerned in the appropriate column when the entry is made. After making the entry in the 'Tab' Sheet Bill Clerk either tick, initial or draw a line through the bill indicating that it has been entered on the 'Tab' sheet. It is then filed for future reference.

When a posting error or omission is detected, it is rectified by means of an adjustment. When an error is caused by an omission or under-charge, the amount of the omission or the undercharge is entered against the room number in the service column concerned and it is back dated as necessary. When the error is caused by an overcharge, the adjustment is made by entering the amount in the Allowances Column. At the same time it is essential to record this amount in an Allowance Book. An adjustment of the total of the service concerned is usually made on the Summary Sheet if and when necessary.

Checking out a Guest

When a guest who is leaving the hotel wishes to settle his account, separate lines are drawn diagonally through the room number, the name of the guest and the number of sleepers. The Bill Clerk has to ensure that there are no further charges are posted to the room being vacated.

Chance Trade

This refers to all cash business, in particular, meals, drinks, beverages and other provisions, which are entered in the appropriate column on separate lines. These entries are made near the bottom of the 'Tab' sheet so that they do not get intermingled with the room numbers and guests' name.

Vertical Tab Sheet

Room No. Date....

Name

No. of Adult

No. of Children

Terms

Rate

B/F

Apartments

Breakfast

Luncheon

Afternoon Teas

Dinner

Morning

Teas

Beverages

Wines

Spirits & Liquors

Beers

Minerals

Telephones

V.P.O's

Misc.

Total Debits

Cash

Allowances

Ledger

Bal. C/F

Folio No.

Total Credits

Column

1. Room No.
2. Name of Guest.

3. Terms, *e.g.*, room and breakfast or fully inclusive. Rate—Charge per person.
4. B/F—Balance brought forward.
5. Apartments—charge for apartment per night.
6. Breakfast—charge for any chance breakfast.
7. Luncheon—charge for any chance luncheon.
8. Dinners—charge for any chance dinner.
9. Early Tea—charge to guests for morning teas.
10. Beverages—charge for teas, coffee or other beverages.
11. Wines—charge for any wines at meals.
12. Spirits, Liquors—charge for liquor taken.
13. Beer—charge for beer.
14. Minerals—charge for minerals water.
15. Telephone—charge for any telephone calls made.
16. VPO's—visitors paid out—Any monies paid on behalf of guests.
17. Misc.—Any sundry charges to the guest may incur, *e.g.*, laundry, taxis.
18. Total Debits—Total of all charges made to the guest's bill.
19. Cash—Any cash, cheques or payments made by Credit Cards made by guest.
20. Allowances—Any allowances made to the guest which will be educated from their bill.
21. Ledger—Any amount which is transferred to ledger account.
22. Balance c/f—Amounts carried forward to the next day's tabular ledger.

23. Total Credits—Total of all payments, allowances or transfer to ledger.

24. Folio No.—Any ledger folio.

City Ledger

City ledger is a ledger in which debtors accounts or accounts receivable other than those maintained in Visitors Tabular Ledger are opened. In India many hotels use city ledger for maintaining the accounts of the following types of debtors:

(a) Guests who checkout without settling the bills.

(b) Credit Card holders.

(c) Air lines who are allowed credit facilities.

(d) Travel Agencies wno are allowed credit facilities.

(e) Government Departments allowed credit facilities.

In small hotels only one city ledger is maintained for the above types of debtors. But in large hotels for the different category of debtors individual ledgers are maintained.

Ledger for Individuals

In this ledger the account of those debtors are opened who had been staying in the hotel but checked out without settling their bills. Such guests are divided into two groups:

(a) Guests who check out without settling the bill but with the permission of the manager and with an understanding that the payment would be remitted by a specified time.

(b) Guests who check out without settling the bill and without the permission of the manager of the hotel. They slip away without bringing their departure to the knowledge of hotel employees.

In some hotels for both types of debtors only on ledger is maintained but some large hotels maintain delinquent ledger for debtors of group (b). As soon as the guest checks out without settling his bill, his account is debited in this ledger and credited in the Visitors Tabular Ledger to close his account in the Visitors Tabular ledger. After specified time when the payment is received his account is credited with cash or bank.

Ledger for Credit Card Holders

It is a ledger in which in which accounts of Credit Card holder are opened. Here Credit Card holders mean those digni taries who do not stay in the hotel but are allowed to have their meals in the hotel on credit. They are the dignitaries who are issued these cards by the hotel itself. They are different from the Credit Card holders who are issued cards by the Banks, Dinners Club or other establishments. Each card is separately numbered and bears the holder's name and signatures. When guest is served meal etc. on credit and presents his card, the employee of the hotel must ensure that the card is not out of date. The credit card holders' account is debited. Periodically the bill is sent and when the money is received his account is credited.

Ledger for Travel Agencies

A separate ledger is maintained for the Travel Agencies. Generally, it is kept in loose leaf form. If a guest comes through some travel agency then the travel agency takes the responsibility of the payment of the bill according to contract. The bills, after taking the signature of the guest, are sent to Travel Agency. Periodically a summary is prepared and sent to travel agency. Immediately its account is debited and on receiving the payment the account is credited.

Ledger for Government Departments

Government Departments are also allowed credit facilities. Parties and banquets are arranged for them. The government department is debited for the charges and the bill is sent to them. When the money is received it is credited in Government Department's account.

HERITAZE HOTEL LTD.
South Ext., New Delhi
City Ledger

Account No.2 Folio No.2.............

Account of .... Authorised Signatory..............

Address .... Paying Authority..............

Date	*Bill No.*	*Room No.*	*Authority Reference*	*Particulars*	*Folio*	*Debit*	*Credit*		*Dr. Cr.*	*Balance*	*Remarks*
	Cheque No.	*Date*	*Bank*			*Amount*	*Commission of Discount*	*Payment*			

Creditors Ledger

Creditors ledger is a part of the personal ledger. It is a ledger in which the accounts of creditors are maintained. By creditors we mean persons or establishments from whom the hotel purchases goods on credit and to whom the hotel has to pay the money. As soon as the Bill and Goods Receipt Voucher is received in accounts department the creditors account is opened in the ledger and credited with the necessary amount. The payment is made on the basis of the purchase sanction.

When the payment is made the creditors account is debited. Some hotels call it Suppliers Ledger.

Impersonal Ledger

It means ledger maintained for impersonal accounts. Impersonal ledger is divided into two groups-Trade Ledger and the General Ledger.

Trade Ledger

Trade ledger is kept for maintaining all revenue and expenses account. In this ledger all such accounts are opened which have a direct relation to trading like purchase, sales and expenses etc. It is a ledger where double entry of personal ledger is completed. This ledger feeds the data to Profit and Loss Account.

General Ledger

General Ledger is a ledger in which especially the accounts of assets and liabilities are opened. It is often desired to preserve the continuity of Assets and Liabilities accounts for a number of years, therefore for individual asset and individual liability a separate ledger is maintained in loose leaf form.

Thus, primary books are those books where transactions are immediately recorded after these have taken place. In an hotel large number of customers come daily, seminars and parties are held. It is, therefore, of utmost importance that these transactions are recorded immediately before it is too late. For those guests who stay in the hotel 'Tab' sheets are used whereas for the guests not staying in the hotel city ledger is prepared. Entries of customers who checked out without setting their bills are recorded in separate ledger, opened for this purpose. A separate ledger is maintained for the guests who are served meals and services; but the Air lines or travel agencies take the responsibility of the payment. Creditor's ledger shows the amount that the hotel owes to outside suppliers. Trade ledger is maintained tc record all revenue and expenses account. Accounts of assets and liabilities are opened in the General ledger. It is in the interest of big hotels to maintain these books to minimize errors and chances of misappropriation of funds.

SECONDARY BOOKS OF ACCOUNTS IN HOTELS

The survey of accounting practices of second ary books of accounts reveal that there are no standardised practices in five star hotels in Delhi. After a thorough investigation, it is being attempted, through this chapter, to suggest the guidelines for developing an appropriate model of secondary books of accounts to cope with the needs of Five Star Hotels in India.

In a hotel where so many transactions take place daily, it is imperative to maintain special records for them called subsidiary journals or books. These journals serve the same purpose as general journal. However, the totals of journals are posted to in the ledger accounts once each month instead of posting the individual transactions. The subsidiary journals are set up in such a fashion that frequently occurring transactions of similar nature will be journalized in only one journal. Most of the hotels have a subsidiary journal for income, one for cash received, one for cash paid out, one for purchases and so on.

Accounting for Restaurant and Bar Sales

Sales in the restaurant are first recorded when the waiter takes the order for food or liquor. He writes the order on a guest check. The guest check is priced and totaled by a food checker, waiter or cashier. The customer eats his meal and is presented with his totalled bill by the waiter.

He pays his bill or changes to his account at the restaurant cashier's counter. The restaurant cashier makes an entry in the restaurant cashier's sheet (Table 1). The restaurant cashier's sheet is really a journal because it is a book of original entry. However, it is one of special columnar journals because it records only sales of food and liquor. The charges sales are immediately sent to the front office to be recorded on guest bills. It is done at once because there is a possibility that guests may check out of the hotel soon after eating. The cashier totals and balances the restaurant cashier's sheet after all the customers have left the restaurant. The formula for balancing it is cash + charges = food sales + beverage sales + sales tax. He verifies that all guest checks are accounted for by checking the numbers of the checks received with the list of numbers of the checks issued to the waiters. The checks, cashier's sheet, and money taken in are brought to the front office and turned over to the front office cashier. The front office cashier records the amount received on the front office cash sheet (Table 2).

The totals of the restaurant cashier's sheet are later posted to the summary sales journal. Many restaurants, in some hotels, do not use a restaurant cashier's sheet, but instead use a cash register of some type. Accounting for restaurant sales using a machine is no different from the manual method. The machine does all the pricing and adding, and the totals come from the machine simply by pressing the total buttons. There are obvious advantages to using the machine. Of importance to the accounting is the machine's greater accuracy and better control.

Accounting for Room Sales

Guests checking into the hotel fill out registration cards showing name, address and other information the hotel wants for its records. The room clerk uses the information on the registration cards to prepare guest bills, room rack cards, information rack cards and check-in notices for various departments in the hotel. The room rack card is particularly important for the accounting department, because the room clerk's daily revenue will be prepared from the information on it. A registration card, rack card and room clerk's daily revenue report are shown in Tables 3 and 4.

Table 1

The Totaled Guest Check and The Restaurant Cashier's Sheet

No. of Cks.	*Table*	*No. of Persons*	*Server*	*Book & Check No.*	*No. of Cks.*	*Table*	*No. of Persons*	*Server*	*Book & Check No.*
			Tax					Tax	
	Please Pay Cashier					Please Pay Cashier			

No. Person	Name	Check No.	Waiter No.	Cash	*Charge*	*Food Sales*	*Beverage sales*	*Sales Tax*	*Sunday*

Table 2

Cash Sales Posted to the Front Office Cash Sheet

Room No.	Account No.	Name	Receipts		Room No.	Account No.	Name	Disbursements	
			Guests	Others				Detail	Guests
						Recapitulation			
						Total Receipts			
						Disbursements-Guests			
						Disbursements-House			
						Total Disbursements			
						Deposit			

Table 3

Registration Card

Arrived	*Room*	*Rate*	*Clerk*	*Departure*

Remarks:

Each evening the room clerk on duty prepares the room clerk's daily revenue report from the information on the rack cards. The revenue report is verified by the night auditor with the revenue he has posted to guest folios, and it is sent to the accounting department along with other information from the front office to be posted to the summary sales journal. All room sales are treated as charges to guest accounts, even though guests may pay for rooms at the time of check-in.

Accounting for Telephone Sales

Date ....

Name ....

Street ....

City ....

All long distance calls going through the hotel's switchboard are entered on the telephone traffic sheet.

Money, Je vels and other Valuable Packages, must be placed in the Safe in the Office, otherwise the management will not be responsible for any loss.

Table 4

Room Clerk's Dally Revenue Report

Room No.	*No. Person*	*Room Rate*	*Tax*	*Room No.*	*No. Person*	*Room Rate*	*Tax*
100				200			
101				201			

102	202
103	203
104	204
105	205
106	206
107	207
108	208
109	209
110	210
111	211
112	212
113	213
114	214
115	215
116	216
117	217
118	218
119	219
Total	Total
	Total First Floor
	Grand Total

The operator prepares vouchers (Table 5) for the calls to be charged to guest accounts and sends them to the front office.

Table 5

Name .... Date......19......

Date .... Room or Acct. No. ....

Symbol.............Amount ....

Do Not Write In Above Space

Person Called		*Time*	*Charges*
Name		Hour of call	Toll
Street		Disconnected	Tax
City		Connected	Service
State	Phone No.	Minutes	Total

HOLD FOR CHARGE LONG DISTANCE

Name .... Room or Acct. No. ....

Operator ....

The telephone traffic sheet is totaled (Table 6), verified by the night auditor and the totals are posted to the summary sales journal. The front office cashier will post telephone charges to guest bills.

Table 6

Long Distance Telephone Traffic Sheet

Date........19.....

				Distribution			*Total*	
Voucher Number	*Name of party Calling*	*Room No.*	*Place Called*	*Phone Co's charge*	*Tax*	*Our Service Charge*	*House Called*	*Guest Charges*

The Summary Sales Journal

All the sales records are sent to the accountant's office, audited by the day auditor, and recorded in the summary sales journal

(Table 7). The journal has at least 31 lines one for each day of the month. Each day the sales information for that day is put on one line in the sales journal. At the end of the month, the sales journal is totalled and balanced and the total figures are posted to general ledger accounts. The room sales column, total food sales column, total bar sales column, and telephone sales column are posted as credits to their sales accounts in the ledger. The sales tax column is posted as credit to the sales tax payable, a liability account. The total of accounts receivable column is posted as a debit to the accounts receivable ledger account and the total of the cash sales column is posted as a debit to an account called exchange. Cash sales are not posted to cash ledger account because all cash sales were also posted to the front office cash sheet and will be recorded in the cash ledger account through the cash receipt journal.

Table 7

Sales Journal

Charge Room	*Soles Bar*	*Total beve-rage*	*Tele-phonic Soles*	*Soles Tax*	*Grand Total*	*Cash soles*	*Amount recei-vable*

Accounting for Cash Receipts

Money received from guests is first recorded on the front office cash sheet (Table 8). Money received as a result of cash sales in the various departments is turned over to the front office cashier and recorded on the front office cash sheet. Front office cashier also receives money from guests paying their bills, from people sending their money in as advance deposits on rooms and other people paying money to the hotel. All this is recorded in cash sheet. Receipts from guests checking out or from advance deposits are recorded in the guests column of the front office cash sheet.

Table 8

Front Office Cash Receipt

		Receipts					Disbursments			
Room No.	*Acct. No.*	*Name*	*Guests*	*Other*	*Room No.*	*Acct. No.*	*Name*	*Detail*	*Guest*	*House*

Recapitulation ....

Total Receipts ....

Disbursements-Guests ....

Disbursement-House ....

Total disbursements ....

Deposit ....

In some hotels, the front office cashier will also give out small amounts of money for guests. Gratuities that the guests charge to their accounts will be given to employees out of the funds of the front office cashier's bank, as well as any other money for such things as collect packages, services performed by outside firms for guests etc. These disbursements are recorded on the right hand portion of the cash sheet. The cash sheet is usually audited by the night auditor and the day auditor.

Most hotels now use a posting machine to record charges to guest bills, as well as cash received or paid out.

The Cash Receipts Journal

Information from the front office cash sheet of all of the cashiers is audited and summarized by the Chief Cashier and posted to the cash receipts journal (Table 9). One line of the journal is used for each day's receipts. The journal is totalled each month the columns are posted to general ledger accounts. The cash sales column will total the same amount as the cash sales column in summary sales journal. From summary sales journal the column is posted as a debit to exchange account. The same figure from the cash receipts journal is posted as a credit to exchange account. The exchange account is a wash account; that is, equal debits and credits are always posted to it.

No......

Date.......19......

Table 9

Cash Receipt Journal

Date	*Day*	*Cash Sales*	*Accounts receivable*	*Sundries*		*Total Receipts*	*Advances to guests*	*Net Receipts*
				Amount	*Expenditure*			

The accounts receivable column is posted as a credit to accounts receivable. The sundries column is used for other ca£h receipts that the hotel might have, such as bank loans or new investment in business. The advances to guest column represents cash dibursements by the front office cashier on behalf of guests. It is posted as a debit to accounts receivable. Finally, the net receipts column is posted as a debit to cash.

The Allowance Journal

Many guests who check out of the hotel challenge charges put on their bill. They forget about phone calls they made, complain about being overcharged for their room or in some other fashion object to paying for part of the charges. Sometimes the hotel makes a mistake. It is possible to post a charge to the wrong account and have the error go undetected until the guest checks out. Sometimes the manager gives complimentary rooms to special guests after a charge has been made for the room. For whatever reason, when the hotel agrees to give credit for charges on a guest bill, it is necessary that an allowance voucher (Table 10) be prepared and signed by the department manager. Such approved allowance vouchers are examined by the night auditor and the income auditor.

Table 10

Allowance Voucher

No......   Date......19......

REBATE OR ALLOWANCE

Room No. ......   Card No. ....   Amount ....

Name of the Guest ....

For ....

APPROVED

....

Clerk   Manager

In case of local telephone call allowance, the bill clerk or the cashier is given the power to give such allowances if he is satisfied with the statement of the guest. However, it is a good rule that he should prepare a combined allowance voucher for the day's allowances and must obtain the approval of the proper authority.

Accounting for Purchases

Purchasing Food and Related Items

The largest amount of money spent by hotels—with the exception of payroll is on food. It accounts for 20 to 25 per cent of the total expenditures, and the steward or purchasing agent will have the responsibility of ordering these goods. It is very important that

(1) the food ordered be of that kind and amount as needed,

(2) it is purchased at the lowest possible price consistent with the quality desired,

(3) only the food ordered is received, and

(4) that the right amount is paid for the food received by the hotel.

To achieve the above objectives the accounting system will have certain built in controls. The steward and chief decide on the menu. Usually they plan for several days in advance. Then market quotations for the perishable items are called. Purchase specifications are the specific requirements of the hotel for each item. In case the articles are purchased from the Central Government or State Government or Government undertaking or Autonomous bodies of Government, it is not necessary to call for quotation.

In case of quotations the purchase department ensures that the quotations received correspond to the required specifications including quality, make, quantity required, the date of supply, mode of delivery etc. In case of provisions and food stuffs the samples may be tested by the medical officer before accepting the quotations. If the quotations are accepted, the purchase department issues purchase order. Four copies of the purchase order are made by the purchase department according to the practice of most of the hotels. The original copy is sent to the supplier, one copy to the stores, one copy is sent to the Accounts Department alongwith the sanction order of purchase of goods and the last copy is retained in the order book.

Receiving Ordered Goods

Normally all goods received by the hotel are accompanied by an invoice for that order (Table 11). The goods are received using the following procedure:

(a) All goods are weighed, counted, or otherwise verified to ensure that the amounts received are as ordered and that the invoice show the proper weights or counts.

(b) All goods are inspected to ensure that the quality of the goods meet or exceeds the purchase specifications of the hotel for each item.

(c) Prices are checked to determine that the amounts charged are the same as those quoted on the quotation.

(d) All fresh meat is tagged with a meat tag.

(e) The invoice is stamped with an invoice stamp and the clerk puts his initial on it.

(f) The receiving clerk's daily report is prepared showing which items went to stores and which items went to the kitchen for immediate consumption.

Table 11

Our Order No.......

Customer's Order No. Phone........

Terms: Net........

Date..............

Sold to:................

Quantify	*Unit*	*Item*	*Price*	*Total*

The receiving clerk's daily report form is one of the subsidiary journals and is used to initially record the purchase of foods (Table 12). The total of the bill is put in the total column, and the items are distributed on the receiving clerk's daily report to stores or direct to kitchen. Those items sent to stores are debited to food inventory and items sent directly to kitchen are immediately charged to food expense. The sundries column is used for those items received by the receiving clerk that are not food.

All fresh meat is tagged with a meat tag. Fresh meat has a tendency to loose weight while in storage due to loss of moisture. It is, therefore, important that the date of receipt of the meat is put on the tag as well as the correct weight so that shrinkage can be properly accounted for by the food controller.

Table 12

Receiving Clerk's Daily Report

No. ....

Date.....19.......

Qty.	*Unit*	*Description*	*Unit Price*	*Amount*	*Total Amount*	*Purchase Journal*		*Sundries*	*Distribution Detail*
						Food direct	*Food stores*		

The Purchase Journal

Each day the invoices and receiving sheets are turned over to the accounting department to be entered in the purchase journal (Table 13). This journal is similar to sales summary journal. There are several columns for inventories and many columns for the most frequent expenses. Any purchase or expense that cannot be categorized in one of the designated columns is entered in the sundries column along with an explanation of the expense or asset it should be charged to.

Hotels also receive many invoices by mail. For example, electric bill comes once in two months. These are entered in the purchase journal and the appropriate column is debited with the proper amount. Many miscellaneous purchases are made by personnel of hotels. Copies of the invoices for such purchases are brought to the accounting department. The invoices are put in a file and the total is entered when the monthly statement arrives. This procedure saves making many entries and is currently used in many of the hotels.

At the end of the month the purchase journal is totalled and balanced. The total of the amount column is posted as a credit to accounts payable. Rest of the columns are posted as debits. Some of the debits are asset accounts and some are expense accounts. Individual amounts in the amount column are posted as credits to specific accounts payable ledger accounts.

The Issue Journal

Food received by the storeroom clerk is checked in placed on shelves. The clerk usually stamp the price of each item on the container so that its cost can be determined later on without having to refer to the invoice. He also enters the date and the amount of goods received on the stock record card. As food is needed, a requisition is prepared and signed by the department head. The storeroom clerk issues the food and other supplies to the department after entering the requisition into the issue journal. Food issued to the

Table 13

Purchase Journal

Stores												Expenses
Date	*Creditor*	*Amount*	*Food*	*Liquior*	*House Keeping*	*Food Exp.*	*House Keeping exp.*	*Repairs & maint*	*Heater, light & power*	*Office supplies exp.*	*Admn. and genl.*	*Sundaries Detail Amount*

kitchen immediately becomes an expense to the hotel. At the end of the month, physical inventories are taken to examine the accuracy of accounting records.

In all the hotels, the accounting system has some in built controls. The sale of food in the dining room is controlled to verify that all guest checks are accounted for. No item offood is given to a waiter without a written order. The sale of liquor in the bar and dining room is controlled in the same manner. However, control of liquor sales is more difficult because often the same person who mixes the drinks also writers out the order and takes the cash.

The daily transactions are verified by the night auditor. All sales must be posted to guest accounts or collected as cash because the night auditor makes certain the total charges and cash sales on his transcript of guest ledger agrees with the total sales of each department. The control of raw food is accomplished by rigidly enforcing the ordering, receiving, storing and issuing routine.

Thus, the accounting records for purchases are set up to ensure adequate controls. Food is one of the most often purchased items in a hotel and the routine of purchasing food must be rigorously followed if adequate control over purchasing is to be maintained. The steward and chief determine the menu, and purchasing department orders perishable items on the basis of the menus for the coming period. Quotation list of suppliers are checked before placing the order.

All received goods are entered on the receiving clerk's daily report and that information is transferred to purchase journal. Other bills are also entered in the purchase journal as they are received. At the end of the month, the purchase journal is added and the totals are posted to ledger accounts.

As goods are issued from the store, requisition are completed and signed by the department head. The requisitions are entered in the issue journal. At the end of the month, the issue journal is tol-,alled and totals are posted to ledger accounts, crediting the appropriate inventory account and debiting the appropriate expense.

The storeroom clerk maintains a perpetual inventory of all goods under his control. At the end of the month, he takes a physical inventory and the count is compared with the book figure.

Accounting for Cash Disbursements

The last subsidiary journals involve the payment of cash. Bills received are first recorded in the purchase journal. When bills are paid, cash account is credited and payable account is debited. The journal used to record these transactions is called the cash disbursements journal (Table 14). It has several columns. The amount column is posted as a credit to the cash account. The cash discount column is posted as a credit and is posted to cash discount ledger account. The cash discount ledger account is deducted from expenses while determining profit. The remainder of the accounts are posted as debits. The sundries column is used when a cheque is written or payment is made for an item that is not already set up as an account payable.

The Petty Cash Journal

The hotels purchase many items for cash as well as by cheque. Infact, the accounting office has a petty cash fund for the items which are purchased for cash. These purchases are of small amounts and are made at local stores. The journal used to record these purchases is called the petty cash journal (Table 15), Cheques are written and recorded in are of small amounts and are made at local stores. The journal used to record these purchases is called the petty cash journal (Table 15). Cheques are written and recorded in cash disbursement journal for money placed in the petty cash, fund. Payments from petty cash fund are made when purchase receipts are received. They are immediately recorded in the detail column. The headings on the petty cash journal varies from hotel to hotel, but certain headings are common to all hotels. Frequently used columns

Table 14

Cash Disbursements Journal

Date	Paid	Clerk	Credits		Debits		Petty cash	Sundaries	
			Amount	Cash Discount	Accounts Payable	Payroll Payable		amount	detail

Table 15

Cash Disbursements Journal

Date	Detail	Received	Total disbursed	Food expenses	House-Keeping supplier exp.	Postage exp.	Office supplies exp.	Gas & Oil exp.	Repairs & ment.	Sundaries	
										amount	detail

are food expense, housekeeping supplies expense, postage expense and office supplies expense. At the end of the month the journal is balanced. The total of each column is debited to appropriate account.

Thus, the cash disbursement journal is used to record the payment of cash. The journal enables us to credit cash account and debit liability, expense, or asset accounts. Small purchases made with cash are recorded in the petty cash journal. Each purchase is entered in the petty cash journal and distributed to the appropriate expense account. At the end of the month, the journal is added and totals are posted to appropriate ledger accounts.

□

9

Room Occupancy Rate Management

Room service is a specialized form of foodservice that transforms hotel guest rooms into private dining rooms. The basic procedures in room service are the same as for any kind of table service. The guest places a food production order. Food is then delivered to the guest's table. Finally, the bill is presented to the guest after the food is served. But this is where the similarity ends.

Logistically there are several differences in guest room service versus dining room service. In room service, the order taker and the server are two different people. This division of labour necessitates a communications system, especially since the server usually does not have an easy opportunity for a second trip to the guest's table if some part of the order is inaccurately communicated. Finally, in dining room service, the food server or service assistant cleans and resets the table immediately after the guest leaves. In room service the server may or may not return within a short time. In many hotels the rule is for housekeeping department staff to place the equipment in the corridor outside the room. Although it may sit for some time just outside of the room, the dirty foodservice equipment is eventually retrieved either by the room service staff or the food and beverage steward.

Room service is also somewhat similar to home food delivery. For both of these types of service, food is delivered to remote settings for consumption. Consequently, time and food temperature become difficult service control factors. Also, both of these service systems utilize separate personnel to take the order and to serve it.

However there are differences here as well. In guest room service, the flatware, silverware, all extra food items, and possibly even the table itself must be delivered, whereas in home delivery, customers are usually capable of providing some of these items themselves. Therefore, the preparation of the room service order requires a well-designed staging area. In addition, where home food deliverers usually use automobiles to transport the food to the customer's doorstep, hotel room service wait staff must transport all of the additional food and service equipment on foot and up, down, or across great expansive hotel complexes.

Segmentation of the hotel market has created a whole class of hotels with limited or no food and beverage service. Many hotels provide only breakfast for room service. Because of labour and equipment costs and the difficulty of forecasting sales, room service is typically the least profitable department in any hotel's food and beverage operation. Some hotel provide order forms for guests to complete before retiring. This gives the food and beverage department some advance notice as to production requirements for the next morning, which helps reduce labour cost. Other hotels with limited food service capability and no room service are now providing some form of buffet style breakfast in the hotel.

It is very probable that in the coming decade only the largest full-service facilities will provide any form of room service. We will therefore describe the organizational structure of a room service operation in a full-service hotel. Usually, at least in a property of one thousand rooms or more, the room service department operates with autonomy under the umbrella of the food and beverage department. The director is responsible for menu design as well as the appropriation of service equipment. He or she ultimately bears the responsibility for maximizing revenue and controlling expenses within the department. Operationally, the director is responsible for appropriation and control of all production and service equipment as well as human resources management and quality control within the department.

Human resources management may be the biggest factor affecting quality control and profitability. In large hotel the room service department may operate a separate food preparation line. The operation may even run 24 hours per day. This requires staffing cooks, service personnel, and supervisors for three shifts. Room service technology is very labor intensive.

Although systems vary across hotels, most allow for one person to do nothing but take room service orders (Schmidt 1987). Another person is responsible for setting up the room-service cart with all utensils and service equipment. The room service waiter, or possibly in larger operations a setup person, adds butter, condiments, salads, and all other required food items based on the food order. Lastly the hot entree is added. For control purposes a room service captain expedites this final step.

Pre-setting or carts adds speed to the service process and is possible whenever accurate demand forecasting can be done. For example, breakfast orders can be accurately forecast by allowing guests to order room service breakfast at night before retiring. In addition, many frequent-guests plans offer free continental breakfast as a perk. These orders can be forecast from front office records.

Room service forecasting is generally based on house count, the number of rooms in the hotel. For example, in some hotels room service for breakfast may be as high as 25 per cent of the guest count. However, the market for room service can vary depending on the type of people in the hotel, check-in and check-out times, and the activities that the guests are engaged in. For example, when a hotel is filled with a group consisting of mostly women, even during dinner, room service use may be as high as 15 to 20 per cent of the guest count. Other groups may have large numbers of late check-ins after the dining room closes. If room service operates after dining room hours, the service may be used. In addition, if businesspeople are required to do large amounts of work/entertaining in their rooms, room service demand can increase.

In-house service charges [note: some hotels deliver of premises] can be one to three dollars per cover. Yet, even with the extra revenue, it can be difficult to break even in the room service operation. The labour cost ratio can be higher than in banquets or the dining rooms. Also, room service requires extensive equipment. For example, a hotel that generates $4,000 to $5,000 in room service revenue per day may require over 300 portable room service carts and coffee pots.

Loss of the smaller pieces of equipment through theft such as silverware, plates, and pitchers can be high. In an effort to reduce losses, some hotels send servers back to the room to pick up the equipment rather than waiting until housekeeping cleans the room the following day. This also helps in pest control. Nonetheless, it requires additional labour and training.

Delivery time varies with demand. For a complete meal during a peak period a guest may wait as long as 45 minutes. However, the market has come to expect faster service. Most hotels attempt to keep delivery times to less than 35 minutes. This can be more difficult than one might expect. Unlike most home delivery operations, menus are usually not limited to a few items. Having to transport more elaborate service equipment also strains delivery time.

Once room service was an expected part of the product/ service mix at any midscale hotel. Now, it is becoming more the purview of full-service and luxury properties. Still, in those properties large enough to have a completely separate room service division, the food and the service can be as elaborate and as elegant as in the finest of dining facilities.

HOSPITALITY TIPS FOR HOTEL AND MOTEL PERSONNEL

DO'S and DON'TS of hospitality

* Do make all of your guests feel welcome. Greet them pleasantly and take the attitude that they are guests in your own home.

* Do be attentive, alert, and cordial, but don't be too "forward."

* Do be courteous and cooperative at all times.

* Do have a general knowledge of your community and the surrounding area.

* Do know the telephone number of the Tourist Bureau or Chamber of Commerce and the most direct route there, so that if there are questions you cannot answer they can be referred to the Tourist Bureau.

* Do know where "services" can be located.

* Do talk up local events.

Front Office Personnel

* Do make him feel at home. Your first contact with the guest is very important. Use a pleasant tone of voice, smile easily. Be cooperative and courteous. Use his name several times, there is no sweeter music to the visitor.

* Do be attentive, alert, and cordial, but not to "chatty."

* Do make complimentary references to guest's home town, particularly if they have traveled a great distance, such as "glad to see you've traveled so far to visit us, Mr. Smith."

* Do make casual inquiry if the guest has visited your community previously, or has stopped at your place of accommodation before. If not, then offer any assistance you may deem advisable.

* Do inquire if the guest is expecting mail or messages.

* Don't be abrupt, no matter how busy you are.

* Don't send your guests away if your establishment is filled. Help them if you can, or direct them to the Tourist Bureau.

Porters and Bell Boys

* Do take pride in your work and have a desire to serve others.
* Do handle the guest's luggage with care.
* Do offer assistance, when necessary, to guests arriving by car, regarding parking areas and regulations.
* Do make a quick check in the room to see if towels, glasses, etc. are in order.
* Do know the dining room hours, and services provided.
* Don't talk in front of guest doors with other members of the staff.
* Don't give a grunt for an answer when asked a question.
* Don't chew gum.

The Ten Commandments

1. Remember the traveler has been invited. You are a representative host.
2. Put yourself in the traveler's place—then treat him accordingly.
3. Do not measure your helpfulness by what the traveler buys directly from you.
4. Find out the visitor's vacation tastes, then direct him to the things he will enjoy in your area.
5. Point out, in addition to attractions in your area, some entirely different attractions elsewhere and nearby the city.
6. Be genuinely pleasant, cordial, friendly, and enthusiastic.
7. Be attentive; give the visitor a chance to talk and ask questions.
8. Do not belittle other states, areas, or cities.

9. Be sure the information you give is correct and that it is understood.

10. If you cannot accurately answer a traveler's questions, refer him to your Chamber of Commerce or other tourist information center.

Checkout

A recent survey by an international hotel and resort chain revealed that two of the top ten peeves that business travelers had about their experiences involved the checkout process (Merrick 1990). Their complaints centered around the length of and inflexibility of checkout times. The checkout procedure is usually the last contact the guest will have with the property. This procedure is the final opportunity for the hotel to ensure the guest leaves with a positive memory or aftertaste of the service experience that was provided (Barrington and Olsen 1987). If the guest has had a particularly bad experience, checkout is the last chance to alter the guest's perception of the hotel by providing a positive experience in order to generate that all essential repeat business. Conversely, if the guest had a good experience, there is a need to perpetuate it by ending his or her stay with a smooth easy checkout procedure. Bear in mind that people tend to remember their most recent experiences more vividly than those that occurred in the past.

Basically the checkout procedure consists of three elements:

(1) the guest vacates the room,

(2) the guest settles the bill, and

(3) the guest departs the property.

Vacating the Room

Just when the guest decides to vacate the room may be governed by several factors: travel plans, checkout time, housekeeping pressure, bell staff availability, and/or post-checkout service provided by the property.

The chief factor that determines when guests decide to check out centers around their business or travel plans. Naturally they want to check out in ample time (but not too early) to keep their next appointment, whether it is driving to the next destination or catching a flight home. Probably the next most important factor governing departure is the formal checkout time, which often conflicts with the guest's travel plans.

The official checkout time is usually posted at the front desk, on the registration card, and on the inside of the guest room door (along with the room rate and emergency procedures). This time can range anywhere from 9:00 AM to 2:00 PM, but is normally around non. In most cases, this time is established by the hotel for its purposes, not for guest convenience.

Although the hotel generally desires to accommodate the guest in any way possible, the rooms must be vacated in order for the housekeeping staff to have them ready by check-in time, which usually starts at about 3:00 PM. Most hotels will allow the guest to make arrangements for late checkout, depending on the volume of reservations that day. A few will attach a fee for late checkout (depending on policy or projected occupancy). When a hotel is projecting a sellout, upon check-in, guests are often required to sign a statement confirming their departure datc. The law varies from state to state on the right of eviction of "stayovers" (guests who continue occupying a room beyond the anticipated checkout time).

Several properties are enhancing guest satisfaction by offering flexible checkin/out times (Seeger 1990). One hotel in Miami allows guests to check out up to 6:00 PM without an extra charge. The thinking is that since 80 per cent of the guests check out by noon, the needs of the customer will be served with little problem to the hotel. A hotel in Dallas rents rooms on a 24-hour basis, similar to car rentals. With this system guests can check in and out at their convenience. This system was well received by the guests because they could make and receive phone calls, take a shower, change clothes, have a convenient and safe place to store their luggage, and their children could use to pool all afternoon while they were in meetings. Many hotels are extending late checkout options to their frequent-stay and weekend special guests. Basically they add extra hours to the weekend by extending the checkout to as late as 8:00 PM on Sunday. This presents little problem because the rooms are not scheduled to be cleaned until Monday morning when most of the housekeeping staff return to work. Finally these flexible checkout times eliminate bottlenecks created when too many people check out at the same time.

Other minor factors affecting the checkout time include.

1. The availability of the bell staff. Experienced travelers plan their checkout time when they know the bellmen will not be busy.

2. Persistence of housekeeping. There are occasions when the guest does not hang a do not disturb sign on the door, and the housekeepers keep knocking until the guest feels compelled to leave and let them do their work.

3. Post-checkout service. If the hotel offers other services to the guests who are not leaving until many hours beyond the checkout time, such as complimentary baggage storage and a place to freshen up before departure, the guests will tend to take advantage of these services and opt for an early checkout.

Bill Settlement

The night auditor updates the guest folio between 11:00 PM and 7:00 AM in order for the hotel to be able to present the bill to guests when they are ready to check out. Depending on the property, the guest has several check-out procedures available.

The simplest and least troublesome method is to check in and out at the same time. With this system the guest pays cash in advance when checking in and simply leaves by the agreed upon time. Of course this method only works in a property where no other, except pay-as-you-go, services are provided. Such a system precludes any amenities including telephone service.

The regular checkout procedure is to go the front desk at the end of the stay, request the bill, and satisfy the account. Although this method is personal and facilitates the handling of all problems on the spot, the major drawback is the extra time involved if the guest is unlucky enough to pick a busy time.

Many hotels offer an express checkout service allowing the guest to avoid the long lines at the from desk. The most popular method of express checkout is one in which the bill or folio is slipped under the guest's door by at least 5 AM on the morning of the scheduled departure date. If the bill is correct the guest gives tacit approval by doing nothing, simply departing by checkout time. Of course this system is only available to guests with prior credit approval.

For a number of years, selected Marriott hotels have offered a popular checkout procedure using the television. In this system the guest turns to the appropriate channel and simply follows the directions. Within minutes of completing the transaction, a printed statement is available to be picked up at the front desk. Not only are guests able to use the system for checkout, but they may also use it to review their folio at any time during their stay. As with most systems, this one is not infallible (Grimes 1991). It seems that in order to save time, a female traveler used he TV to check out at 6 A.M. and then went for her usual morning walk. When she returned her magnetic key would not open her door. By this time the hotel was very busy with heavy elevator use and long lines at the desk. When she finally got to tell someone of her problem, she was already late for an appointment. She discovered that the computer had changed the code for the door key and she had to be checked back in again. Luckily her bags were still in the room. Hopefully the consequences of the self-service checkout procedure will be explained to future guests.

Payment Options

As in most sales situations the hotel guest has a variety of options when paying the bill, such as cash, check, credit card, transfer to another guest account, or direct billing. Of course any hotel will take cash at the time of checkout, but cash in advance is another matter. A guest who pays cash in advance would not be allowed to make any other charges. This arrangement is more convenient in a facility where services are limited to sleeping rooms only. However, even the most basic property has a telephone and probably movie rentals in the room. In this case, the guest would be asked to pay for additional services when rendered.

Most hotels are reluctant to take a check for all the obvious reasons, not the least of which is the fact that most guests are writing checks on out-of-town banks. Normally, the only way a lodging facility will take a check is to use a check approval organization. Travelers' checks are different and, with proper identification, are treated the same as cash. Most properties have strict policies on handling checks and when followed there is seldom a problem. Be mindful, however, that just when the industry thinks it has the perfect system, along comes another scheme to defraud.

The most popular and widely accepted form of payment is by credit card. It is nearly impossible to rent a car without a credit card, and most hotels would like to move in the same direction. The credit card is so popular with businesses because the risk of extending credit is shifted from the hotel to the issuing institution. Normally when the guest checks in, his or her credit card is imprinted, and, by signing the guest registration card, the hotel has a "signature on file" thereby enabling the hotel to collect charges made by the guest even if he or she fails to sign the charge slip.

Another common method of satisfying a guest account is direct billing to a third party, which is transferred to the city ledger account. This method allows local companies who do frequent business with a hotel to set up an account for their clients or employees. These accounts are usually invoiced on a monthly billing cycle. An infrequent method of third party billing occurs when a guest's charges are transferred to another guest's account. Of course this method requires authorization from the account being charged, who must in turn adhere to the hotel's policies.

Settlement Problems

When the guest checks out the bill is presented for verification of charges. Fre quently there are discrepancies on the bill because many people are involved in reporting the charges, such as restaurants, lounge, gift shop, parking, telephone, and movies. These charges are then posted to the guest folio by the night auditor. Computers may be used to automatically post the charges at the point of sale but no system is foolproof and mistakes are made. Erroneous charges on the bill can be a real source of tension between the hotel and guest, especially telephone charges. Since deregulation many local and long distance telephone companies are vying for the lucrative hotel business. Each have varied rates and surcharges, which are not disclosed to the guest until he or she is shocked by the bill. For example, some companies automatically charge for a call after so many seconds. Therefore a guest may let a phone ring ten times with no answer and hang up, only to be surprised to be charged for a completed call. These and other phantom charges need to be resolved for guest satisfaction.

An increasingly popular method of dealing with guest satisfaction is called "empowerment", whereby lower level employees, such as desk clerks, have the authority and responsibility to solve problems without management intervention (Brymer 1991). If mistakes are made the desk clerks may adjust the bill, offer an upgrade on the next visit, or ask the customer what would satisfy him or her and try to act accordingly.

Departure

After the guests check out they are expected to make no more charges, surrender their room key, and leave to premises. These events do not always occur immediately, therefore checking out does not sever all guest-host relationships. Although no charges are allowed after checkout, a guest may have just charged breakfast to his or her room and those charges were nct posted in time to present the complete bill. As a result of this problem, the clerk should always ask if there were any recent charges that do not appear on the bill. The hotel relies on guest honesty in this case but, if charges appear later, the hotel must go through the ccmplicated process of collection. Point of sale computers that post charges immediately have all but eliminated this problem.

The guest is not expected to surrender the key immediately upon check-out. The time interval between checkout and departure seems to be a gray area that is not formally stated. The checkout procedure should trigger a signal to the housekeeping department that the room is ready for cleaning. The only delay in such cases may be when the guest retains the room key to do any last minute packing or to wait for a bellman. Guests can leave the key in the room, give it to the desk clerk, place it in a special key drop, or, if they forget completely, they can mail it back to the hotel. With disposable electronic cards gradually replacing keys, their return becomes moot.

Finally when the guest checks out a guest history card should be created listing all pertinent information about the guest. As one hotel executive once said, "It's amazing that I call for a pizza delivery, give my phone number, and they ask if I would like the large pepperoni like I got the last time." The hotel business has a lot of catching up to do (Greger and Withiam, 1991).

❐

10

Marketing Functions

For most hotel companies, it was only during the 1980s that the word "marketing" became anything more than a euphemism for sales. Indeed, in the competitive landscape of the not too distant past, most activities that related to putting guests in rooms could be accomplished by an aggressive and knowledgeable sales staff. In today's competitive environment, this has become impossible.

Hotel companies that have designed a sophisticated inventory of hospitality services need a similarly sophisticated scheme for letting their clientele know about their services. For most hotel companies, true marketing has now evolved to reflect their own sophistication as well as that of guests and potential clientele.

Business travellers, travel agents, and meeting planners who represent and book group and convention business are well educated and informed consumers. To serve this clientele, hotels have had to develop marketing efforts and product segmentation to first interest the market and then to allow people in that market to make intelligent choices from among competitors. Marketing is thus an umbrella term that covers a number of strategic and tactical activities designed to tell the clientele the "story" of the hotel's services and to encourage that clientele to make choices based on how one hotel's marketing message compares to alternatives. In any given hotel or hotel company, marketing includes: a range of sales activities; public relations; advertising in all media; design of symbols and images; and, increasingly, the departments of convention services, reservations, and perhaps catering. Research also plays a major role in designing marketing strategies and tactics.

Managers understand the range within which these data may be interpreted and applied. Successful managers and high-quality organizations will always be seeking information and data that allow them to make accurate decisions and design effective marketing and/or managerial efforts. These data can take a number of different forms, but for the most part they deal with the various characteristics of the hotel's target market that affect its choice of hotels. Hotels will find mechanisms to accumulate the following sorts of data about their guests and potential guests:

(a) **Geographic.** What sorts of communities are represented; what parts of the country or world; how far do they travel.

(b) **Demographic.** Age, sex, occupation, income, ethnicity, family, education.

(c) **Psychographic.** Client's self-image; social or peer group; lifestyle; personality traits.

(d) **Behaviouristic.** Is hotel choice a routine or special occasion; what does guest seek in terms of quality, service, economy; user status (non-user, ex-user, potential user, regular user, first-time user); usage rate (light, medium, heavy); loyalty.

While many of the specific details or programmes included under the marketing umbrella can be farmed out to agencies that specialize in advertising or public relations, the hotel's strategic marketing plan has to come from within the hotel organization itself.

If marketing, as it has been said, is the promise, then it is the hotel's employees who keep that promise. This is particularly important with the group market, represented in large part by meeting planners. In the Rutherford and Umbreit study, of the 316 critical incidents gleaned from 52 separate MP interviews, over 100, or 32 percent, had the convention services manager (CSM) as its central focus.

In recognition of the central importance of the CSM in keeping the promise, many hotels include convention services as a functional component of the marketing department.

The professionals in these departments design their activities specifically to make sure that the efforts and promises of the sales department and marketing messages are delivered to the group while it is on the premises of the hotel. Michael Adams's article on "a day in the life" of such a manager provides graphic evidence of the importance of this position. It also gives us a detailed look at the responsibilities that are important for this professional to master in participating in the hosting of such an event.

All in all, the strategies, tactics, activities, personnel and concepts described by articles in this section provide an overview that only hints at the importance of effective management of the marketing function.

Marketing is perhaps the most written about topic in hospitality literature. Because there is such a diversity of opinion it can be argued that there is no one "right" way to market, nor is there any single piece of literature generally considered seminal to hotel marketing. The reader is urged to consider the references used by contributing authors and the suggested readings, and to actively peruse recent hospitality journals to achieve greater understanding of this fascinating process and by extension, its management.

We've seen great changes in the travel industry during the 1980s, with mergers, acquisitions, niche marketing, and brand extensions. With all this activity, the consensus is that the travel industry is maturing. While that may be true, there's no likelihood that change will slow down.

On the contrary, we will see tremendous proliferation of travel services and experimental products and services. With the pressure of competition, many of these new products will fail. Companies that are now dabbling in the travel industry will either have to make a serious long-term commitment or disappear. If you think the competition is tough now, just watch how severe it will be in a few years' time.

In most parts of the world, travel and tourism is one of the largest and fastest growing segments of the economy. Ironically, because of its fragmented nature, the travel industry has never been given the recognition it deserves.

As travel becomes more central to the lives of more of the world's population, its contribution to the world economy is better recognized. Consequently, travel is attracting more capital investment and more sophisticated talent.

Marketing will be a key to success in the 1990s. Lip service and slogans will no longer substitute for a real understanding of the marketplace. No longer can we merely respond to market demands. Instead, we must anticipate them by reading Market conditions better and faster than before. The hotel industry is making great strides in this direction. It is moving rapidly from an operations-driven industry to one that is marketing and consumer-driven. The importance of marketing is apparent, as more CEOs are drawn from the ranks of marketing departments rather than from operations.

If hotel companies are to survive what we call the "no-nonsense 1990s," they must be consumer-driven. Armchair marketing is dead. Instead, companies must gain a better understanding of the wants and needs of their consumers and how best to communicate with them. In so doing, marketers are discovering a sophisticated buyer—one who is well informed and intolerant of slow, boring messages.

The velocity and amount of information that is being disseminated to consumers is growing right along with their ability to consume it. The growth of broadcast media, particularly television, is largely responsible for this acceleration. In industrialized nations, the generations born after World War II have grown tip largely watching TV. Others, without access to TV, have listened to the radio.

As programming and technology improved, viewers and listeners discovered that, compared to print, they are being exposed to more information, more quickly, more vividly, and sometimes more accurately with broadcast media. Generations discovered they could hear about an item faster than they read about it and view a video on it even more quickly.

But television has not replaced newspapers or radio in the marketplace. Instead, people are doing all three reading, listening, and viewing—thereby consuming far more information. In this process, time has become a precious commodity.

People are generally unwilling to concentrate on slow, complicated, or boring messages. Sometimes even the velocity of televised information is too slow, and people zap through programmes, using the remote control on their videocassette recorder. With split screens, viewers can browse more than one programme at a time. This behaviour shows conclusively that the mind can comprehend things much faster than we can speak.

As a result, the communicators and advertisers of the future will need to experiment with an efficient new visual and verbal language that can be quickly and easily understood. In print advertising, messages will have to be more simple and similar to billboards, with shorter headlines and more powerful visuals.

Data-base Marketing

As the hotel marketplace becomes more competitive and complex, merely identifying and chasing market segments won't be enough to get the business. We will need to refine these segments further into narrow "slivers," so we can target microsegments. The age of data-base micromarketing is made possible by improved technology. The hotel industry has long been able to capture information about its customers through the registration process. Only in recent years have we seen significant strides in this area. With advanced computer software, hotels will be better able to capture and tabulate customer buying patterns and preferences. With this data base, hotels will be better able to target their marketing and ensure customer satisfaction with the product.

Even as the travel market grows larger, becoming a mass market, hotel companies will have to become more selective about which segments of that market they pursue. Armed with their data base, hotel companies will begin to position themselves against microsegments.

By refining profiles of their customers by using geography, demographies, psychographies, and buying patterns and preferences, hotels will discover nuggets of business opportunities for which they can compete effectively. Moreover, with a deep understanding of their customers, these hotels will be able to tailor their facilities, services, and staff training to their guests' needs. We are convinced that hotel firms large and small that are committed to developing customer data bases will be the ones to compete effectively in the 1990s.

Yield Marketing

With the development of data-base marketing, hotel companies will gain a weapon that will benefit revenues, which will constantly be under pressure. Many hotels are already developing yield-management systems that are appropriate to their operations. Yield management can be extended to marketing to create what we have termed "yield marketing." To do this, hotels will need to link their sales, marketing, and reservations systems with their property-management systems. This will be possible because small computers are becoming steadily more flexible and powerful. Yield marketing will link customer responses with the hotel's advertising and promotional efforts. With such a system in place, your hotel will be able accurately and quickly to measure and even anticipate the effectiveness and efficiency of marketing investments. As advertising and sales costs climb, a system like yield marketing will be essential in helping hotels achieve higher returns on advertising and promotion.

Human Resources Management

During the 1980s, individual hotels and entire hotel chains did whatever they could to differentiate themselves in the consumer's mind. The proliferation of various hotel brands and products was a large factor in this differentiation effort.

In the 1990s, we expect advertising to be an important differentiating factor. The look, quality, style, and tone of properties' advertising will help estabilsh a distinct personality or identity in the marketplace. This personality will also send a signal to employees as to what the hotel stands for.

As facilities and amenities are duplicated from hotel to hotel, consistent staff service and attitude will become substantial differentiating and competitive factors. Hotels that can attract, train, motivate, and hold their employees will have a decided competitive advantage. With the tightening of the labour market, retaining talented employees will be more challenging.

The role of human resources managers will become critical, and all hospitality firms will have to develop innovative recruitment and motivational programmes. Hotel managers will have to open two-way communication lines with employees, place more emphasis on a work atmosphere that increases the quality of output, and give greater recognition to the fact that all staff members affect the guest service experience.

First Blush

But all these efforts can easily be wasted if a critical factor is overlooked-namely, the person who doses the sale. The hotel industry spends hundreds of millions of dollars to develop beautiful and elaborate advertising campaigns to get potential customers to do one thing. That thing is to dial the number of the hotel's reservation desk or system. And who does that customer talk to when he or she calls for a reservation? Almost always, the least seasoned, perhaps lowest paid member of our sales staff answers the' call.

In most cases, the reservationist is the first employee to talk to the customer. Shouldn't this person be the most motivated and best informed member of our staff? If not, all the merchandising efforts in the world will not close the sale. Companies like Disney are leading the way in employee training, so that every staff member is immersed in company culture and ready to serve the guest in an appropriate fashion.

Bonding

Once the new customer has been won, hotels face the challenge of keeping that customer. It costs hotel companies five to six times as much to win new customers as to keep them. But today's notoriously fickle customer has little brand loyalty. To promote more loyalty, hotel operators are beginning to realize they must stay close to their customers, listen to them, and satisfy their wants and needs.

By personalizing the guest experience, we can build the customer's loyalty and create repeat business. Advertising, too, must become more important and relevant. As advertising plays an increasing role in winning new customers and keeping the old, the credibility of the message will determine its underlying effectiveness. We must place our message and our hotel name in the context of our customers' lives. The closer we can relate the hotel to 'our prospect's lifestyle, the closer that person will feel to the hotel, the more effective the advertising message will be, and the stronger the brand loyalty. Burleigh Gardner calls this "bonding," and we see evidence of it in a greater number of consumer advertising messages.

Hotel advertising seems to be lagging behind consumer products in attempting in getting consumers to bond to the hotel brand. That job will fall not just on advertising campaigns but on all levels of hotel employees. These are the challenges of the 1990s: Give the consumer your message and be quick about it. Deliver on your promises in such a way that the consumer is aware of an open, two-way communication with your establishment, bring employees into the picture by understanding their needs. Pay attention to micromarketing and explore the possibilities of yield marketing.

Selling to Group Markets

Selling to group markets in the hotel business is both an art as well as a science. The science side deals with applying the principles of marketing and management to hospitality selling. Product positioning, market segmentation, target marketing, and sales management are all practiced in hospitality group market sales, just as they are selling strategies in any industry. The "art" reflects the reality of intuition, common sense, good judgment, and decency in dealing with customers, clients, owners, employees, and the community-at-large. In other words, management theory usually works but must always be weighed by good instincts and "using your head."

Clients and Customers

Selling hotel space means considering the needs of both clients and customers. Clients are the persons responsible for planning the event—be it a company's annual sales conference, a group holiday tour, a national medical association convention, or a family reunion. Customers are the people who actually attend the event. These include the conference attendees, the association convention delegates, the individuals who purchased the holiday tour package, or the family members attending the family reunion.

Hotel sales managers deal primarily with clients. It is their job to find out the needs of the potential clients and their respective customers, and then to determine whether the hotel can fulfil those needs. These needs typically include the hotel guest rooms, meeting rooms, banquet facilities, hospitality suites, and so forth.

Location of the hotel, access to airports and highways, recreation facilities, and service amenities are also common criteria that clients consider when booking with a hotel. Once the meeting is "booked," it is the job of the entire hotel management team to ensure that the needs of the client and their respective customers are, indeed, met.

Market segments for hotel sales may include associations and conventions, corporations, government, education, sports, medical, incentive travel, and group tours. Though not an exhaustive list, each group represents a major market in hotel convention sales. Following is a brief description of each.

Group Markets

The needs of a meeting planner, an event coordinator, a tour broker, or a football coach travelling with his team do vary. Thus, the group market is segmented by various types of groups that share common needs. In turn, most hotel marketers identify one or more of these group market segments as their specific target market(s) for their respective hotels. This not only helps the hotel to be better positioned in the marketplace, it also gives the hotel sales staff focus in its selling efforts to identified target market needs.

Association and Convention Market

Of the major group markets, associations and conventions are probably the most widely written about, read about, and known about. They range from small regional associations such as the New England Rose Growers Association to meganational associations such as the 12,000-member American Bankers Association. Associations meet regularly, most often on an annual basis. Throughout North America these meetings are commonly known as the "annual convention." The association and convention market can be further segmented by the type of organization. These include trade associations, professional associations, and the "SMERF" association grouping, which includes social, military, educational,religious, and fraternal organizations. Because of the largely non-profit nature of SMERF organizations, they tend to be more price-sensitive than the trade and professional associations.

Corporate Market

Corporations of all sizes hold various off-premise meetings, conferences, and conventions. Typical locations for these meetings are hotels, resorts, and conference centers. The various types of corporate meetings include sales and marketing, training, management, professional/technical, and stockholder. They can range in size from 10 to 1,000+ attendees meeting annually, semiannually, or quarterly. Some larger corporations have professional meeting planning departments that plan all the company's meetings, whereas others leave the job of meeting planning to the department head or division head who is calling the meeting.

Government Market

Many hotels specifically target the government market largely because of its sheer size. For example, almost 15 percent of the U.S. workforce is employed by local, state, and federal government agencies. Most government off-premise meetings are educational seminars and/or training programs. Government meeting planning is quite different from that of the private sector; special attention needs to be paid to specific government regulations and restrictions, per diems, and special budget and billing procedures. The Society of Government Meeting Planners addresses the specific needs of meeting planning for all levels of government.

Education Market

The education market for hotel convention sales is an often misunderstood market, most likely because it is quite broad and has component parts in other major markets. The education market includes secondary and higher education institutions such as private schools and public universities, education associations such as the National Association of English Teachers, and corporate education and training seminars.

The main reason for the education market's potential as a selected target, market is its breadth, its repeat business potential, and its willingness to meet during traditionally slow periods. First, the education market is broad in scope and cuts across many industry sectors, including profit and non-profit organizations. Second, the repeat business potential is strong, especially from large institutions with a multitude of divisions and activities. Targeting a university, for example, would include soliciting business from the academic units, the alumni office, the division of continuing education, and so forth. Third, and perhaps most important, many education-oriented conferences meet during the summer months, which is typically a slow period for corporate, trade, and professional association convention activity. As noted earlier, the education market is price-sensitive as well. Thus, "matching" the price needs of this market will help fill empty guest rooms during an off-peak summer period.

Sports Market

Professional and collegiate team sports constitute the major portion of the sports market. Professional individual sporting events such as golf and tennis and amateur sporting events such as figure skating championships are also part of this growing market. A key aspect for soliciting the sports market is understanding the specific needs of the coach and/or sponsor of the event.

Typical requests include close proximity to where the sporting event is taking place, special menus and meal times, unusual checkin and checkout times, extra security and privacy, large guest rooms, and special billing procedures.

Medical Market

The medical market is comprised of health care professionals in medicine and related disciplines attending seminars, symposiums, and workshops for their particular field. Sponsors of these conferences include universities, private institutions, medical associations, clinics, and the like. Research and technology, in particular, have spurred tremendous growth in the medical meetings group market where there is a pressing need to keep pace with the latest advancements in the medical profession.

Particular needs of the medical market for hotel marketers to consider include a short booking lead time, high-tech audio-visual equipment, and guest rooms accommodating work/study space, for instance, large desks, good lighting, and quiet.

Medical meetings meet often and regularly, and their meeting planners are very meticulous in their demands. Though sometimes considered difficult to deal with, they usually respond quite favourably to a professional approach in assisting with their meeting needs.

Incentive Travel Market

Incentive travel is a reward to salespeople, dealers, distributors, and employees by management. It offers travel for goals and/or achievements reached over a specified period of time. Incentive travel is largely a motivational tool and management often hires professionally managed incentive travel companies to develop and implement their programmes.

The incentive planner is looking to develop a programme that will provide a memorable experience for the participants. Thus, criteria such as an exciting destination, variety of entertainment options, creativity in food and beverage functions, and recreation alternatives are important for the hotel and site selection decision. The incentive travel market is a lucrative one and hotels offering attractive destinations actively seek this business.

Group Tour Market

The group tour market is huge and complex. In this market one can be dealing with a number of players, including wholesalers, retailers, tour brokers, and travel clubs. Because of its complexity, most hotels that target this market usually have one or more sales managers who specialize in it. In essence, the group tour market meets the needs of individuals who wish to travel fol pleasure with other groups of people. Instead of setting their own itinerary, they seek the help of a professional travel planner who assists with the selection of an itinerary. The itinerary may be a prepackaged tour offered by a tour wholesaler, a travel club developing its own itinerary, or simply a charter to reach a predetermined destination at a discounted price.

The Sales Process

Target marketing is essential for successful selling to group markets in the hospitality industry. Once target markets have been identified it is important to understand the basic tenets of the sales process. The five major steps of the sales process are given below:

1. **Open the Relationship.** Current accounts, prospecting, leads and referrals.
2. **Qualify the Account.** Determine needs and wants both tangible and intangible in past and present.
3. **Present the Message.** Provide "solutions" to "problems" through features and benefits offered by the hotel.
4. **Close the Sale.** Ask for the business and "book" the account.
5. **Service the Account.** Deliver as promised.

Open the Relationship

The obvious first step is to open a relationship with a potential client. There are numerous sources and the best place to start is with current accounts. Trace dates or tickler files are commonly used by sales managers as a reminder to periodically check with regular accounts about upcoming meetings, events, or newly planned conferences. Other sources include prospecting, leads, and referrals. Prospecting is calling on potential clients who have not met previously at the hotel but have the potential to do so. For example, if a new division of AT&T recently relocated in an area, a sales manager from the hotel should make a sales call to learn about their off-premise meeting activity, who plans the meetings, and where the meetings typically take place. Prospecting is often times initially done by phone and then followed up with a personal sales call to identified potential clients. Leads and referral are opportunities for potential business from an outside source.

Qualify the Account

Qualifying a potential account is twofold. The current needs and wants of the meeting planner must be identified. This includes both the physical as well as the psychological needs of the meeting being planned. The physical needs refer to the largely tangible aspects of the event such as number of persons attending, duration of the conference, number of guest rooms required, number and size of meetings and banquets to be scheduled, and so on.

Present the Message

Once the needs and wants, both tangible and intangible, have been identified, the sales manager is now in a position to present the message. This is usually done in person at the hotel and then followed up with a letter of proposal or letter of agreement.

This letter of agreement includes all pertinent items discussed during the negotiations such as dates, rates, number of guest rooms to he reserved, major food functions, and credit policy. Once both parties have signed the letter of agreement it then becomes a contract.

A key point in presenting the message is that the sales manager provide "solutions" for the meeting planner's "problems.". The tenet of marketing is that you—the supplier—can provide the consumer with what he or she needs. In hotel sales it is the facilities and services of a lodging establishment that are provided to house, feed, and entertain the attendees of a meeting, conference, or convention. The meeting planner sets the objective(s) for the meeting, not the management of the hotel. However, it is the job of the hotelier to ensure the meeting planner be given the facilities and services to help meet those objectives.

"Book it" is hospitality sales vernacular for closing the sale. It means that a signed contract from the meeting planner has been received by the hotel and that reservations for the guest rooms, meeting rooms, and banquet functions are "on the books." The event may be scheduled for two months away or ten years out. And it may have taken anywhere from two weeks to two years or more to open the relationship, qualify the account, present the message, and dose the sale. Nonetheless, it is now booked and preparation for servicing the account begins. Servicing the account may or may not be the job responsibility of the hotel sales manager. In larger hotels, the account is often turned over to the convention services department. However, the sales manager continues to keep in touch with the client even if he or she now shares joint responsibility with a convention services manager assigned to the account.

Service the Account

Servicing the account entails collecting all the many details that need to be pulled together prior to the event taking place. These include such items as specific meeting room setups, audio-visual requirements, VIP lists, suite accommodations, food function menus, rooming lists, billing instructions, credit arrangements, storage of shipments to the hotel, ground transportation requests, schedule changes, and so forth.

A few weeks prior to arrival a convention resume is developed outlining the specific details for the group. It is an internal document disseminated to all department heads in the hotel. For larger groups and/or complex events a preconvention meeting is often held. Here, the meeting planner confers with key department heads to review the convention resume, clarify any questions that arise, and go over the inevitable last minute changes.

Client-finding

Marketing is all about getting and keeping a client. Sales is charged with getting a client-finding out who needs what and where the "fit" fits. Hotel operations is charged with keeping a client by delivering a product or service that meets and exceeds customer expectations. In other words, we want more than just a satisfied customer, we want the customer to return again, again, and again.

Relationship Marketing

Relationship marketing is very much involved with getting and keeping a customer. It views a sale as part of a process, not as an isolated goal to be obtained. In relationship marketing the customer is viewed as an asset of the firm. As an asset, the customer becomes as important to management as does the building, the equipment, the inventory, and the employee.

Strategic Analysis

The primary purpose of strategic analysis is to give planners a platform from which to review the significance of their firm's market situation and to think about options in dealing with it. Strategic analysis consists of the SWOT analysis (strengths, weaknesses, opportunities, and threats) and the strategic analysis questioning sequence.

The SWOT analysis is the detailed search and listing of factors from the situational analysis that might or will impact the business's strategy. Strategic marketing is based on the SWOT analysis. The process by which SWOT factors are derived is to carefully review the internal analysis for strengths and weaknesses, and the environmental analysis for opportunities and threats, and to then record, in the appropriate category, every factor that has a reasonable possibility of affecting the shortand long-term future of the firm.

The secondary purpose is to identify and analyze potential or actual threats that could hurt the business, and weaknesses in key areas that may need to be upgraded to allow the business to compete more successfully. Collectively, weaknesses and threats are often referred to as "problems." On paper, most weaknesses can be corrected; but in the real world, a business may have to live with some imperfections or less than exemplary skills or assets.

FUNDAMENTALS OF MARKETING

Marketing in a hotel operation is an essential management function that directly affects the success of a business. The American Marketing Association defined marketing as "the process of planning and executing the conception, pricing, promotion and distribution of goods and services to create exchanges that satisfy individual and organizational objectives".

Hotel business directly produce and provide customers goods and services that satisfy the need for food, beverage, and entertainment. The producer is directly accessible to the consumer, creating a proximity that allows restaurant management to identify and respond to customer needs.

In most retain situations, the producer of the product is far removed from the consumer. In the restaurant industry, the producer is directly accessible to the consumer.

The consumer wants to inform the producer in the retail marketing chain of needs that could be satisfied or changes that would make a product more salable (Figure 1). In order to do this, it is necessary either to pass backward through the chain of product distribution or to find a way of reaching the producer directly. The restaurant distribution chart gives the producer and consumer direct access to one another. A decision is made to develop a restaurant business, it is necessary to identify and understand consumer needs. In this chapter we will discuss the application of market survey

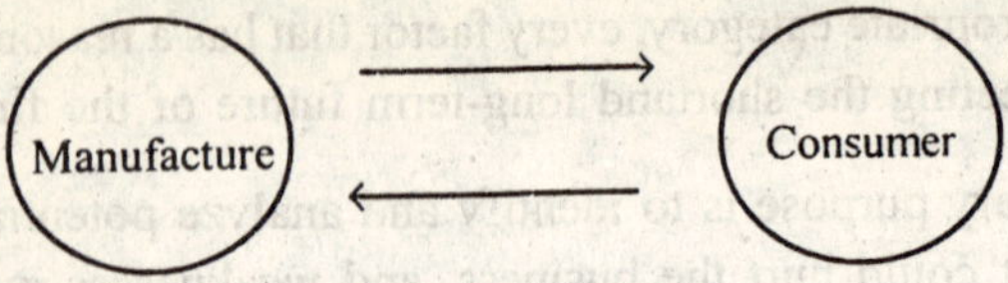

Fig. 1. Restaurant industry marketing distribution chart.

information to meet the needs of the target market. Marketing methods and techniques that are essential to developing a good marketing programme are the marketing cycle, the food service marketing mix, and the marketing campaign. Identifying marketing opportunities is the key to successful product/service development.

The Marketing Cycle

The marketing cycle is a series of four steps that are used to create and evaluate products and services. These steps, as outlined in Figure 2 are the following:

1. Identify consumer needs.
2. Develop products and services to meet needs.
3. Generate consumer interest to purchase or use product/ service.
4. Evaluate financial success and consumer satisfaction.

These steps must be performed in the sequence indicated to bring a product or service to market successfully.

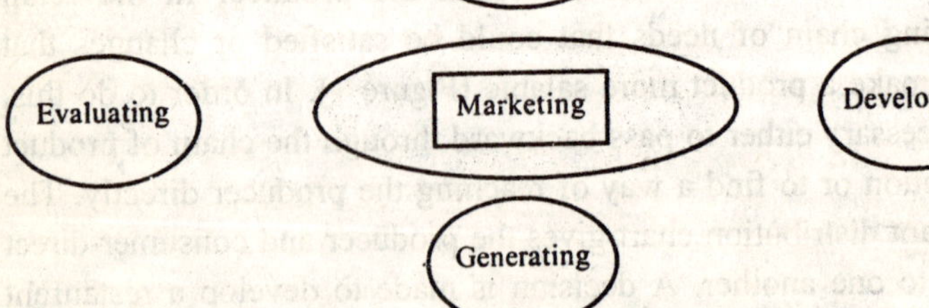

Fig. 2. Marketing cycle.

Identify Consumer Needs. A consumer need is identified when management recognizes a service or product that is not currently being offered. Need is usually recognized when a product/ service is requested by the consumer or offered by other restaurant operations.

Healthy dining is an excellent example of a customer need that has been identified by foodservice operations. Restaurant managers use the resources of local hospitals to create menu items which are developed to meet nutritional guidelines. A number of restaurant associations across the United States have developed healthy dining programmes.

Develop a Product or Service. Developing a product or service to meet consumer needs requires that management thoroughly understand consumer needs and accurately identify the perceived value of the product or service.

It is essential that the selling price be determined before the product specifications are outlined. The cost of producing the product will directly affect the selling price. If consumers are not willing to pay the price, then the product will not be financially successful. Market research is an effective method of identifying perceived value.

Generate Consumer Interest. Generating consumer interest is achieved primarily by applying market research information to determine a target market at which is directed a variety of interest-generating advertising media. To achieve the desired response from the target market, it is necessary to develop a marketing campaign.

Marketing campaigns plan a series of events, promotions, and advertising placements. The objective of these activities is to reach established goals of increased revenues and/or customer counts.

Evaluate Success. The success of a product or service is evaluated in terms of both financial and customer satisfaction objectives.

Financial success is judged by determining whether management's original financial objectives for the product were met.

Customer satisfaction is gauged by analyzing customer reaction to the product or service. A good way of recording customer reactions is to provide comment cards. To use this marketing information effectively, management needs to establish a policy of sharing the comments with employees and responding directly to them. Favourable and critical comments should always be passed along to staff. Sharing problems identified by customers at general staff meetings often produces solutions that are employee-generated. Acknowledging customer complaints and providing an incentive to return increase the perception of professionalism and interest in the restaurant.

THE FOOD SERVICE MARKETING MIX

To set the marketing cycle in motion, three major factors regarding the product must be established. These factors, called the marketing mix, determine where the product will be presented to the customer, how the customer will be informed about the product, and what price the product will be assigned. To address the food service industry, however, the traditional marketing mix must be adjusted to in corporate the service component that is essential to food service products.

Table 1

Marketing Mix

Marketing mix	Food Service marketing mix
Product	Product/Service service component in combination with food product
Place	Presentation theme concepts, atmosphere, location, staffing and menu·pricing scale
Promotion	Communication menu design, advertising, promotion, customer comments and server communication
Price	Various pricing models

Food service products, especially in restaurant settings, require an element of service in order to reach the customer, changing the first marketing mix element to Product-Service. Presentation incorporates factors such as theme and staffing as well as location. Price is an important factor in the presentation of the food product, often determining customer acceptability. Promotion includes the application of marketing methods and the communication skills required to sell food product directly to the customer.

MARKETING OPPORTUNITIES

Successful entrepreneurs and marketing specialists are individuals who recognize an opportunity to satisfy a need or create a product or service. Their ability to do so is often aligned with circumstances that indicate the probability of success. These circumstances are primarily related to demographic or environmental issues.

The "1991 Foodservice Forecast" published by the Bureau of Foodservice Research states, "The final ingredient which continues to create opportunities for foodservice growth is perpetually changing demographics (population characteristics). These factors, coupled with price increases for food to be prepared at home rather than food consumed away from home, will continue to create opportunities for the industry."

The demographic issue identified as having the major impact on the food service industry will be the' aging of the baby boom generation, which will increase the average age of the entire population. According to the Bureau of Labour Statistics:

Consumers in the age bracket between 34 and 54 years old spend over 30% more on foodservice than other age groups. This segment of the population will grew by 11.3 million Individuals (a 32% Increase) by the year 2000. The United states will experience a period of unprecedented personal wealth over the next twenty years, directly associated with this demographic transition. Services that make life easier will experience gains.

The use of restaurants and other food service operations is no longer an extravagant drain on the family budget but a necessity. In

1991 food service industry sales were over $256 billion, accounting for 45 percent of all dollars spent on food. This figure may reach 50 percent by the year 2000.

The demographics that can and are affecting the food service industry merit continual review by owners and managers, who must be able to observe, analyze, and forecast shifts and trends that will affect their customers and business.

Often referred to as external environmental factors, demographic characteristics are of several types. In Table 2 all of the environmental factors that are traditionally included in industry marketing analysis are outlined. Those factors which can have a specific impact on the restaurant industry are highlighted.

Table 2

External Environmental Factors

Social-cultural	*Economic*	*Technological*	*Ecological*	*Competitive*
Life-style changes	Interest rates	New products	Environmental	Number of competitors
Life expectancies	Deficits	Patent laws	Waste management	Strength of competitors
Birth rate	Gross national product	Industry R&D	Public image	Market entry
Growth rate	Unemployment levels		Safety of product	Market exist
Family arrangements	Energy sources	Computer technology	Packaging procedures	Market growth
Consumer activism	Inflation rate			Market share
Shifts in Population	Money supply			Foreign competition
Changing women's roles				

Some of the factors currently having a profound impact on the restaurant industry in the sociocultural category are life-style changes, family arrangement, and changing women's roles. Economic factors include unemployment levels as well as energy sources and costs. Competitive factors are number and strength of competitors, market growth, and market share. Radical economic changes in the 1990s are affecting the entire world economy. Restaurant managers should seek out and use information that interprets and indicates how these factors will affect a community to develop a marketing plan. Market survey information often provides strong indicators of how a community is reacting to national and world trends.

As demographic changes reach the community level, managers can identify opportunities to react with products or services which reflect the needs of their customer base. Market research information often provides the data to support the development of marketing opportunities.

1995 Meal-period highlights

Breakfast

* More than one out of five (20.7 percent) of all individuals over eight years old consumed a commercially prepared breakfast at least once during a week.
* On the average, individuals consumed 0.5 breakfasts away from home in a week.
* The average individual skipped 1.6 breakfasts in one week, making break fast the most frequently skipped meal.

Lunch

* Almost six out of ten (56.8 percent) individuals ate lunch prepared away from home at least once a week. This makes lunch the meal most frequently consumed away from home.
* Individuals consumed, on the average, 2.1 lunches away from home per week.
* The average individual skipped lunch 0.6 times in a week.

Dinner

* The average individual consumed 1.2 diners away from home in a week.
* Among individuals over age eight, 53.5 percent consumed at least one commercially prepared dinner in a seven-day period.
* Individual skipped, on average, only 0.1 dinners in a one-week period.

MARKET RESEARCH

Market research information can be gathered from a variety of sources. Competition surveys such as seen in Chapter 2 and 3 offer information about the average check, menu items, beverage prices, and facilities of restaurants that are in direct competition for the same customer. Understanding how much the customer is willing to pay for a product or service in a competitive setting gives management a strong indication of acceptable pricing.

To apply this information to an indIvidual restaurant business, management must identify *(1)* the average household income of current customers and *(2)* the availability of customers within targeted income averages. Management can use market research information on average per person check totals to help identify which category of overall sales volume matches their operation. By comparing national average checks with current sales volumes, consumer spending trends can be analyzed to find out whether the customer's perceived value of menu items is higher than what is currently being charged. The results of interpreting this type of market research information could also cause management to change the focus or concept of the overall menu programme.

Father analysis of the current marketplace of restaurant dollars focuses on research concerning the composition of the average household. By understanding how households allocate food service dollars, management can identify the target market for marketing efforts for their operation. Table 3 indicates household spending patterns on food consumed away from home.

Table 3

Household Expenditures on Food away from Home by Household Composition-1989*

Household composition	*Size*	*Income***	*Average annual expenditures*	*Percent of food budget spent*	*Annual per capita expenditures*
All households	2.6	$3.308	$1.762	42.4%	$678
Husband-wife only	2.0	$37.183	$1.977	45.1	$988
Husband-wife with children	3.9	$43.576	$2.326	41.1	$596
Single parents with children	2.9	$17.416	$1.190	34.8	$410
Single person and other households	1.6	$20.260	$1.248	46.2	$780

* Of all household groups. singles allocated the largest proportion of their total food budget to food away from home.
** Income is before taxes.
Source: Bureau of Labour Statistics. Consumer Expenditure Survey. 1989. National Restaurant Association.

Tablc 4

Percentage of Aduit Restaurant Visits

*Percent of adults visiting types of establishments once a week or more, by age and marital status, 1991**

Type of establishment or service	*Single, under 45 years old (%)*	*Single, 45 years old or older (%)*	*Married, under 45 years old (%)*	*Married, 45 years old or older (%)*
(1)	*(2)*	*(3)*	*(4)*	*(5)*
Tableservice, average check $10 or more	25	17	16	21
Tableservlce, average check less than $10	42	35	28	35

(1)	*(2)*	*(3)*	*(4)*	*(5)*
Fast food, eaten Inside restaurant	41	17	25	19
Carryout	44	26	36	17
Self-serve cafeteria or buffet	24	13	13	19
Delivery	20	6	11	3
Supermarket, convenience store, or deli-eaten same day	28	21	12	14

* Singles under 45 years of age were the most frequent customer at almost every type of establishment or service.
Note Check size is per adult.
Source: National Restaurant Association
Restaurants U.S.A. Washington, DC, Vol II, No, 10, Nov. 91

If this information is matched to the information in Table 4 management can conclude that single persons less than 45 years of age patronize full-service restaurants with average checks of $10 or more 25 percent of the time, while single persons over 45 patronize full service restaurants with average checks of $10 or less 35 percent of the time. Married couples over 45 frequent restaurants with average checks of over $10 more often than married couples under age 45. From this information we can conclude that married couples without children spend more per capital on restaurant during than any other market segment.

THE MARKETING CAMPAIGN

The marketing campaign is the application of the marketing cycle phase, generating customer interest. Creating promotions, planning advertising materials, and developing a formal media programme are elements of a marketing campaign. The food service marketing mix provides the information that is the foundation of any marketing campaign.

The development stage of a marketing campaign requires establishing the most effective way of creating customer interest. A variety of methods for advertising and promotion are available.

Internal methods of promotion include special events incorporating holidays or specialty cuisines. In-house advertising can be accomplished by table tents and cards, posters, banners, and a server communication programme.

The most effective use of advertising media for a restaurant business focuses on newspaper ads and radio time. Newspaper ads are generally timed to appear on days of the week which have been identified as those when readers are looking for entertainment information. The same principle applies to identifying radio time that reaches the established target market.

Community goodwill is an important component in generating customer interest. A business's involvement in local activities of all types creates good public relations and often free advertising in the form of media coverage.

The final phase of the marketing campaign is the evaluation of the success of the programme. Success is determined by how well management's objectives are met. If the primary objective is to increase sales, success is measured by the amount of increase in revenues. If the objective is to increase customer attendance, success is measured by the total increase in customer counts.

Alternative methods must be developed to measure customer satisfaction. One of the most effective is tracking customer return rates. The number of repeat customers is an accurate indication of the satisfaction levels of customers. Management establishes a return rate target goal and methods by which to track if. If the return rate falls below the goal level, then measures are taken to evaluate product and service in order to increase repeat customers.

An effective marketing plan in generally developed around an established outline. Owners and managers who are not familiar with formal marketing plans would be advised to seek professional assistance.

FRANCHISING FOR FOODSERVICE

The franchise is found in all types of businesses today, from restaurants to laundromats, from tax preparation services to auto parts stores. However, no franchise is more well-known than foodservice franchising. Mention the word "franchising" and images of the Golden Arches (McDonald's), Burger King, Kentucky Fried Chicken, Bob's Big Boy, Bonanza Family Restaurants, and Nirula's immediately come to mind. But franchising—is much more than these popular images. Franchising is a very old concept that has become so popular that sales currently account for over 50 percent of total retail sales. A big portion of those sales is foodservice.

Concept of Franchising

Franchising is a concept that describes one method in which goods and services reach the customer. A franchise relationship must be formed between two companies. The company that owns a trademark (such as McDonald's Golden Arches) and a method of doing business (how to make and sell hamburgers and other fast-food items the McDonald's way) is the franchisor. The company that buys from the franchisor the right to use its trademarks and to operate a business according to the franchisor's guidelines is the franchisee. The word franchise is sometimes defined as a right. Because that right is owned by the franchisor, the franchisee pays for it. Franchising, thus, is a way of doing business that benefits both the franchisor and franchisee.

The word franchising comes from an old French word that means "freedom from servitude". The idea underlying this work is tnat by owning a franchise, the franchisee is freed from the bondage of working for someone else as an employee. The franchise becomes a business owner with much of the same self-reliant, decision-making ability as an independent business-person who starts a firm from scorch. The primary difference, however, between a franchisee and an independent businessperson is that the franchisee has a legal, contractual relationship with a franchisor that requires him to do business as the franchisor instructs him. An old saying in franchising is "You're in business for yourself, but not by yourself. An independent makes all decisions independently".

The franchisor benefits from this relationship through the opportunity to expand the business at a much lower cost than otherwise. The franchisee invests much of tha money for his or her store, but the franchisor controls the product, the service, and how the franchisee presents them to the customer.

This way of franchising is called the business format franchise, which is the way most foodservice franchises operate. A business format franchise is one in which the franchisor sells two essential rights to the franchisee: *(1)* the right to adopt the image or identity of the franchisor (this may be the official trademark of the company, such as the Wendy's girl, the Golden Arches, or the way the letters are shapped in Baskin-Robbins, or the colour of a building.); *(2)* a fixed way of running the food service outlet. The franchisor will instruct the franchisee on all aspects of operating. In some instances, the franchisee must do it only one way. To illustrate:

1. How to cook a particular dish. In Nirula's, employees are told that to make a pizza properly, exact amount of ketchup and cheese must be applied in spiral form to the base-no exceptions.

2. Where to buy food and the equipment to make the food. Franchisors spend a great deal of time with the companies that sell to franchisees to ensure that what they ship to the franchisee meets very strict standards. Franchises must purchase from these approved sellers.

In some instances, the franchisee may make decisions without asking the franchisor. Some examples include.

1. How much to charge for menu items.
2. How much to pay employees.
3. Advertising purchased in the local market. While the franchisor buys television and radio advertising the franchisee may decide to hand out flyers or offer a special in a coupon book.

History of Franchising

Franchising can trace its origins to the Middle Ages when the Catholic Church and local government granted tax collecting franchises.

Tax collectors (franchisees) made their rounds, sending their revenues to the Church or government body (franchisor), but keeping a percentage for themselves. In 1562, the Council of Trent banned this form of taxation because it seemed to breed corruption. In the eighteenth and nineteenth centuries, the legislature and monarchy of England granted franchises to noblemen, giving them complete authority over large geographical areas to develop their personal wealth in exchange for their unwavering support.

In the United States, the first franchise businesses started in the mid-1800s. McCormick Harvesting Machine Company began franchising around 1850 (Justis and Judd 1989. The Singer Sewing Machine Company started during the 1860s. Other companies to employ franchising were General Motors (1898), Coca Cola (1899), Rexall Drugs (1902), and Western Auto (1909).

Foodservice Franchising

In 1925, Howard Johnson started an ice cream business. He used franchising to expand this business and a chain of restaurants throughout the East Coast. In 1940, his outlets were the first to be build on a freeway (then called a turnpike). His early efforts now boast over 200 restaurants nationwide.

In 1955 within about three months of each other McDonald's and Burger King began what was to become a revolution in foodservice franchising. McDonald's from southern California and Burger King from southern Florida have become international giants in the fast-food business. Also during the 1950s, Kentucky. Fried Chicken and International House of Pancakes began their operations. Most of the growth in this field occurred in the 1970s and 1980s.

The history off food service franchising has demonstrated a pioneering influence on how all types of retail franchising are conducted. Foodservice is a competitive business. To remain successful, franchisors and franchisees have had to be innovative and creative. For example, jack-in-the-Box in the 1960s was the first retail business to use computerized cash registers. Burger King was the first to use highly sophisticated, computer software and hardware for employee scheduling, inventory control, and other analyses. McDonald's was the first to install playgrounds. These are just a few examples. Each day, foodservice franchise participants continue to make history.

Types of Foodservice Franchises

Many types of operations come under the category of foodservice franchises. Some of the categories overlap, but the typical ones are:

1. **Fast-food Restaurants.** These are the most recognizable of the foodservice restaurants. They specialize in quick service and relatively limited menus. Examples are Burger King, McDonald's, Kentucky Fried Chicken, and Taco Bell.

2. **Full Service, Family Style, or Coffee Shop Restaurants.** These outlets specialize in a full menu, food cooked to order, table service, and they cater to family business. Many orient their menus to serve breakfast 24 hours a day. Examples are Denny's TGIFridays, and Ponderosa steak house.

3. **Ice Cream Parlors.** Baskin-Robbins made this category famous. Now, other companies, such as Dairy Queen and Swensen's, serve primarily ice cream and desserts.

4. **Retail Baked Goods.** These companies differentiate themselves by serving baked goods cooked fresh on the premises. Located in various size malls, companies such as Davids' Cookies and T.J. Cinnamons serve cookies and cinnamon rolls.

5. **Retail Food Store.** Hickory Farms is a well-known example of this type of foodservice operation. They sell traditional, specialty, and gift food items such as exotic cheeses, meats, and fruit preserves.

6. **Doughnut Shops.** A type of fast-food operation, their menus are primarily for breakfast and snacks. Their "entree" is a wide variety of doughnuts. Winchell's and Dunkin' Donuts are the most famous.

7. **Other Categories.** Ethnic, limited and full menu, nutrition, and drive-in/drive-thru are just some of the other categories that usually overlap the previous six. For example, Benihana of Tokyo is a full service, ethnic (Japanese) outlet, Rally's is a highly limited menu, fast-food hamburger restaurant, and Heidl's Frogen Yozurt is a nutritionally based, limited menu, fast-food operation.

Merits and De-merits of Foodservice Franchises

Foodservice experiences the highest rate of failure of all retail businesses. Some statistics show (Justis and Judd 1989) that 80-90 percent of restaurants are bankrupt within the first five years; other types of businesses have equally dismal prospects. Franchising helps brighten up these pessimistic numbers. In the mid1980s, only 3.3 percent of all types of franchises were discontinued for any reason. The statistics seem to suggest that franchising a restaurant has important advantages that substantially increase the chance of success of the franchisee over an independent operator.

Merits

Some of the most important advantages of franchising are:

1. **Recognized Name** and logo (for example, International House of Pancakes, Ronald McDonald).

2. **A Reputation.** When we decide to eat at a particular franchise, we do so for many reasons, one of the most important of which is that we know what to except (the quality of a Sizzler steak, seafood, or salad bar).

3. **Technical Assistance.** An individual does not need any experience in foodservice to be a foodservice franchisee.

In fast, some franchisors prefer minimal experience because novices go into the business without any preconceived notions about how to operate. The franchisors are the experts in their field, having done substantial research about what their customers want. They use this knowledge and their experience to give advice and provide operational manuals on how to do the simplest tasks (for example, how to mop a floor) and the most difficult challenges (for example, setting up a food inventory and a cost control system).

4. **Quality Control Standards.** The standards for performance that the franchisor imposes on franchises are beneficial because they ensure that consistency exists from restaurant to restaurant regardless of location or ownership. This consistency is good for business so that a customer who goes to a Ponderosa steak house in Las Vegas, Nevada, will visit the store in Blacks-burg, Virginia.

5. **Lower Costs.** Franchisors train their franchisees to operate their foodservice outlets much more efficiently than that of an independent outlet. Franchisors have developed systems for everything, and that means saving money. The franchisor also sets up special buys with suppliers so that the cost of purchasing equipment and inventory are much lower.

6. **Opportunities for Expansion.** Many franchisors grant territories so that franchisees can have more than one store. With their help and assistance, the franchisee can expand his or her success to multiple locations.

Demerits

Some of the most important disadvantages of franchising are:

1. **Restrictions on Franchisee Decision Making.** Some people have difficulty making decisions that are restricted by someone else (the franchisor). They do not want

another person telling them what to do. Individuals are advised that franchising may not work for them. "Being in business for yourself, but not by yourself" is not for everyone.

2. **Franchisor Power Issues.** Franchisors are often perceived as being too powerful and too involved in the franchisee's business. That perception may come from too many visits from their personnel, insensitivity to the differences in needs of franchisees in different locations (for example, not allowing ethic items on the menu in an ethnically concentrated area, or requiring that buildings be protected from frost in desert locations), or disagreements over whether a termination of a franchise is really fair. This disadvantage may be nothing more than a difference of opinion between franchisor and franchisee, or it may be more serious. Disagreements always happen, even in the best relationships; honest and open discussion are the best solutions.

3. **Inconsistency of Standards.** The larger the chain of foodservice outlets the more difficult are the efforts to ensure that the standards are the same at all stores. Customers often do not understand the different owners may operate differently; they have a reasonable expectation that their food, service, and cleanliness will always be the same.

4. **The Perception that Franchises are Failure Proof.** They are not. Many franchisees believe that the reputation and the assistance of the franchisor is all that is necessary for success. Occasionally, the franchisor's literature is misleading concerning the amount of work required and the possibility for success. People need to be realistic. The foodservice business is one of the most difficult and time consuming, even in the best of all worlds. Prospective franchisees need to read all of the available literature and

then visit locations and talk to franchisees in their restaurants about the requirements for a successful operation.

Trends in Foodservice Franchising

Many of the innovations in retail business have come from the pioneering efforts of foodservice franchises. A few have already been identified. The following are some of the significant trends that appeal to be forming today.

(1) Non-traditional Franchising. The number of good locations is shrinking and their costs are rising. Competition is more intense, and the price of effective advertising continues to grow. These factors have caused franchisors to look for places to build their restaurants that are different from their traditional, free-standing positions. Fast-food and limited menu outlets are now ground in airports, malls, zoos, hospitals, train stations, gambling casinos, school campuses, and many other unusual places. Experts agree that these non-traditional places work well for several reasons:

(a) The captive consumer is already three for a different reason and will want to eat;

(b) Other competition is limited or non-existent; and

(c) Changes in how a city grows may be unlikely to affect sales.

(2) International Expansion. As the economic of the world interact more and people of other countries want to try more Western goods and services, international foodservice franchises are becoming more popular. Most of the major fast-food and many of the other major foodservice franchise organizations have expanded to every continent except Antarctica. Recently, the McDonald's franchisee from Canada opened the first fast-food restaurant in Russia. Others are following. These foreign locations are among the busiest in the franchise chain. Look for the well-known signs in whatever country you travel for a familiar taste of home.

(3) The Labour Shortage. Foodservice franchisees have traditionally hired teenagers to do most of their jobs. An ample number of them and other young people were always available because of the baby of World War II and the Korean War. In recent years the number of people under 21 years of age has been decreasing as the number of foodservice outlets have been increasing. In some areas, franchisees are running out of traditional young employees to hire. To solve this problem, franchisors and franchisees have been recruiting retired senior citizens, housewives, and college students. They are finding that these new employees work well with teenagers and provide a maturity and longevity to their work force. Some of McDonald's advertisements feature senior citizen workers. Another approach that franchise operators are taking to meet this challenge is to continue to automate their businesses. New equipment is being developed to reduce the number of employees that the franchise has to schedule.

(4) Other Trends. Other trends and challenges that face foodservice franchise operators are:

(a) **Limited Menu Versus Expanded Menu Decision.** Rally's Hamburgers, a relatively new franchise compalily, boasts a menu with only a few items so the quality is high. Other major chains add new menu items in the hopes of adding more customers.

(b) **Legal Issues.** In some states franchisors are being given more power to tenninate their agreements with franchisees. In other states, the law is more franchisee-oriented. The la\vs also differ vastly in how much information the franchisor must offer to people who want to become franchisees. Overall, the legal issues are confusing and varied throughout the country.

(5) Synthesis. The objective of marketing a hotel operation is to serve customers food and beverage products that satisfy their needs at a price perceived as having a fair value. In order to reach this objective it is necessary for management to follow the four steps in the marketing cycle. To set the marketing cycle in motion, the food service marketing mix must be determined. When the format for product or service, presentation, and communication has been established, marketing activities can be initiated.

Market research is a valuable activity in any marketing effort. Market research information identified needs and opportunities in the marketplace, qualifies the target market, and provides the data to support product/service development.

The marketing campaign is the application of market research information combined with data from the food service marketing mix. The activities or a marketing campaign generate customer interest in a restaurant business, its products, and its services.

❐

11

Purchasing and Stores Management

NATURE OF PURCHASING

Purchasing is here defined as the buying in of goods to enable an organisation to function in accordance with its objectives.

So, in respect of both the costs involved and the attainment of quality objectives, this is an area which must receive continuous attention from management.

In retailing organisations and in many manufacturing concerns purchasing is the assigned responsibility of managers who operate at a senior level and have their own clerical support and organisation-often extensive.

In the hotel and catering industry, particularly in the commercial sector, a frequently met feature of purchasing is the division of buying responsibilities among departmental heads such as chefs, housekeepers, bar managers, restaurant managers and control office supervisors. While this may be necessary because of the departmentalised nature of many of the purchases, it is suggested that special care may be necessary to ensure that this divided responsibility receives supervision from senior management to ensure that:

(i) purchases are made which do support the organisation's objectives.

(ii) clerical procedures are designed and used to facilitate control over purchasing.

(iii) those members of staff with purchasing responsibilities have received sufficient instruction in good purchasing practice to enable them to carry out their responsibilities effectively.

Also, the importance of good relationships with suppliers is of obvious benefit to any organisation which depends upon the availability of goods of specified quality and reliability from outside sources. It is the way in which the purchasing and subsequently the accounting functions are practised which will determine the type of relationships which will be formed with suppliers. The day-to-day contact between the organisation and its suppliers is not conducted by senior management, but by their agents—order assemblers, despatchers and drivers on the suppliers side and the purchase clerks, good receivers and storekeepers of the receiving organisation. This emphasises the importance of having purchasing policies and procedures which are designed to create mutually satisfactory commerce between supplier and receiver and provide documentary evidence that procedures are being followed.

Purchasing a Procedure

The variety within the hotel and catering industry regarding sectors of the industry and unit size within sectors makes for difficulty in discussing the extent of the responsibility of any member of an organisation who carries out purchasing duties.

The aims of the purchasing function are:

(i) to buy goods which give the best value for money and which are consistent with the quality standard and company image required.

(ii) to ensure that the organisation actually receives the goods ordered and to be paid for.

(iii) to ensure that goods purchased are put to the use for which they were bought.

(iv) to make payment for the goods received in accordance with the terms and conditions of trading agreed with the supplier.

Thus, the purchasing procedure could be summarised by nothing that it covers the ordering, receiving, storing, issuing and paying for goods received.

Ordering of Goods

Ideally, the ordering of goods should be governed by use of an official order form signed by an authorised member of management. The order should be made sufficiently in advance of the need for the goods so that any difficulties such as non-availability, price change or altered pack sizes can be satisfactorily settled without causing disruption to the work of the organisation.

Having said that, it must be recognised that the hotel and catering industry experiences situations where unexpectedly high demand, or the organising of functions at unusually short notice cause the ordering procedure to be set aside. Telephoned orders and even using the organisation's own transport to collect goods required in a hurry will then occur. If there is an observed tendency for this to occur frequently then it indicates the need for an overhaul of whatever method of forecasting demand is in use. Where any short-circuiting of the ordering procedure arises there must be a routine for making sure that as quickly as possibie after the non-standard order has been made, the correct document and authorising procedure must be followed and used as proof of order and confirmation to the supplier.

It is not uncommon to find, particularly in small to medium-sized hotels, that difficulties which are experienced in passing suppliers' invoices for payment are mainly caused by ordering procedures having gone by the board in times of crisis. Thus, a reasonable aim for an ordering procedure to have is control over payments to suppliers. This aim will be assisted by documentary evidence from the ordering system to actual receipt of goods being paid for.

The larger establishment will need order forms in sets, sequentially numbered for security and with copies distributed to departmental manager, control office and goods receiving section. The procedure could then include instructions to goods receivers that no goods are to be accepted in the absence of an order and to the manager with responsibility for purchasing, that the order must be checked for price and clear statement of any special terms or discounts which have been negotiated with the supplier. On receipt of the goods, the receiver would check the physical delivery against the order, make any alterations necessary and pass the retained copy of the supplier's delivery note with the copy order to the control office to be used for checking the invoice before payment of it.

Goods Receiving

Once the actual goods arrive, control over them changes from a paperwork procedure to a physical activity. The goods must be thoroughly checked against the order before acceptance documents are signed. If the volume and value of items such as meats, fish and poultry are high, then accurate weighing equipment may be a necessity at the goods receiving point. Any slackness in goods-inward checking is observable by the suppliers' drivers, and while they are no more dishonest than any other section of the population, the temptation to profit by such slackness may well be irresistible.

Having checked the goods, the next stage is to move them into secure stores, registering their receipt on the bin-card, cardex system, computer memory or whatever system is in use for stock recording. In one institutional catering situation, pallets of food stores were frequently left in the goods receiving bay after checking and instances were noted of members of the kitchen staff taking items directly from the pallets for use in the kitchen. Itis fairly easy to see why, in this establishment, stock checks were seldom able to reconcile shelf stocks with stock records.

Storing and Issuing of Goods

The two aspects of storing which are of concern to management are firstly the provision of storage spaces which are physically suitable for the stocks as regards space, ventilation, temperature, humidity, cleanliness and secondly, security.

Fields of study such as food production and food science deal fully with the first aspect and some indication of possible losses because of poor security have been described in the previous section.

Payment for Goods

Suppliers' invoices should be checked for quantity, price and description of goods before payment is made. This does not imply that there is likely to be a conscious attempt to defraud by the supplier, but simply that genuine mistakes can arise and that part deliveries will require noting and including in the receiving establishments' system for progressing the delivery of the rest of the order.

Many years ago, a large British departmental store saved themselves a lot of money by dismantling their procedures for checking invoices because it was costing more to maintain them than the money recovered by the discovery of invoicing errors. This could be a factor to take into consideration when designing a system of invoice checking, but it is as well to remember that a large and powerful organisation whose suppliers are likely to be on their best behaviour in dealings with that organisation, but, lesser organisations may not enjoy the same respectful treatment.

Stock Control

The term 'stock control' is used to describe a system of ordering in which the prompting of an order is effected by the amount of stock of an item held in the stores.

The reason why stocks of goods are required at all is so that processing, or any other work dependent upon those goods, can continue uninterrupted by lack of materials. What stock control attempts to do is minimise the total costs related to stocking goods and materials of all kinds.

The costs related to stocks arise from:

(i) ordering costs (clerical labour involved in preparing an order, stationery costs, telephone costs incurred in progressing orders or other queries on orders, and postage costs per order)

(ii) stockholding costs (rent, rates and power and costs of storage space, storekeeper's wages, insurance (if related to stock values carried) and, largest cost of all, the cost of the capital tied up in stock value).

The first group of costs are stated as a sum of money per order and the second set, a percentage figure of the average stock-holding value.

These two components of the total stock costs move in opposite directions. The more items ordered on one purchase order, the less is the ordering cost per item, but as order size increases the average number of items held in stock increases and the stock-holding cost, therefore, becomes higher.

One of the principal aims of stock control is to determine the number of items to order at one time so as to minimise the total of these two costs. This number of items is often known as the Economic Order Quantity (EOQ).

Evaluating Quantity Discounts

Some suppliers offer a discount on goods ordered over a specified amount. In effect, such a discount is a reduction in the cost of the goods concerned. The cost per unit of stock is a component in the calculation of the EOQ, and a reduction in the cost has the effect of increasing the size of the EOQ. To evaluate whether the offered discount is worthwhile, or not, the sources of saving from taking up the offer must be weighed against any increase in costs there may be. It is only if the savings are greater than the cost increase that the discount should be taken up. The savings result from the lower cost price and (because greater quantities are ordered) reduced ordering costs.

The increase in costs arises from the greater average stock which would be carried and, hence, higher stockholding costs.

The use of the EOQ Formula

As in all quantitative techniques, the answers given are dependent upon the validity of data used in the formula. The cost per order is relatively straightforward, although careful thought is required to identify all the costs associated with issuing an order. Stationery and clerical labour are obvious costs and easily computed, but allocating order-associated telephone, delivery and receiving costs may need a more prolonged data collection period before a realistic cost figure is identified.

The stock-holding cost is also made up of several parts, for example stores upkeep, handling costs of stores in storage, deterioration and, perhaps, some part of the insurance costs. But, by far the greatest cost is that of the capital which is tied up in stock. It may be company policy to require, say, at least a return of 12½% on any investment made. This could, then, be the base figure for the stock-holding cost to which could be added the other costs mentioned above to arrive at the final figure. It is convention to state the stock-holding cost as a percentage of the average stock value for an item because, clearly, there is a strong relationship between the value of the goods in store and the stockholding costs as outlined.

Even with modern facilities for data processing, the up-dated calculation of EOQ measures for every item of stock would not be done by most managements. An approach which is used to reduce the number of calculations involved is to classify the range of stocks according to the amount of capital tied up in each item and establish, say, three classifications: high-value stocks for which EOQ is used, medium value stocks whose maximum and minimum stock levels are continuously supervised, and low-value stocks which are operated on maximum and minimum value levels without absorbing an unwarranted amount of management time.

A further advantage of the study of stock behaviour and associated costs is that it should emphasise to management that significant costs can be needlessly incurred in this field. The true cost associated with ordering is often underestimated until the procedure for its discovery is carried out and, in many cases, the cost of supporting the capital invested in stocks is unappreciated until investigations of this nature are made.

Materials Management

The aims of materials management are to:

(i) ensure that the materials purchased are fit for the use intended.

(ii) minimise the materials cost by controlling their use and treatment.

The 'fitness for use' aim depends for its achievement on full specifications both of the use and the materials concerned. A simple example of the development of these specifications is the purchase of new floor covering. Consideration of use would require clarification of where the floor covering is positioned, what density of traffic it will be required to withstand, the type of decor into which it must fit and the length of time estimated before its renewal. A full specification of use is an aid to making a good decision on the actual purchase. In this example, the supplier would be in a position to advise on durability and types of covering to choose from if appraised of the full facts of the situation.

In the case of food purchases, the expertise is normally available within the establishment as to the purchasing options open. However, this is not to say that management can rely upon the best purchasing decisions being made as a matter of course in this area unless, once again, constructive thinking produces specifications to act as guidelines. The training and experience of a particular chef may be such that he considers no ingredients but 'the best', nor does he make use of the many pre or partly prepared ingredients available. This may be a case for the chef's manager to investigate and, in company with the chef himself, establish and agree the cost saving specifications which the chef may have ignored. In the course of an investigation of this type, a high quality and expensive frozen meat dish was being bought in and the hotel had both kitchen labour capacity and freezer capacity to spare. The decision to make better use of both underutilised resources by making the dish on the premises reduced costs and provided a product comparable in quality to the bought-in dish.

Value Analysis

The technique of value analysis has been developed to assist in the formulation of specifications which, while meeting in full quality requirements, yet aim at minimising product costs. Many companies form value analysis committees to investigate fully all aspects of production, materials to be used and so on. In hotel and catering situations attentions could be directed to the ingredient lists for major menu items and the skill of the committee members would be exercised in seeking lower cost, substitute foodstuffs, or re-assessing ingredient specifications to achieve the same customer satisfaction at lower cost.

On the housekeeping side, the quality of materials available and their range of prices would be investigated against the background of what is required of the materials purchased. For example, if the policy is to change decor in the public areas of the hotel every five years, then perhaps paying for qualities of carpeting with twice that life expectancy might be reconsidered.

Similarly, all recurrent, significant expenditure on materials could be investigated by committees constituted of people able to contribute to the matter under discussion and clear as to the purpose of the exercise the reduction of costs coupled with the maintenance of required standards.

As is the case with all techniques of this nature, preliminary identification of areas where its application would be worthwhile is essential. The individual item's unit cost is not always the best indicator of the applicability of value analysis. What must be looked for is the total expenditure on a given item. One unit of glassware or crockery does not bulk large in an establishment's accounts, but a study of total, annual replacement costs may well indicate scope for cost reduction. In this example the value analysis group could identify sources and causes and breakages, the robustness of the glassware and crockery in use and then go on to a survey of what goods are available, 'shopping around' to find a desirable combination of durability, appearance and acceptability. It can also be seen from this example that a well directed investigation has the potential to yield benefits in operating methods such as the handling and safeguarding methods to be used when dealing with breakable items. This aspect could emerge during the investigation into the incidence and causes of breakages, when clear identification of causes can often go a long way towards establishing cures.

Control Aspects of Materials Management

In the earlier chapter on control, reference was made to analysing sequences of activities and seeking for possible sources of loss, or wastage, in order to develop control systems designed to minimise these. This approach is clearly applicable to the management of materials from the stage of making the decision to buy from a particular supplier right through to the usage of the bought materials.

In the case of foodstuffs, the management aim is to ensure that proper care and storage are standard practices so that no avoidable waste takes place before use. During processing, trained staff and the correct, well maintained machinery and equipment should assist in obtaining the yields and numbers of portions from given amounts of food inputs.

There is also a significant amount of capital invested in linen, furnishing fabrics, carpeting and other floor coverings, cleaning materials and equipment, glassware, crockery, cutlery and so on. All these items should be purchased according to good, purchasing practice and their management not left to chance. Stock checking is an obvious way to initiate control, but, further management action to achieve lower operating costs is highly desirable. Additions to costs are caused not only by pilferage, but careless handling and the lack of correct care and maintenance routines. After the years of formal instruction in accommodation management which have been available to entrants into the hotel and catering industry, there must by this time be many members of the industry's management who have the training to identify shortcomings in this area and, given time and opportunity, the ability to devise systems of materials management which could achieve cost reductions when thoughtfully applied.

The problem in all industries is the harnessing and direction of the know-how to be found among all levels of managers in order to achieve a fully controlled operation. This does not happen spontaneously, but must be consciously engineered, having as the start point the relevant objectives of the organisation and moving via systems and procedures, tailored to the needs of the establishment, towards the boal of full use of all resources.

Standards setting for the Control of Wastage

Standards set for food and labour cost control have been described earlier and it should be apparent that the standards for the utilisation of foodstuffs come into this field of materials management. It would be useful to be able to establish standards which would assist in the control of the costs of all materials, and the purpose of this section is to illustrate how this may be done.

If bed-linen costs are taken as an example, the task is to arrive at a workable guide for management to enable them to recognise whether the actual costs incurred are in line with those expected. The 'expected' costs are the result of the attempt to set a standard for bed linen costs by the approach described below:

(i) Identify the costs involved bed-linen purchases, laundering and linen repairs.

(ii) Obtain linen stock figures by physical stock check, noting numbers in use, in linen store, laundering, repair and on order.

(iii) Using room occupancy ratios, seasonally expressed if necessary, and taking into account the frequency of linen changes, calculate usage of bed-linen during average weeks.

(iv) Working from current stock figures and basing usage on a proper rotation of bed-linen stocks, calculate laundering costs, assess probable repair costs and assess the number of articles to be scrapped as outworn. (This assumes that the laundering and repair costs of bed-linen are recorded for subsequent comparison with those calculated.)

From this collection of information and calculations it is now possible to assess the expected costs of purchasing, laundering and repairing bed-linen and to use these as a standard against which to compare the actual costs. Note that the calculations are based upon an expert view of the wearing quality of the bed-linen and the sound management of stocks. If the standard is a significantly lower figure than actual costs, then an investigation should be undertaken to discover if present practices are responsible for the adverse variance.

Variety Control

Wide varieties of goods and services offered for sale bring intheir wake increased costs caused by the need to carry extensive stocks. Extensive stocks of goods increase those expenses associated with monitoring stock levels, re-ordering and the physical reception and storage of many different commodities. In addition, a wide range of activities is demanded of staff in support of an output of wide variety. This can reduce productive efficiency by a loss of time in preparing and clearing away before and after short production runs.

In a small number of cases, where an organisation is set up to provide 'anything the customer asks for', wide variety presents no problems because the prices of goods and services are high enough to yield satisfactory profits. In the more typical commercial organisations and in the non-profit-making sectors of the hotel and catering industry, unnecessary variety has often grown more by accident than by design.

The following notes describe a procedure for identifying and controlling excessive variety.

Simplification, Standardisation and Specialisation

Simplification, in the context of variety control, is the process of reducing the number of types and varieties of a product to eliminate unnecessary variety.

Before a product or range of products can be simplified, it is necessary for management and the technical experts in the area concerned to agree upon the standards required for the products with regard to quality, composition, method of processing and method of measuring how the products compare with standards.

An example of this type of standardisation could be the examination of a menu, not necessarily with the aim of reducing the variety offered to customers, but for reducing costs and labour in the preparation of menu items.

This examination would require the presence of the managers responsible for the kitchen and menu design and any others in a position to contribute to the discussion. The intention would be to examine ingredients lists, checking that standard recipes are established using the minimum number of ingredients to achieve the desired results. This may be assisted by considering the use of pre-prepared mixes—one stock item instead of several. Also, although restriction of customer choice is not the start point of these variety control discussions, it is clear that a useful contribution may be gained by the availability of figures reflecting the popularity of the various items on the menu. If the demand for certain menu items has declined, then perhaps their exclusion from the menu could achieve a reduction of unwanted variety causing little or no adverse criticism from customers.

The outcome of this exercise should be reduction of unnecessary stock items achieved by standardizing recipes which are agreed upon as producing the right quality of dishes and a total menu which meets the needs and wants of the customers.

It should be noted that this approach does not prevent the development of new dishes for addition to the menu. The design of a new menu item would be controlled by ensuring that the increase in the number of items stocked is at minimum, and then the reception of the new dish by the customers would be monitored to predict whether its popularity is such that the drawing power of the restaurant is enhanced by its continued inclusion in the menu.

This same approach can be applied to any area where uncontrolled variety is causing excessive costs.

The specialisation appearing in the heading of this section refers, in this context, to a policy decision being taken by management to concentrate activities on producing a restricted range of products or services. The advantages of so doing arise from:

(i) reduced costs of administration (fewer stocks, easier ordering, fewer suppliers).

(ii) possible development of greater expertise on fewer activities.

(iii) a lesser range of skills required by the staff, so producing easier recruitment and, possibly, lower wage costs.

(iv) the opportunity to build a sound reputation as a specialist supplier of the particular goods or services offered.

Examples of specialisation in the hotel and catering industry include restaurants specialising in fast food or sea-food, hotel groups which offer a bar-be-cue menu, hotels which market short-stay accommodation for tourists and concentrate on accommodation rather than the provision of food.

Pareto Analysis

A technique which is useful to identify items or stocks which, respectively, are responsible for the bulk of sales revenue or stock value is the construction of a Pareto curve.

Taking stock items as an example, the curve is constructed as follows:

1. list the stock items in descending order of annual usage

2. cumulatively total the column

3. calculates the percentage each item is of the total
4. plot the items (x axis against percentages (y axis)

It is now possible to determine the items which represent, say 80% of stocks, those representing the next 15% and those which make up the last 5%. Clearly, this presents a good guide to the concentration of control systems on stocks the items representing the 80% of stocks to receive the closest attention, the next 15% less elaborate control systems and the last 5% the simplest procedure possible.

Pareto analysis can be carried out in similar fashion for revenue earning items, or items' contributions to profit. Here, the analysis directs attention to the array of products which represents a very small amount of revenue, or profit, disproportionate to their numbers and the labour and administration time absorbed by them. These products are the identified candidates for the simplification process. If demand for anyone of them is static or declining, if the profit margin is not exceptionally high and if there is no other pressing reason for keeping it (such as to satisfy an important customer) then consideration should be given to dispensing with it.

Sources of Supply

The importance to effective purchasing of a thorough knowledge of both individuals suppliers and various sources of supply is clear. The selection of the source of supply depends upon the size of the operation and the type of commodity being sought. The buyer for a large organisation using considerable quantities of vegetables, fruit and meat would probably buy at the appropriate market and would develop good relationships with the traders who best met his particular standards on quality and price. The buyer from these sources must, of course be experienced and knowledgeable about the goods being purchased. Smaller organisations might use wholesalers specialising in these goods, selecting the ones with whom to trade by visiting premises and noting those aspects which indicate the efficiency, hygiene and quality level of the warehouse.

The cash-and-carry warehouses are a further source of supplies. Some of the larger cash and carry operations have developed sections especially for caterers and also carry wide selections of non-food items which may be of interest to the hotelier. The disadvantages of this form of buying are that the buyer must supply his own transport for the goods and the account is settled at the time of buying.

Whatever source or sources of supply are used, it is the duty of the buyer to be continually vigilant as regards the number of suppliers with live accounts and the price and quality of all goods being bought. Too many suppliers, spreading the purchasing power of the organisation thinly, reduces the influence of the buyer with all suppliers, making it more difficult to develop relationships which advantage the buyer's organisation.

In Summary, It may always work the case that a supplies of good standing provides quality merchandise and is reasonable on the prices. The buyer should make all reasonable efforts to ensure service, quality and prices are acceptable to the buyer.

❑

12

Restaurant Development

Restaurant operational styles are of three major types: quick serve, family style, and full service. Within these three categories are restaurants which offer a wide variety of service styles from self-service to French service. Buffet, take out, and banquet service are some of the variations.

All of these categories of operational styles are operated as both independent and franchise businesses. To be better able to understand the development and current status of these restaurant operations as businesses it is important to understand the difference between an independently owned restaurant operation and a franchise restaurant operation.

Independent Ownership

Independent ownership may be by an individual or a chain. Both individual and chain restaurants can be operated by a single independent owner. The distinction between individual and chain is the intentional duplication of a restaurant operation into more than one unit.

Many successful restaurateurs have taken a proven restaurant and found locations which will successfully support a duplicate of that operation. Early restaurant entrepreneurs such as Howard Johnson and Bill Marriott provide excellent examples of the successful application of this practice.

Howard Johnson found a highway intersection location to be highly successful. When major interstate roads replaced the original two-lane highways, his company moved quickly to provide roadside restaurants where customers had always found them, along major travel routes.

After founding the first Hot Shop in Washington, D.C., Bill Marriott and his wife, Allie, would locate major intersections in the Washington, D.C., area along routes which were heavily traveled. Opening Hot Shoppes in these locations provided the basis for the Marriott Corporation, which today operates hotels and restaurants internationally.

Independent restaurant operations are free-standing units. These operations may be owned and managed by individual owners or groups of investors. Owners may be involved in more than one operation and often borrow successful ideas an incorporate them into another restaurant, depending on the theme, cuisine, and location. Some owners choose to put all of their energies into one restaurant. The Hilltop Steak House in Saugus, Massachusetts, has consistently been one of the highest-volume single-unit operations in the United States. Averaging over $8 million annually, this restaurant seats 1100 and serves a limited menu which concentrates on highquality beef dishes. Customers have been traditionally standing in line for a quality of food and service that they know will be consistent with their expectations. Independent restaurant operations are financially based on the resources of owners and/or investors who expect a percentage of any profits made as a return on their investment.

Chains

Corporate giants have found that takeovers of smaller corporations have often yielded a chain of restaurants. Depending on the primary objective of the corporation, the chain may be sold off or absorbed into the company. Food-related companies such as General Mills have developed their own restaurant chains and kept then under corporate ownership rather than turning then into franchises. The Olive Garden restaurants are a direct development of General Mills Corporation. These restaurants are financed by the parent company, which in turn receives all of the profits.

Franchise

> Franchising is a method of doing business whereby a parent company (the franchisor) grants (*via* a franchise agreement) an individual outlet owner (the franchisee) the right to market its products and services while using the parent's proven name, reputation and marketing techniques.

Restaurant franchises are duplications of successful restaurant operations which are sold to individual owners or investors. An owner may have more than one franchise. Companies that sell franchises may also continue to own and operate some units for the parent company. These are called company-owned units and are not classified as franchives.

Popeye's Famous Fried Chicken and Biscuits began in New Orleans, Louisiana. A fast-food restaurant that specialized in high quality fried chicken quickly found success with southern customers. Adaptations of coatings and additional aspects of regional southern cuisine helped to expand the number of units in the Louisiana area. When Popeye's founder, Al Copeland, made the decision to offer this successful restaurant format to other interested investors, he retained the company's ownership in a number of units. Franchise owners are sold a complete duplication package consisting of a building structure, signage, equipment, decoration, training, paper supplies, and recipes. Franchise owners must agree to follow company guidelines to ensure consistent product quality and customer service. Failure to do so can result in their franchise licenses being legally revoked.

Financial arrangements generally include an initial franchise fee and require a cash investment by the investors. The parent company also receives a royalty on the earnings of each franchise. The amounts of fees and percentages of royalties range widely from one company to another, depending on each company's history of success.

RESTAURANT OPERATIONAL STYLES

Quick Serve. Quick serve is the 1990s food service industry tenn for what has traditionally been called fast food. In the 1960s and

1970s the development of the fast-food restaurant chains, McDonald's, Hardee's, and Burger King, specializing in a variety of hamburger items and french fries initiated a wave of self-service restaurant chains that included Taco Bell, Kentucky Friend Chicken, Long John Silver's, and a host of others representing specialty foods and cuisines.

These operations follow the basic format of providing limited seating in a casual atmosphere for customers who order at a self service counter to "eat in or take out", In the 1970s drive-through windows were added to many of these operations, allowing customers to order over an intercom system located in the parking lot and drive up to a pick-up window for their orders.

The growth of this segment of the industry was in direct relation to the growth of the population group represented by the "baby boomers," or post-World War II birth group. Today this group is about to become the senior citizen population of the United States and still represents the largest and most important consumer group in America. As the baby boomers began their families, the demand for inexpensive food served quickly in a caused atmosphere suited, for families with young children reacted very favorably to the fast-food restaurant style.

In the 1980s this same customer group now began to look for more variety in fast food menu offerings as well as healthier items and methods of preparation. Fastfood restaurants responded in part by producing salad bars and prepackaged salad items. In 1990 McDonald's Corporation was the largest purchaser of iceberg lettuce in the United States, according to the California Iceberg Lettuce Association, clearly showing the favourable reaction of the general public to these menu offerings.

The McLean Deluxe hamburger, developed in cooperation with the National Beef Council, represents a major attempt by McDonald's Corporation to present food items in response to the needs of their customers. Chains such as Wendy's introduced a self-service buffet bar offering Mexican and Italian cuisine items as well as salads. Pizza

Hut developed a line of pasta dishes to augment their traditional pizza/sandwich menu. Breakfast became an addition to many of the specialty hamburger and fried chicken chains in an attempt to recover slipping customer counts.

By the end of the 1980s the increase in two-income families dramatically changed the life-style of the American family, creating an increasing demand for foods to take out to eat in. The take-out window was, in many operations, doing as much volume as the walk-up counter. In Sharon, Pennsylvania, the Quaker State and Lube Restaurant does close to $1 million of business annually in orders of chicken wings from their one drive-up window.

Fast-food restaurants were beginning to turn into casual family-style restaurants on their menu boards but remained self-service in their operations. As the industry began to recognize the impact of the development of the take-out segment of their operations and other trends, adjustments were made to the marketing plans of a number of restaurant chains:

1. *Quick-serve* was developed to define casual family-style dining which could represent fast-food, fast-food/family-style service combinations, or family-style service alone.

2. *Take out* becomes a stand-alone restaurant concept.

3. Menu items that could be preprepared in a fast-food kitchen setting that also responded to the demand for healthy eating concerns were identified.

Pizza Hut Corporation has created a lone of Carry-Out units which sell and deliver pizza as well as selection of menu items from the fed roof Pizza Hut restaurant menus. No customer seating is provided and drive-through windows are generally available. The company excepts to have 3000 of these units located across the United States by 1995. In addition, Pizza Hut pizza will be made available to food service vendors in all segments of the industry from airlines to sports stadiums. This addition to their marketing strategy now allows the traditional Pizza Hut restaurant to co-ncentrate on casual family-style service in a quick service setting with the fast-food line shifted to the Pizza Hut Carry-Out unit.

Family-Style. Family-style restaurant operations are represented by food service operations offering booth and/or table service in a casual setting. A combination of buffet and table service can provide labor-cost-reducing opportunities while giving customers variety in visual presentation as well as menu offerings. Independent as well as chain and franchise restaurants incorporate this service style into their overall operations.

National chains such as Big Boy's and Howard Johnson's are examples of familystyle operations. Theme and cuisine restaurants such as Chili's, the Ground Round, and Bennigan's are blends of family-style/casual dining. Family-style dining restaurants can offer alcoholic beverages but in the majority of cases do not. Operations that offer breakfast/lunch services are often operated as independent restaurants whose owners work as chef managers. Delicatessens with table service, cafeteria-style steak houses, and coffee shops are also examples of the variety of family-style operations.

Full Service. Full-service restaurant operations are designated as those restaurants offering sit-down table service. A full-service restaurant is not defined by its price but by the type of service, atmosphere, and menu selection offered to the customer.

Menus in full-service restaurants generally offer a variety of course selections from appetizers to dessert and include alcoholic beverages. Pricing of menu items can range from mid/low to expensive, depending on the theme, cuisine, and location of the restaurant. Fuel-service restaurants are generally independently or chain owned. The Chart House is an excellent example of a chain-operated full-service restaurant. The company operated sixty-two units nation-wide in 1989. These restaurants often confine themselves to dinner service only with location as a primary feature. They are located on a waterway whenever possible to emphasize the water navigation chart theme expressed in their signage, name, and menu cover. The atmosphere is casually upscale, and the menu offers a full course selection of regionally specialized items. In Philadelphia, Pennsylvania, the Chart House is located on the Delaware River adjacent to the city. The architecture of the restaurant devotes all ofthe window space to water views. The lower level is a lounge and raw shellfish bar with dining on the upper level. Operation begins at 4:30 p.m. and caters to an after work and social clientele. The average check without alcohol is $15.

The economic recession of the early 1990s is affecting this segment of the restaurant industry more than any other. Full-service restaurants which flourished during the 1980s saw as much as a 50 to 60 per cent decline in their customer counts in 1990 and 1991. Michael Hurst, former president of the National Restaurant Association, noted that the roots of this severe downtrend lie in major changes in the dining out preferences of the baby boomers who represented a large percentage of the previous customer base for this restaurant style. Mr. Hurst noted, "Through the 1980s, this influential market segment sustained an interest in chic, experimental, high-priced dining establishments, but a variety of factors-aging, family building, a loss of confidence due to the 1987 stock market crash-has created another revolution in taste within this group. Today, baby boomers are looking for less elaborate meals in homelike surroundings and at lower prices."

The result of this change in customer needs and demands is a dining style called casual style. Full-service restaurants are adjusting their decors to reflect a less formal, comfortable atmosphere. Menu offerings are being revised to include simpler food items with less labor-intensive preparation. American regiol1al foods prepared by "home-style cooking" methods are returning to full-service restaurant menus in place of highly developed food ingredient combinations and plate presentations.

This change in menu offerings has also allowed the menu pricing structure to be lowered to attract customers who are feeling the constraints on both business and personal spending for entertainment.

Healthier menu offerings include a wide variety of fresh seasonal greens and vegetables. Poultry has become the most popular low-cholesterol source of protein. Turkey and chicken are appearing in both traditional and experimental forms on restaurant menus. Cooking methods also reflect healthy dining concerns as stir-fry, steaming, and grilling take precedence over deep-fat frying, roasting, and use of heavy sauces.

Healthy dining programmes for full-service restaurants are the result of the combined efforts of local hospitals and areas restaurant associations around the United States. Restaurant menus indicate items which have been planned under the supervision of hospital dietitians to respond to a variety of dietary concerns, including low-cholesterol and low-sodium cooking. Restaurants provide nutritional breakdowns of the menu items for customers. This awareness of healthy dining concerns among restaurant customers responds to the basic needs of both middle-aged and senior citizen customer groups.

Concept Dining

In the 1980s the increased costs entertainment combined with rising menu prices created a concept called the destination restaurant. Operators realized that customers were, for economic reasons, being forced to choose whether to go out for either dinner or entertainment rather than combining both in one evening. As a result, restaurants which offered both a dining and an entertainment package began appearing in a wide variety of themes and concepts. The Air Transport Command is one of a number of theme restaurants currently operated by Specialty Restaurants of Anaheim, California. The restaurant combines a casual-style, ful-service restaurant with an entertainment lounge. In addition, the World Wat II theme of the restaurant incorporates a location adjacent to the runway at a small airport which allows diners to watch airport traffic. Nineteen forties music and memorabilia combined with interior design features complete a package which provides entertainment for families as well as couples over an extended dining time period.

Cuisine themes can also provide entertainment as well as a dining experience. Oriental restaurants which incorporate grill top tables into their facilities design offer guests the opportunity to watch their meal being prepared at the table. Table seating allows a number of guests to sit around one large table top so that customers are often seated alongside complete strangers.

Traditional full-service restaurants can incorporate light entertainment into their operations in a variety of ways. The Guest Quarters Hotel in Valley Forge, Pennsylvania, takes advantage of their bar area to promote late evening attendance by offering a piano lounge atmosphere adjacent to their dining room, providing popular much for easy listening and customer participation. A singing bartender adds more interest. This relatively low-key and inexpensive form of entertainment retains dining room customers for after-dinner drinks as well as drawings new customers for light late evening entertainment. The result is a steady volume of customers for a high-profit food and beverage area that might otherwise run high labor costs and low sales.

Setting up a Restaurant Business

It is elementary to the success of any restaurant business that owners and managers define a target market and develop a customer profile. This step is necessary for both established restaurants and start-up businesses in the planning stages. A target market is that segment of the pool of available customers who have been identified as the strongest potential customer base for a business and toward whom all sales efforts are aimed.

Determining a target market requires the preparation of a market survey to outline the geographical community and its population with the objective of identifying a pool of customers. These prospective customers are them analyzed to identify needs within the group that will be met in the format of a restaurant business.

Market Feasibility

The term feasibility refers to how practical a project or an idea is or how easily an objective might be accomplished. When considering a potential foodservice project—whether that project is developing a new restaurant, purchasing an existing property, changing the focus or direction of an existing restaurant, or bidding on a foodservice management contract—a marketing feasibility study must be completed prior to making the "go-no go" decision regarding the project.

The objective of a comprehensive marketing feasibility study is to determine whether the market potential is appropriate for a proposed project. The study is similar to a market research project in many ways and must be completed prior to the completion of a financial feasibility study that would be the basis for the final "go-no go" decision on the project. Essentially the market feasibility study should ask these questions: *(1)* Is there a market for this business in this area? *(2)* If so, how extensive is this market? and *(3)* What is the potential for capitalizing on this market at this location?

To answer these questions, a complete market feasibility study consists of the following components:

1. An analysis of the current market and the growth potential of the market area.
2. An assessment of the potential site(s).
3. An analysis of the competition (both direct and indirect) relative to the total market potential.
4. A determination of the facility (including type and size) that would best satisfy market demand.

Ultimately, the decision regarding the project is based on the financial feasibility or the project's ability to generate a profit and provide a return to owners or investors on the funds they invest in the project. The comprehensive market feasibility study provides the data base for many of the estimates considered in the financial feasibility analysis.

Market Analysis

The location for a foodservice facility must be evaluated on the basis of the potential access it affords the operator to customers. The population available as potential customers must be described in such characteristics as population demographics, employment statistics, and major employers in the area. It is necessary to examine the market potential of the current population, but it is necessary to evaluate the future market, as well, if the market feasibility study is to be complete.

Trading Area

Generally a foodservice facility draws its customers from a particular geographic area, called the trading area for that operation. The size of a facility's trading area varies markedly. It may range from only the clientele of a particular organization housing the foodservice facility (that is, the children attending a particular school and eating in the school cafeteria) to a one to three-mile radius that often defines the trading area for a fast-food facility or a family style restaurant. It may even extent to a 30- to 40-mile radius or more for a fine dining facility with an exceptional menu or an unusual and attractive location.

The trading area is usually divided into primary and secondary areas with the primary area generating at least 50 per cent of the facility's business. Generally, unless the operation is located in or near a major traffic-generating location, such as a shopping mall or a hotel, about 50 per cent of the foodservice's revenue will be generated by the population that is within a one-mile radius of the property. When preparing a market analysis for an existing property, the trading area can be determined from studies of the current patrons. A good approach for this analysis is to ask customers where they were just prior to coming to the foodservice facility and plotting their responses on a map of the area. In a new facility, however, it must be estimated from studies of the patrons of other operations.

Population Demographics

Once the trading area has been defined, the demographics, or the characteristics, of the population within that area must be identified and analyzed. The products and services offered by the foodservice facility must match the wants and expectations of the potential customers within the trading area if the operation is to be successful. Demographic data that should be collected for the study includes:

1. Average age of the population
2. Average family size
3. Disposable income level
4. Educational levels
5. Ethnic backgrounds
6. Housing density
7. Housing values
8. Population density
9. Ratio of homeowners to renders
10. Ratio of males to females
11. Ratio of marrieds to singles
12. Types or housing
13. Types of occupations
14. Type of religions
15. Unemployment statistics
16. Types of employment

Neighborhood Descriptors

Many features of the neighborhood surrounding the proposed project site can significantly impact the market potential. Such features can also be important influences on the type of operation that would be successful in this trading area. Examples of these features include the following items:

Population base Diversity and Stability. It may be difficult to find a product base that will be attractive to the required number of customers if the surrounding population is composed of very diverse ethnic groups, for example. Also, in a neighbourhood that is experiencing rapid change, a popular concept today may be quickly rejected by the new population making the potential success of the foodservice facility short-lived. A stable, reasonable homogeneous population represents the most desirable population base.

The Neighbourhood Appearance. The appearance of the neighbourhood may give some indication of the amount of discretionary funds available to the area population. Discretionary funds are the dollars persons have "left over" after paying for their fixed commitments such as rent or mortgage and utilities. These funds are available for them to spend as they wish, including for the purchase of food prepared outside the home. A neat, well kept neighbourhood may indicate a population base with sufficient discretionary income to support a foodservice establishment. Fer example, in New Delhi the restaurants located in south of Delhi are thriving with good business whereas the restaurants located in other areas are striving for business.

Other area Businesses and Activities. The presence of other businesses or activities in the area is an indication of the type and amount of traffic flow that might be expected. Facilities such as retail shopping centers, athletic, cultural, or entertainment centers, and office or wholesale centers may bring potential customers to the trading area. In many instances, these businesses and activities may complement the products and services offered by the foodservice establishment.

Public Institutions. Public institutions also influence the customer traffic in a trading area and should be considered in the market analysis. Public institutions are facilities such as schools, day care centers, colleges, and universities, governmental services and buildings, and military bases. Public institutions not only influence the volume of customer traffic in the area but they may also significantly determine many of the characteristics, such as age, educational background, or leisure time interests, of the potential customer population.

Psychographies

Psychographic considerations are those that picture the personality characteristics of the population. These considerations may also reflect the psychological factors that affect the population's behaviour patterns. For example, considerations of concern to the market analysis would be the lifestyles of the trading area population and that population's spending patterns.

Much information is required for the market analysis as well as for the subsequent phases of the market feasibility study, and it is available from a variety of sources. Some of the many sources that might be used to generate the statistics and other information needed for this study.

INTERPRETING THE MARKET FEASIBILITY

Understanding the key factors to be assessed in interpreting market survey information is essential to use this major marketing tool effectively.

Community Needs

Primary to any decision involving developing or changing a food service operation is accurately determining the need for a new restaurant or changes in a restaurant in the community as a whole. The general economic health of the community is an essential indicator of what the response to different styles of food service operations will be. Using the information gathered the following questions can assess the current and future economic health of the community:

1. Was there a decline or increase in population growth within the past 5 years?
2. Is the population growth in the next 5 years expected to decline or increase?
3. Are the majority of households families or single persons?
4. What is the average family size?

5. How many two-income families are there?
6. What is the percentage of family households with three or more persons in comparison to the number of two-income families?
7. In what range does the highest percentage of household incomes fall?
8. In what range does the highest percentage of the married population fall?
9. What is the largest population group by age?
10. What is the average per capita income?

The answers to these questions will tell you whether the population is increasing or declining and in what income level and age range the largest customer pool lies. These answers, combined with an analysis of the competition within the community, will produce an overall picture of the prospective business climate.

Customer Needs

As discussed previously, demographic information on a potential customer base can be broken down into the following demographic categories.

1. Age
2. Average income
3. Family size
4. Sex
5. Marital status
6. Occupation
7. Level of education

Segmentation is the breakdown of information into categories. It allows management to identify key factors about potential customers which would make them a more effective target market. To complete the exercise, management determines some common characteristics which identify their customer base. For example, customers may be light or heavy alcoholic beverage drinkers, sports oriented, frequent travelers, casual or sophisticated in their dining habits.

The combination of consumer characteristics and demographic information will create a customer profile that will identify a target market profile:

Customer profile + Demographic information = Target market.

This target market profile can now be broken down further into a segmentation of the frequency of customer use.

The frequency with which a customer will return to a restaurant is a good indication of his or her reaction to marketing efforts. The pattern of use of a restaurant also provides additional marketing information for the customer profile. Tools for measuring this information are often indicated by the method of payment that is most commonly used and the purpose of the customer's use of the restaurant.

Restaurant operations who develop customer mailing lists can qualify their users by categorics and target specific mailings and promotional activities to them. The three general categories are: heavy user, medium user, and light user. By combining such additional information as family size, average check amount, beverage consumption, and purpose of visit these customers can be targeted for specific marketing efforts.

A major identification of a segment of the market concerns what customer needs management can identify and create products and/or services to fulfill. The fastestgrowing segment of the food service industry is takeout. A combination of changes in the family profile, work patterns, and eating styles has increased the demand for high-quality food products that can be purchased fully or partially prepared and taken home for consumption. The profile of this customer might be the following:

Family size: 2-4

Average age: 35

Sex:female

Average income: medium to upper

Frequency: heavy user

Method of payment: check or credit card

Profession: career-oriented

Management can also this information as the basis for future plans and decisions about changes in concepts, promotional activities, menu programmes, hours of operation, and staffing.

Labour

By completing the labour source analysis you will identify the availability of various labour pool in your geographical area. By comparing increases or decreases in availability of labour with forecasts you will also be able to perceive how well you will be able to fill the labour requirements of your restaurant.

The percentages of available labour within age ranges indicate the type of average employee you win have. High school students turn over quickly but have a high energy level. College students are seasonal and transient. Older employees are reliable and interested in their jobs. Their employment records are stronger than those of the other two groups. This population group is also more receptive to lower wage scales because this is a second income in many cases supplementing pensions and social security payments training programmes provide an instant pool of employable personnel as well as a resource for training your employees.

By comparing the needs based on objective analysis with the available labour pool, management can make a realistic analysis of whether the demand of the restaurant will be met by available workers. If there needs cannot be met, then management must adjust the operation of the restaurant to match the available skills of the labour market.

Competition Survey

In addition to the information on the competition survey management can look to the recent development of other restaurant operations an indicators of the needs of customers and the community as well as trends in economic health. The current trend toward company-owned units of corporate chains rather than franchises provides professional marketing information to independent owners and managers. Southwest Cafes, Inc., offers five different Mexican theme restaurants. Each restaurant concept answers the need of a different target market. Some offer higher-priced menu items and full service dining. Others offer midrange pricing with an appropriate menu item selection. Yet another offers a quick-service atmosphere with low-range menu pricing. Interior decor and seating match the level of menu item selections and range of pricing. By recognizing which market this company is trying to reach in establishing new restaurants, management can incorporate this information into their new development strategies.

A thorough survey of the competition also allows management to compare menu item listings and prices. This comparison often reveals market saturation of cuisine trends, dining styles, and theme concepts. By comparing the number of available customers with the current competition management can assess how competition could affect future business and decide whether the community will support the restaurant concepts and changes being envisioned. Market saturation of direct theme and menu ideas provides management with the opportunity to create a different approach to the original plans or change to different dining styles and levels of cuisine. It is also possible to identify a window of need that the competition is not filling and develop a concept to answer that need.

❐

13

Arrangement of Kitchen and Dining Room

KITCHEN

We started with that little moan because it is time now to consider that engine-room of any restaurant, the kitchen. It is the kitchen which dictates everything about any eating-place. It dictates the size of its dining-room and the number of 'covers' which can be served. It dictates the style and type of restaurant you are going to run, and it dictates the type of customer you are going to welcome. Everything about your kitchen is going to tell everyone else what exactly it is that makes you attractive to some and repellent to others. It seems that, because the kitchen is 'behind the green baize door' in most people's minds, it is also a place where no human being would wish to tread. Most odd.

Take the average fast food outlet and, why be coy, what about a Little Chef? Now, to say there is any element of the cooking of great food in such a place would be straining credulity overmuch. Yet the kitchen is in full sight of every customer, it is invariably clean, the staff are invariably clean as well, there is no smell of greasy chips, old fat, unclean hot plates, spilled and congealing gravy, long burned-on food. And this in a country crawling with environmental health officers armed with manuals of regulations needing fork-lift trucks. But perhaps that may be the problem—no health officer has ever been a chef. If he had, or was, perhaps our kitchens would get better and our food attain a general level of acceptability.

Open Kitchen Door

The truth of the matter is that great kitchens come from men and women who know about and understand food, or from organizations which have so cleverly targeted their market that they are able to insist on certain standards being observed by all who work for them. And in this context we put the vast majority of the fast food outlets. We surely sure they have problems with cleanliness, with staff, sometimes with supplies or disagreeable customers, but those problems rarely seem to rub off on me, as a customer travelling the country on business or pleasure.

We are on about a great many so-called restaurateurs who seem to feel that what is out of sight is also out of mind and has nothing anyway to do with their customers. They could not be further from the truth. Although we are by no means an apostle for the 'open-plan kitchen on view to all school of thought, we are an exponent of the belief that a kitchen, your kitchen, should be open to all if necessary and not just to the environmental health officer once you have shoved the dog-bowl under the sink and the dishcloths into a cold oven. It is, yet again, an attitude of mind. A closed kitchen is a closed view of the catering trade.

One of our great happinesses, when we had a hotel and restaurant in Scotland, and again in southern England, was that a great many of our better guests always seemed to end up in the kitchen—as our relatives and we do when we are in France. And inability to pay the bill is not the reason in either case. Our guests, customers, felt somehow at home, at ease, and it was a measure of our success that we were able to convey this to them.

Planning the Kitchen

The first thing to do with the kitchen in your new premises is nothing at all. To avoid expensive mistakes, you are going to need a long, hard look at your new operation and the sort of place you intend to run. It is no good, for instance, calling in a plumber (at about £12.50 an hour) or, for that matter, an electrician at about the same price, to do just the 'odd job or two', and then about a year later calling them both back to undo what they first did and do something else. Please do not yield to that temptation, however inconvenient it might be one day in the future because you have got busier and more successful.

Once again: research, reconnaissance, planning is the way to start, as it is the way to go on.

Now we are not assuming you are opening a great restaurant with marvellous 'classic' cuisine and delicate patisserie right from the start. For that you would have to go to a great restaurant in Britain, or a fairly good one in France, to see how they order such things. And unless you are made of money, we are not suggesting either that you call in a specialist kitchen-designer who is an expert in commercial kitchens. The first thing you have to do is study and plan the workflow.

Your kitchen is the wrong shape, for a start, and it is far too small or too big. In any event, none of the 'services', such as water, gas, electricity, is anywhere near where you want them. Exactly, but how do you know where you want them until you have discovered exactly what your problems are? Apart from the specialised 'fast food' operations, the average kitchen starts as being a mess and goes on getting worse. For the most part, if you have taken over an existing business, it will be inconvenient if not downright grubby, and if you are starting up anew, it will be sadly lacking in everything you feel you must have, (Bad thought. 'Must have' is not something you can know about until you have put at least a toe into the water.) Of course you can go to one of the many very good kitchen equipment suppliers who also offer a kitchen planning and advisory service, for the most part free if you order their equipment. And, remember, you do not always have to buy such equipment: leasing it could be a better proposition for you. On the whole, we have nothing but praise for such companies but they must know in detail what you are intending to do. It is obvious, is it not, that a fast food operation needs equipment very different from that of a traditional restaurant, apart from certain basic items, and certainly the suggested layout may be different? Yet the work How will remain much the same: preparation, cooking, serving and keeping warm, collection for the dining-room, clearance from the dining-room, an area for plate-cleaning and stacking, along with cutlery and glasses, washing-up of such items and racking for storage after washing-up, or for redistribution again for further customers, and a pot-wash for the larger cooking utensils. The law also states that you must have a handwash facility with soap and clean towels in the kitchen, as well as at least two sinks, for vegetable preparation and for other uses. Quite simple, really. The trick is getting it all in, because you need work surface, a cooker or two, storage areas, waste bins and a lot more besides. And where is the refrigerator going to go and what about the deep-freeze?

Yet chefs like us often say that too big a kitchen is worse than too small a one—it merely increases the leg work. There are basically two types of kitchen layout—that in which the cooking is done around the outside (the walls, in other words) and the centrally placed 'island' cooking site, or 'piano' as the French call it. Both systems have their advantages, but the island site almost certainly needs a bigger area for it to work properly, otherwise people tend to bump into each other and might cause serious accidents. Accidents are endemic to kitchen work. They are mainly of the 'cutting' type (very often because knives are too blunt, as opposed to being too sharp) and, of course, the scalding type. But slippery floors take their toll as well, not because they are wet and clean but because they are wet and greasy. Cleanliness is very much preferable to godliness in any kitchen.

Choosing Equipments of Kitchen

Do not decide for yourself until you have seen the incredible equipment now on offer. Even if you cannot, regretfully, afford it from the start, just to look and learn is a joyful experience. And that takes us to the next point. Where do we go to get an idea of what we might need or would dearly like to have? The easy answer, indeed the only answer, in our opinion, is to go to the catering exhibitions which are held alternately in London, Olympia, and Glasgow, Kelvin Hall, early each year. The dates of these main exhibitions are well heralded in such trade magazines as the Caterer and Hotel Keeper. There are many other exhibitions too, both in the major cities and in smaller provincial towns, at which a considerable range of equipment and food products are displayed. They are without question Wonderlands of ideas, both established and innovative, and for the most part the demonstration staff on every stand are knowledgeable, helpful and courteous.

These exhibitions will give you a basic idea, out perhaps you cannot afford everything you see. Then, as we mentioned before, discuss the possibility of leasing certain items, which will free what money you have for those other, essential cash items which will always crop up. And if leasing is not possible, try the second-hand dealers. In practice, we found that very little good second-hand equipment was available, but there are one or two specialist firms in London which have quite large selections, and some do exist in major provincial towns.

Main tourist centres, such as Bournemouth, often have such outlets and, of course, there are auctions in various parts of the country which are advertised in the trade press. The only problem with auctions is that you want to know very definitely what you are looking out for, and roughly how much it should be worth, so they should be approached with caution.

But in any event, once again, you must know the sort of operation you are going to run. Write down the main requirements for such an operation and if necessary contact the Catering Equipment Distributors Association, who will be pleased to help about your local suppliers.

Another source of help and one much to be admired is a firstclass catering suppliers. Once again there are two or three in London, certainly a very fine firm in Glasgow and others dotted about the country. But you will be better off if you concentrate on your nearest provincial city Birmingham or Manchester, for example, if you are not near Glasgow or London.

These shops sell everything from vast commercial equipment, suitable for hospitals or institutions, to smaller pieces of equipment which you might even find in your own domestic kitchen.

Air Cleaning Equipment

There is one item of equipment which we have mentioned in passing but not dwelt upon it is almost always forgotten in average kitchens, it is always an afterthought, if it is considered in the first place, and yet it is, to me, jolly nearly as important as a sink or a cooker. It is ventilation or air-cleaning equipment.

How often have you got out of your car in a pub car-park, say, and been assailed by that awful stench of chip oil? How often have you gone into a restaurant to be greeted first of all by that smell? The franchise agreements for such places are very strict about cooking-smells, and we always feel that. if they can get rid of them efficiently (when most of their operation is frying or grilling), why cannot other establishments? Quite honestly, the answer is simply that the owners or such places do not, themselves, notice how frightful their property smells. An inn and restaurant we know not far from where we live used to have owners who were very strict about how their place smelled and even went so far as never to serve chips, because their extraction equipment was fairly non-existent. Most customers commented, as we did on entering, that the hallway always smelled so good, of enticing food being cooked, and the dining area so good, of polish, fresh flowers and wood fires. The important point about the smell of that place was the word 'enticing' it made you hungry just to go in there. Now the same place has new owners who do not seem to worry about it. One of our friends said she was not going back there any more—she had hung her coat in the hallway and, when she collected it on leaving, it stank of old chip oil and had to go to the cleaners before she could wear it again. We thought it very sad, but very typical.

There are a number of systems on the market, and firms which specialise in 'tailoring' ventilation of a kitchen to your own requirements.

The filters have to be kept clean, of course, and the whole thing must be regularly serviced, which is normally done under contract with the suppliers or engineers. But remember that 'extraction' means what it says the warm air goes out as well as the smell, and places can get quite chilly if the extractor is not well regulated. An alternative is the aircleaning system, which we have found very effective, though they tend to sound a little noisy at those times when your restaurant is none too full.

From Floor to Ceiling

Let us, finally, take a quick look at the various items of equipment you may need and set your mind at rest about some of the 'technical' terms you may come across. For all work surfaces, stainless steel is the most practical and easiest to keep clean. It is also the most expensive. Most catering suppliers have 'ready-mades', either with racking underneath or with drawers or cupboards, or a combination to suit your own requirements. There are also firms which specialise in. 'tailormade' work units.

Laminates tend to 'lift' if not very carefully fitted, and the inevitable joins also harbour dirt which does much to upset the visiting environmental health officer. They often look nicer, however, and with care and professional joinery there is no reason to dismiss them out of hand.

Floors should be easy to clean but non-slip. Tiles are very hard on the working feet they are practical, as are most of the surfaces recommended by the dozens of specialist suppliers. In an ideal world, floors would be laid with a 1 in 120 slope to suitable drain-aways, making washing down extremely easy, and where floor and wall meet there should be curved coving for ease of cleaning and protection against bugs and dirt.

Ceilings too should be washable. Wood is frowned on unless very smooth and well coated with high gloss paint, but ordinary plaster is perfectly acceptable, again with gloss paint, as it is on walls, although in areas of heavy wear, such as around a stove, concrete walls with gloss paint are often used. One or two proprietary wall claddings are available which can be acceptable to the health officers and make for a very nice, often decorative finish, in cases where existing walls are in very poor shape or have to be done away with completely.

Equipments for Cooking

Ranges, or 'boiling-tables', to use the catering terms for the domestic cooking-hob, can be had in a number of sizes of four, six and eight 'rings' . Choice of fuel is up to you. Either they are free-standing, with storage space below, or ovens are fitted beneath, again of various sizes; although you will increasingly hear the word 'gastronorm' being used in connection with all ovens and steamers a belated attempt to standardise sizes so that oven trays etc. will fit any item of equipment. There are certain objections to having ovens below boiling-tables, access being high on our list anyway. Nothing is more annoying than having to move aside from a stove just because someone else wants to get something into or out of the oven. We prefer separate ovens, preferably at waist height, with drop-down doors upon which pans can be rested if required, but space and personal attitudes can make this debatable. One word on fuel: if you do not have town gas or natural gas, do bear in mind the liquid petroleum gases which are available, normally Propane, which has a much higher BthU rating than Butane and also a lower freezing temperature, which makes quite a difference believe you me, if you have to cook in places like the Scottish Highlands in wintertime. The cylinders come in various sizes,' or a larger vessel is filled regularly by a visiting tanker, similar to that for oil heating. Automatic change-over valves are a normal fitting so that the gas does not 'die' on-you- in the middle of service. Various 'package' deals are available with LPG suppliers, so discuss these in detail with their local representatives before you make up your mind, especially as not all existing gas equipment can be converted from ordinary gas to LPG.

Britain has been slow to accept thé advantages of LPG, possibly because of supply problems in the past, the proliferation of strictly 'local' gasworks and the fact that not many restaurants existed outside towns and major villages, but its use is becoming much more widespread now, especially in the catering trade, and there is a choice of equipment at one time only the French (inevitably) made gas hobs which came with all three different jets as standard.

There is no ambient surface heat at all on the hob surface or surround, which makes them very safe.

Ovens are too well known to dwell upon. There is little difference between domestic and commercial apart from size, but we do favour the convection or 'fan' ovens now available as they cut cooking-time by as much as thirty or forty per cent and are marvellous for baked products.

Microwave ovens are a different matter. They are still being sold as a primary cooking-tool, and the catering industry, always quick to jump on an easy bandwagon, took them to their hearts, often with disastrous results. They are not, in our very definite opinion and experience, a primary cooking-tool but they ire good for defrosting and for the reheating of certain foods. We think they are much over-rated, and a microwave oven would be very far down any list of mine for kitchen equipment.

Steamers are good for the cooking or 'holding' of certain items, especially vegetables, even though they are designed primarily for the larger, institutional type of demand. Once again, new types are always coming onto the market. Make quite sure, however, that you really do need one before committing yourself.

Grills are another much-debated item. If the heat source is above the food-tray, it is technically a salamander; if below, it is a grill. The widespread availability now of the very heavy, often cast-iron griddle, which is an electrically heated 'hot plate' upon which the food is directly placed, has meant the need for old-fashioned grills has lessened. You can see these working in any fast food outlet, and they are very acceptable to all chefs, although cleanliness once again is the watchword.

Shelves

May we make a plea for shelves, and not cupboards, in kitchens. You have probably seen those depressing, glossy photographs of 'designer' kitchens in the Sunday magazines and elsewhere: all neatly planned with masses of cupboard doors and work surfaces empty except for the obligatory bowls of aubergines and lemons. That is nothing like a commercial kitchen. Indeed, it is nothing like our own kitchen at home. Just imagine that situation in a busy kitchen. In the first place, whenever you want something you are bound to be carrying something else in one hand. You have to put it down, having opened the cupboard door, and then use two hands to get what you want, not forgetting to close the door afterwards. If you do not close that door, someone else will come along and walk into it. Yet time and again we see doors on cupboards even in restaurant kitchens. Forget it all. Go for shelves, open shelves, and, above all, hooks under them and on the ceiling. Hooks to hang every cooking-utensil you can imagine: sieves, spoons, choppers, colanders, saucepans, jugs and the 101 items which make a kitchen so enjoyable to work in. Keep cupboards for foodstuffs, not cooking-tools.

Storage System

Storage is a problem in most kitchens. Very rarely is there enough of it. A good old-fashioned walk-in larder is ideal. Perforated zinc, or a similar small-mesh screen, at the windows, rodent proof, well-fitting doors and good ventilation are all you need, along with stout shelving to take heavy items. Most Victorian houses had such places, and jolly good they were. All too often nowadays food is stored in unsuitable areas just because there is not enough room for a proper 'larder'. The health officers will want to know about where you store foods of all kinds, so make sure any area is kept spotlessly clean. They object to stuff on the floor at least eight inches above ground is required. There are specialist suppliers now of very good wire racking which can be bought and built up on a modular system.

Once again, a catering exhibition will have many such examples. The same goes for wine 'bins' which can be built from 'kits'. Do not keep even red wine in too hot a place.

A steady temperature, about 14°C, is better for all wines, whatever their colour, if you do not have specialised, separate storage areas or wine cabinets. A lot of nonsense is talked about wine. It is better to have one main storage area from which you take red wines into the restaurant, and put some white in a cooler each day.

Water and Washing-Up

Hot drinks need hot water, and small boilers are available for these. They are sold on their hot water output per hour, fifty, a hundred or 150 pints, but they are also quoted in cups or gallons. There are eighteen cups to a gallon. Choose a boiler which is reasonable to your projected need. And while we are on the subject of hot water, your kitchen is going to need: a vast quantity, so make sure your hot water system is able to cope adequately. Nothing is worse than 'running out' of hot water just when you need it most. And it will happen, never fear, unless you have a proper supply. Remember, every meal served needs between one and four gallons of hot water. Dish-washing machines are not always necessary, providing you have a plongeur coping with the dirty plates and cutlery. And you should always try to have a special 'pot wash' area reserved for saucepans, which are extremely unwieldy. Basically, dish-washers are of two types and the type distinguishes their price ticket. The cheapest to buy are of the domestic type. They are 'stacked' with the dirty plates and cutlery and then left to get on with it. This process takes an hour or more, depending on the make of machine. The second, or commercial type, has sets of trays or racks which are stacked with utensils and put into the machine, which then washes and dries them in a matter of minutes. These are going to cost at least £800, possibly more. There is a third type which will probably not concern you at this stage: it consists of a 'conveyor belt system onto which the utensils are placed, the 'belt' taking them through the washing process in one continuous movement until they emerge at the other end, clean and ready for storage. These machines are used in very large restaurants, hospitals and so on. Fay, forget the third type. But consider the difference between the other two: The most common commercial type, which washes in a very short cycle, has a 'knock-on effect in that your stocks of crockery and cutlery need not be too enormous, as it copes with up to 200 items an hour, allowing for five items per meal. If you use the 'domestic' type, you 'lock up' great amounts of your eating utensils for long periods, 'which means you will have to carry very much greater stocks of every item.

Cold Storage System

The only other item worth mentioning is refrigeration equipment. A decent-sized refrigerator in the kitchen is a must and, if you have the space, at least a small deep-freeze to hold items you regularly need, such as stocks, sauces and so on, to be topped up every day as necessary. There should be room for a larger deep-freeze outside somewhere, if you do not have room in the kitchen. Cabinet, or upright, freezers with pull out drawers are less caring about electricity but quick to rummage around in. Chest freezers are economical, but whatever it is you need will always be at the bottom. They are, however, better for large joints of meat and so on. Some of this equipment may well be offered to you for free if your operation requires large quantities of frozen foods. Ask about such concessions when you have become established with a large supplier but do not tie yourself unnecessarily to that supplier alone. It never pays in the long run. It has always been said that no kitchen has enough refrigeration equipment. As you expand, you will probably want a 'walk-in' cold store. They are made in sections and fitted quite quickly by specialist suppliers. You can sometimes get one secondhand, by keeping an eye on the classified advertisement section of the local paper.

Finally, remember that a deep-freeze can also supply you with ice if your operation does not warrant an ice-making machine. We remember once going out to dinner one very hot evening at a local restaurant where the staff were almost proud to tell you that the ice-machine had broken down the previous weekend and the engineer had still not called. They were less than amused when we asked them why they had not thought of making ice in their deep-freezers, which we knew they must have, because of the quantity of 'bought-in' dishes on their 'extensive' menu. A little forethought, and a proper routine, would have ensured that at least on deep-freeze held a large plastic bag of ice-cubes, kept topped up after every service from normal ice-trays.

THE DINING-ROOM

We turn first to the dining-room and the sort of image you wish to create. It is an important image. From the moment your customers walk into your establishment, you proclaim to them exactly what sort of food they are likely to be offered. This condition is, we believe, peculiar to Britain. Most of your customers may seem to care more for the setting than for the food, perhaps, but it is the restaurateur who, over the years, has to be blamed, for it is he who has created the idea that the two go hand in hand, as if by Holy Writ. Much as we would like to say to you: ignore this whole idea that decor is more important than food, to many, if not most, customers, the fact remains that many very successful restaurants have been founded, and thrive, on this whole idea. It is no good our saying that in France, for instance, we have far more regularly eaten very well indeed in places with paintwork peeling off the walls outside, and wallpaper peeling off the walls inside, than in the 'smarter' establishments which are designed largely to lure the unsuspecting within their webs. It is no good in saying that for centuries, so far as we know, the French have ignored paintwork to concentrate on the food and drink. It might well be that paint and paper were too expensive in that country until the arrival of the ubiquitous DIY shops a few years ago. The fact must remain that in Britain the 'face' is more important than the food and that you can get away with culinary murder providing the decorations are presentable.

We are assuming that you are not made of money and cannot afford the specialist restaurant interior designers who nowadays abound and often make their living out of what are known, today, as 'themed' restaurants. Both the designers and the 'themes' cost a great deal of money. We do not necessarily think that all designers are a waste of money (for those with success already achieved) but we do think 'themes' very definitely are.

But you must get used to the technical, modem jargon. A 'themed' restaurant is very often a sure sign of previous design failure among the big chains or, anyway, lack of sufficient profit for the money invested. You have certainly come across what we mean: those places with the odd fishing-net and glass float strung across the ceiling, an oar or two and an old sail artfully draped on a wall. That is, crudely, a 'theme'. It is designed to give the customer a feeling that he is in a place where sea food is of the best. The fact that it is frozen fish and chips, same as you would get in dozens of other places, and more honestly (and probably better too) in a local fish-and-chip shop, is immaterial.

A vast amount is spent on 'themed' restaurants, and it is not too cynical of us to say that it is all a great cod on the general public. We can think of at least a dozen restaurants, each of which has been 'rethemed' in the past ten years and still serves the same old food (badly) as before.

Because they have a great amount of money, the larger chains of outlets constantly do this, and change their brand name too. The big brewers are high on the list, spending thousands of pounds on new decor and ideas while leaving the food sold in their pubs in the same old, soggy state.

Sometimes these fashions come and go with extreme rapidity; sometimes they take ages. You may yourself remember the craze many years back for the destruction of genuine Victorian interiors in pubs and restaurants, particularly by one brewery chain in the Midlands and north of England, which owned a very large number of outlets. After ten years or so, they discovered they had made a mistake and set about recreating the self-same Victorian interiors they had wantonly destroyed, but at enormous cost. And serve them right. Unfortunately, as always, it was the customer who paid the bill, along with the shareholders.

These warnings serve merely to put the dangers into your mind. If, say, you want to run a restaurant specializing in fish of all types, by all means think in terms of making the sea part of your decor. But remember the money it is going to cost. You may be better off keeping your decor pretty ordinars, though attractive, and being content with its lasting for years until success has been achieved. We think that would be a better course; certainly it will be more prudent.

Convenience and Comfort

So much, then, for 'themes'. But there are a number of established 'rules' on interior design with which you should be acquainted. The first is probably the old adage that harsh lighting and hard seats make for quick turnover of customers and that subdued lighting and soft seats make for fewer numbers staying longer and being charged more for the privilege. Once again, you must decide in essence right from the start into which category your restaurant is going to fall, which category you, yourself, wish to adopt. The adage demonstrates the extremes. There are qualifications, obviously, within this statement.

For instance, low tables and chairs, even if very comfortable, make for a quicker turnover of customers, which is particularly suited to a coffee-or tea-shop or something similar. After a time, customers feel psychologically awkward, and they hasten away, leaving the table for someone else. This is not true, however, if you have a bar area where customers can order their drinks and discuss what they are going to eat before going into the dining-room proper. Chairs and tables which are top hard and uncomfortable in those circumstances tend to focus attention on how long customers are waiting for their food. A judicial blend is necessary.

Similarly, seats facing a wall, even an attractive alcove, will not remain filled for long. People are too curious about knowing who is behind them for such arrangements to be popular. A local coffee-bar in our area has just such an arrangement and in the centre of each room is a long communal table. The turnover in customers is very quick, as neither type of seating is conducive to long-stay trade. Whether the owner planned it deliberately that way we do not know-we suspect not, but he certainly achieves an aim of increasing his through—put by not encouraging his customers to tarry long over their coffees, salads and so on. A visit to your catering suppliers will show you a range of furniture suitable for a dining-room. It should be sturdy, able to cope with the constant use which often rough-handed customers will give it, and of correct height for the operation you are planning. It will be expensive, and in our opinion the design often leaves much to be desired. This is particularly important and worthwhile explaining more fully. In an ideal world, an area of two square feet is needed for each customer seated at, a table. Round tables, especially if old or antique, often look nice, but they are impractical as a general rule and those with centre pedestals are often rocky or unsafe as well. If you use square tables, however, it would seem to follow that for four people you would require a table four feet by four feet. But this is not necessarily accurate you can get away with less.

We also gained an insight into the truth of the saying, 'Your table will be ready in a moment, sir,' one lunchtime when that was, literally, the case. Whenever we hear this said in any restaurant, we all tend to collapse with laughter but, alas, the explanation never quite rings true. In France, similar tables are often placed in front of a banquette running round the walls. If your dining-room is suitable, this is an extremely good and versatile design, leaving space in the centre for displays or other dining-tables. Couples will normally sit side by side facing outwards into the room, or, if preferred, they can sit facing each other, as can four people dining together. Apart from the seating, a form of cosiness can be achieved by room-dividers, if you so wish. These divisions can be achieved by plants in long troughs, open-work screens or, as we saw once in a famous restaurant in Limoges, blinds of thin bamboo cane, which hung from the ceiling and could be unrolled at will to divide off, as required, groups of diners at various searing configurations.

We are not, however, trying to write a treatise on interior design we are merely trying to put into your mind a number of ideas which may appeal to you and may be adapted for what you desire. Once again, if you remember our dear old notebook, you will have jotted many ideas down while doing your researches—those that appealed to you and those that did not.

The important thing throughout is to fashion your own restaurant design to that of your type of trade your market, in other words. If you are going for the fast food operation, fixed seating of some discomfort to those built like ourself will suffice. But not if you are planning an up-market operation, obviously. And above all, if you are not interested in fast food and quick turnover of customers, make sure, we beseech you, that there is plenty of room around each table, as well as on it. Lack of elbow-room is not just a matter of comfort for the customer, it is essential for the staff who have to wait at table. We know of one, now very successful restaurant in a southern town which started off by crowding in too many tables. The atmosphere was stifling for the diners, and impossible for the waitresses both in heat generated and in terms of service. The food was excellent, and we regretted that we would never visit the place again because of this over-crowding. The restaurant has now learned its lesson, we understand, and is much more comfortable for everyone. It deserved to do well but took years to recover from an initial, and near-fatal, mistake.

Of course, if you wish there to be a non-smoking area, that is a different matter. Many chains of fast food restaurants have such areas. On the whole they work well. But we notice that virtually all of them have some form of air-cleaning or extraction. In such places we have never found any trace of stale tobacco, nor indeed detected any smell of tobacco being smoked.

As a very broad guide-line, dining-rooms should be 'cool' to look at, as, opposed to 'hot'. Therefore try to avoid the red end of the spectrum. Greens are excellent but virtually impossible to get right first time, as they always seem to turn out too wishy-washy or too harsh. We also know many people who have a positive dislike of green, for psychological reasons we have never managed to discover, but it exists nonetheless. And with all colours, remember it is the overall effect that is important. How does the room, as a whole, look? Cool and inviting, warm and inviting, cold and functionally distant?

Dining-rooms should, if possible, have a temperature lower than that of the rest of the building. They tend to heat up quickly once full of people and get very uncomfortable. So, although they should be pleasantly warm, but not hot early in the service session, try if you can to control the temperature downwards the busier you get, or as the session goes on. This is not impossible; it just takes care and forethought. Most people find their appetite sharpened by a room slightly cooler-looking, and cooler-feeling, than their immediately previous surroundings, which might even be a small bar area inside the entrance. If you have no such area or perhaps do not want a bar, some form of division, say with a screen or two, should be designed to separate, however subliminally, the entrance from the restaurant itself. This is not, of course, necessary in certain operations but it does help to put the customer at ease except in fast food or the 'bistro' type of outlet, though even many of these do, in fact, have such an area, however notional. At its best, interior design is excellent. We remember some years ago reading about a newly opened local restaurant which seemed to make more of its design than its food. It sounded quite frightful, heavy brown tablecloths, brown candles, rich furnishings and drapes in reds and so on. In fact, it sounded so appalling that our relatives and we just had to go. It was quite marvellous, and the work of David Hicks. But only a Hicks could have done with those colours what was achieved. He seemed to have broken every rule, but it worked wonderfully.

Licensing for Restaurant

We have already considered the position regarding a liquor licence, but if you decide to apply for one, you will need to satisfy the licensing justices about its service, as well as supplying plans of the bar and surrounding area. If there is no room for a bar as such, you will need a dispense area where you keep drink and 'dispense' it; hence the name. In Scotland there are, to many minds, curious laws relating to actual bars, which in restaurants have to be no bigger than a certain size, to prevent, it is said, customers leaning on them and thus using a restaurant as they would an ordinary pub. These regulations are not irksome, however, and for the most part it is better for you to have a dispense area, rather than going to all the trouble of applying for a proper bar, for which permission is still hard to obtain. To comply with the liquor laws, whether you have a proper bar or not, remember that you must display a list of prices and a notice stating what size measures are used for spirits. In England and Wales the common size is one-sixth of a gill, in Scotland it is at least one-fifth, but one-third gill measures are quite common they do not believe in anything less than a decent drink! You may even be asked for a 'wee half in Scotland, which is no less than a half-gill, though this tends to happen in pubs rather than in restaurants. The whole question of liquor sales in restaurants was made somewhat simpler by the Licensing Act, 1964, as it specifically defined eating places rather than just 'lumping' them in with other premises where alcohol was sold. Regulations since then have allowed alcohol to be sold throughout most of the trading day rather than just within the old 'permitted hours', as they were called, and restaurateurs wishing to obtain such a licence should have no difficulty. One no longer need face the ludicrous situation which obtained previously, whereby a person eating, because of his job or personal preference, outside pub licensing hours could not have a drink with his meal or was forbidden another glass of wine, say, just because the clock said half past two when he was eating his cheese.

Stations and Still-Rooms

We have considered the overall look and effect of the dining-room, but what of the practicalities? Well, we do not intend to go into great detail about knives and forks, plates, salt and pepper mills and glasses. We would have thought that you do not need us to remind you that such things are necessary but they are going to cost a lot more money than you thought, so be careful to make provision for such items if yours is a new operation. What is often forgotten are the service 'stations'. These are quite simply storage cabinets, for want of a better word, from which cutlery, glasses etc. can be drawn for laying-up tables in the immediate area, and they should contain everything that may be needed by a waiter, or waitress (even ash-trays!). As far as possible, the top should be kept clear and is large enough to take a decent-sized tray, carrying food from the kitchen as well as for loading with dirty plates and cutlery before being taken to the wash-up. Such stations make the work of your staff much easier, as they have to do less walking. It also helps customers, because anything they might want is nigh at hand and no time is lost in fetching it. Unless your restaurant is very large and with a great number of tables, it is not likely you \\Iill need many of these stations. Indeed, just one will often do, somewhere near the kitchen doors, providing it is large enough to do the job by holding everything the dining-room may require.

In the great restaurants of the world there are many such stations, jealously guarded over by a *chef de rang*. who is responsible for all aspects of service to the tables under his station, and perhaps one or two commis waiters who do most of the fetching and carrying.

In fact, to someone like me, the atmosphere and skilled attention of a great dining-room are absorbing, but in lesser places, with ideas, as they used to say, 'above their station', ill-discipline, lack of skill and inattention become irksome to the customer, and restaurants quickly lose their popularity. Do not attempt too 'smart' an operation at first, unless you are extremely skilled and can afford to pay extremely skilled staff. Apart from one or two stations, it is also a good idea to have the equivalent of what used to be a 'still-room', where hot and cold drinks are prepared and where cold first courses, as well as sweets or cold puddings, can be kept for service. This saves time and the weary feet of staff and takes some of the load off the kitchen. Years ago, every restaurant worth its name had a still-room, but the fashion has largely died, owing to the 'wasted' space being needed to earn money or just because there is not enough room. If that is the case; a sort of 'mini still-room' can be set up on your work station, perhaps for a coffee-making machine. Even that alone will save time and tempers in the long run. The object of our hotel exercise, however, us to, make the customers as comfortable as possible and help the staff to be as efficient as possible.

Sixteen-Hour Rule

Throughout industry the myriad regulations and conditions relating to employing people do not apply to those working fewer than sixteen hours a week. There is thus an exploited minority who receive no protection of any kind, and it is onto this minority that the major portion of the catering trade battens-for catering is uniquely suited to 'casual' labour which can thus be manipulated without fear of the law. Coupled with this is the fact that the catering trade is not 'unionised'. Although the TGWU does have a catering section and does try to recruit as many members as it can, the numbers of card-carrying union members is but a tiny drop in an otherwise vast pool of labour.

Now, we are not in any way criticizing the many large hotel and restaurant chains which not only have good union agreements, with proper rates of pay, which they apply to all staff, regardless of whether they are permanent or 'casual' workers, but also treat them with essential and befitting dignity whatever their position in the hierarchy. We are speaking of that other section of the industry, and huge it is when added together: the smaller restaurants, hotels, pubs, tea-shops, coffee-bars and so on. The record for this section is extremely poor and quite inexcusable. We said earlier that the sixteen-hour-rule deprives most workers of any rights under the law. This is not quite true. Even a casual worker, if employed for between eight and sixteen hours per week over a period of five years is entitled after three months further work to receive a written statement as to his or her hours, pay and terms of employment as well as a job description.

In all honesty, we have to say that it is unfortunately rare for 'small' employers to regard this Statement of Employment regulation as anything other than irrelevant. We dare say some employers do, in fact, observe it, and we have just been unlucky, or lacking in diligence, in not having found any, but for the most part the question is either simply ignored or the employers do not even know about it. After all, five years is an unconscionably long time for any 'casual' to be around.

There is, of course, nothing to force anyone to work in the catering trade if he or she cannot stand the heat of the kitchen, as they say, they should get out of it but we find that attitude in this case cynical. The fact is that the trade does suit some people, and it suits a great many of them who are interested in the work, 'enjoy it and are of value to the industry as a whole, apart from being good 'ambassadors' for it. This pool of 'casual' labour for the most part consists of women, many with children, for whom full-time jobs are out of the question. Casual working suits such people, as it certainly suits the employers. But there is no need to exploit them just because the law does not cover them and they hold no union tickets.

MANAGEMENT OF STAFF

Casual Staff

Your new operation is going to require casual staff. What could be easier (instead of making promises you cannot, or have no intention of keeping) than working out beforehand what those hours are likely to be and how much you are going to pay for them? Ah, but so many employers say, how do we know in advance when we shall need such staff? Wednesdays, for instance, may turn out to be slack, and we do not require them on that day. Well, that should be your problem, not the problem of some poor, willing casual worker whose hours and days on or off are constantly being changed, even at a moment's notice. This is simply not the way to behave towards anyone; just because someone is paid by you does not entitle you to chop and change their work hours because it suits you. Such employers are the first to grumble if any of their staff treat them the same way. In a country town near us there is a coffee-lounge-cum-tea-shop. In the window is a more or less permanent notice appealing for staff. Every time anyone goes in there, the waitresses are different only the owner remains a constant factor. Customers find it unsettling, certainly, but what must it do to the owner's nerves and peace of mind? All this because the owner's treatment of staff is notoriously bad those contracted to work, say, on a Tuesday, from 10 a.m. to 5 p.m., are more often than not telephoned the previous evening either to be told they are not wanted after all or to have their hours shortened or changed completely. Yet from this person come the loudest and longest complaints locally about difficulties with obtaining staff in the first place, and then keeping them.

The catering trade is notoriously fickle. One disastrous Monday can be followed by a Monday which breaks all till records. There is no way anyone can foresee what is likely to happen from one day to the next. This does, of course, make it difficult for employers, but surely the easiest thing to do is to explain to a prospective 'casual' what the problems are and then guarantee a certain amount of work and a certain amount of 'shortfall' pay. There is nothing illegal or wrong in this. When we found ourselves in a similar position, we experienced no difficulties, because our own problems had been explained to the members of staff in advance. We guaranteed such people a certain amount of money per week. If they did not work the required hours which that money covered, they would still get paid that amount. If they worked more hours than the guaranteed minimum, they were, obviously, paid extra. And becalise of judicious organization, no 'casual' lost money by being sent home on a 'quiet day rather earlier than they expected. And they were never 'sent home'. They were simply told that, if they wished to go, they could. They regarded it rather like being let out early from school, because they knew they would not lose money. And it 'paid' us in the long run too: we never felt bad about ringing them up or asking them to come in for an extra stint. Because we played fair with them, they played fair with us. Staff loyalty cannot be bought by money, but it can be 'bought' by a generous understanding of their problems and an agreement in advance about the terms of employment.

There was one extra thing: when staff were on duty, they were fed and fed properly, as near to normal meal-times as the catering trade can manage this sounds proper and reasonable, yet is it not the practice among a great many catering establishments. In one restaurant we know, staff are given half an hour for their own lunch-break but they are not paid for that half hour and they are not allowed to eat anything except a bowl of soup and a sandwich or filled roll without paying for it. Staff problems again? You have guessed it. Yet that particular owner complains all the time about the way she is constantly looking for staff because they constantly leave for other jobs. If you are working for a very large organization with a great chain of hotels and restaurants, the hours you work, the meal-breaks you get and the food and payment therefor are laid down and written into the terms of employment. It is usually more than fair and reasonable. Staff know where they stand. But in smaller establishments, such as your own is going to be when you start off, you may not be able to employ many full-time staff, and 'casuals' will suit you excellently. They will suit you excellently-but only if you treat them as human beings from the start with homes, lives and problems of their own. Especially those Upon whom you can really rely, the older man or woman with a sense of responsibility gained from years of experience, not necessarily in catering.

❑

14

Role of Supporting Services

Many reasons contribute in customer's choice of a restaurant. These may be decor of the place, surroundings, menus and their presentation, quality of the food, the cost effectiveness factor, lack of choice etc. All these can effectively influence the customers preferences but more often than not the service provided by the waiting staff has an impact more lasting than any other factor.

The Waiter

All waiters play a virtually important part in the success or failure of the business in which they work. Restaurants succeed mostly because the customers who eat in them leave feeling that they have had a satisfying, enjoyable experience; they tell their friends and come back themselves. It is the waiters, in direct contact with the customers, who create the pleasing, friendly atmosphere and provide the efficient, thoughtful service that make customers feel they have had a good time and want to return. Good waiters can be as important to successful restaurants as good cooks, and in the best establishments cooks and waiters work together as a team.

Good waiters (male or female) are vital to the hospitality industry and enjoy many opportunities for career advancement. Skilled waiters can either build lifelong and satisfying careers as table waiters or they can move to pther positions such as a wine waiter, head waiter, restaurant manager, banqueting manager or catering officer.

The Job of a Waiter

The waiter's job is to work as part of a team to make sure that customers leave feeling that they have enjoyed the food and the whole social experience. To achieve this the waiter must be friendly, efficient, knowledgeable and skillful.

In order that waiters can do their jobs properly it is important for the people preparing the food to understand what the job involves so that they can provide what is needed. The waiter is, as it were, the conductor of the meal, orchestrating its service so that whatever the customers require to satisfy them is provided. If the customers want their food quickly, then it must be served quickly; if they want advice on the choice of food or wines, then the waiter must be able to give it; if they ask for the bill it must be ready quickly and it must be accurate. All this requires the waiter to community effectively with the customers and with the rest of the team in the restaurant, the kitchen staff in particular.

A waiter cannot serve efficiently or sell effectively without a good knowledge of the menu. You must know and be able to describe all the dishes on the menu, what they contain, how they are cooked and how they are served. For example, if a guest were to ask, 'What is the fish of the day?' you should be able to reply something like: It is John Dory, baked in the oven with a stuffing of prawns, garlic and herbs, and garnished with spinach and a delicate white wine sauce.' Later the same guest might ask, 'How do you think the Pecan Tart would do for dessert?' and your reply could be, 'Well, you have just had the John Dory, so I think the Pecan Tart would follows rather well. It is a crisp tart with a rich filling of toasted pecan nuts topped with chocolate sauce and cream.'

Qualities Required of a Waiter

Not everyone has the right qualities to be a waiter. There are many requirements. Many are similar to those needed by the chef. Some are different. The first and most important requirement is the right attitude.

Attitude—a pride in Professional Service. A waiter must enjoy dealing with people and take pleasure in making sure that they are happy. No amount of technical skill will compensate for the wrong attitude to customers, to the job and to workmates. If you feel that service is somehow servile, then waiting is not for you.

Appearance and Personal Hygiene. Waiters work with food almost as closely as the people who prepare it, but also they are continually under the scrutiny of the customers. They must keep themselves perfectly clean at all times. Waiters must be neat, with their clothes as clean as themselves. Hair must be kept tidy and well under control, either short or tied back. Shoes must be perfectly clean (and comfortable). Uniforms must be clean and pressed. Take a spare shirt to work in case the first gets dirty. Do not wear heavy make-up and keep jewellery to a minimum.

Punctuality and Reliability. Service to customers cannot be delayed. If you are not there on time you force someone else to do your work for you. The work will not wait. Make sure you arrive before your shift begins so that you have plenty of time to prepare. Never let your colleagues down by failing to appear for work. If it is absolutely impossible for you to get to work, make sure that you give as much warning as is humanly possible.

Deportment. Never lean or slouch, but always stand and move already and confidently. Even if there is nothing you can do directly to serve a customer, always be doing something constructive, cleaning, tidying and preparing for more customers to come. The waiter's deportment indicates to customers the efficiency of the business. Those behind the scenes can help waiters to keep their cool by taking care to present the food properly.

Loyalty and Teamwork. Never complain about those you work with in front of your customers. The waiter's professional duty is to make sure the customers leave satisfied that they have had value for money. If you have complaints, take them to your superior directly. Remember too that the waiter is part of a team, so be prepared to help your colleagues out. For example, never ignore a customer not in your section of the restaurant, but take the customer's request to the waiter responsible for that section. Always pull your weight in the cleaning and preparation.

Honesty. Waiters deal with money and work in a team with colleagues. You must be completely honest in spite of temptation. If you steal or cheat you will, sooner or later, be found out and your career as a waiter will be finished, even if you are lucky enough not to be prosecuted.

Ability to sell. Waiters are sales people. By selling effectively they can make all the difference between the success or failure of a business. They must be enthusiastic about what they have to sell, and be prepared to get to know their product what's on the menu and how it is cooked and served, and why wines and other drinks there are and what they are like.

Always remember that the customers are the most important people in the business, and nothing is ever more important than serving them.

Food Service Styles

Many factors have effect on how a meal should be served. Some of these factors are:

The Type of Establishment and where it is. Different types of establishment include first class (five-star) hotels, licensed hotels, fully licensed restaurants, cafeterias, snack bars, fast-food outlets, sandwich bars, institutions (like hospitals, hostels, the army, etc.) and catering for transport (for example airlines).

The type and Number of Customers. Families, couples, groups, business peoples, young children, young adults, invalids, etc. all demand different styles of service.

The type of Menu and the Price of the Meal. Types of menu vary according to whether they are a la carte, table d'hote, for snacks, buffet menus, for banquets or for self-service food bars. The price makes a difference too the more customers pay, the more elaborate and attentive service they except.

The Length of Time for the Meal. Take-away customers want their food quickly; office workers at lunch time except to be served (and billed) without delay. On the other hand, people out to enjoy a leisurely dinner in the evening will not want to be rushed.

There are also various basic styles of food service which are found in restaurants of different types, regardless of how formal or informal they are or the kind of customers they cater for. The most common styles are:

(1) Buffet Service. This is really self-service. Customers help themselves from a range of dishes displayed on a buffet table. Sometimes move expensive items are carved to order at the buffet, but often the waiter's role is confined to clearing the tables and serving drinks.

(2) Plate Service. This is the simplest form of table service. All the food is put on the plates in the kitchen, and the waiter has simply to take it and place it in front of the right customer. The principal item in the dish, for example the piece of fish in the case of the John Dory, should be put nearest to the customer, with the vegetables arranged round the main item away from the customer.

(3) Semi-silver Service. The main item is put on the plate, as in part plate service, decorated in the kitchen and then placed by the waiter in from of the customer. The vegetables are brought in a separate container and served with a fork and spoon by the waiter on the customers left-hand side. Customers are asked individually what vegetables they would like, and these are arranged attractively on the plate in front of them.

(4) Part Plate or Family Service. The main item is put on the place, suitably decorated in the kitchen and is then put in front of the customer. The vegetables are brought in a separate container which is placed on the table in front of the customers who help themselves as they wish.

(5) Silver Service. Empty plates are placed in front of each customer and the waiter serves all the food. The waiter is entirely responsible for how the food is served and its appearance on the plate. Customers should be served from the left with the waiter using a spoon and fork.

(6) Gueridon Service. A gueridon is a small table or stand. With gueridon service, the waiter prepare all or part of a dish at a gueridon beside the customers' table. It might be carving roast beef on a special trolley; or preparing some flamboyant dish like crepe suzette. Obviously only highly-trained waiters attempt gueridon service.

There is no one set of rules which lays down what is 'correct' food service in all circumstances, any more than one style of dress is right for customers in all establishments. What would be right for an old-fashioned city restaurant catering mainly for an elderly and well-off clientele would be quite wrong in the informal atmosphere of a pub bistro in a seaside holiday resort.

PRE-CUSTOMER ARRIVAL PREPARATION

Waiters have plenty to do before the customers arrive. These jobs include cleaning and polishing: taking bookings (reservations); setting the tables; and back-up preparatory tasks.

Cleaning and Polishing

There are particular techniques for achieving bright and clean cutlery, crockery and glasses:

(a) Glasses look best if you hold them (already washed!) over steaming the water until the glass has fogged, then dry them with a clean cloth, polishing as you go. The result will be sparkling glassware.

(b) Cutlery should be dipped in hot water them rubber dry with a clean tea towel.

(c) Crockery must also be polished. Rub the sides with a clean cloth before laying it. Be careful not to leave your hand impressions on the crockery in the process.

Taking Reservations

The head waiter is usually responsible for keeping the booking diary or reservations book. However, any waiter must be ready to take bookings if the head waiter is not immediately available.

Reservations are usually made by telephone. When you answer the phone, clearly identify the establishment and politely offer help: Good morning, the Castle Restaurant. May I help you? Listen carefully to what the customer wants. If the customer wants to book a table, follow the 'house rules' of the restaurant. These will usually require you to ask and not the following:

1. The name of the person making the booking;
2. The day, date and issue for which the reservation is made (for example Thursday 19 June at 8.30 p.m.) it is surprising how often people will muddle the day and the date; one is a check on the either;
3. Special requests, for example extra quick service, a guest with particular dietary needs, a bottle of lemon juice or a birthday cake;
4. The number of people corning or the number of covers required (check in the booking diary to make sure that there will be room to take the party at the time requested!);
5. The telephone number of the person making the booking (for conformation, especially for large parties).

Read the detail back to the caller to make sure you have not made a mistake. The details must be recorded accurately and neatly in the booking diary.

Do not keep customers waiting on the phone. Before putting the phone down, thank the customer for the booking. You know their name now, so use it: 'Thank you very much Mr. Rajinder. We'll look forward to seeing you on Thursday at 8.30.'

Even at this early stage the waiter and chef need to work together to give good service. For example, one customer requests a reservation on Friday who is disabled. There are some disabilities that make it difficult to eat certain dishes. The chef might be able to help here by presenting the food differently but only if the waiter finds out abut the requirement and passes it on.

Table Setting

Before the tables can be set they must be arranged to suit the bookings for the meal or the pattern of trade that is expected. Usually the manager or head waiter will decide how the tables are to be positioned. Make sure they are stable. If they are not, a wedge of cork can be put under one leg for stablity. Iftablecloths are used they must be put on the tables.

The place for each diner is called a cover. (The work 'cover' is also used to mean the number of people dining or the number of meals sold). It is usual to set only a basic cover before the guests have arrived and made their selections. The middle of each cover should be marked with a 'centre guide' round which to position the cutlery, crockery and glassware. The centre guide could be a plate or an unfolded napkin.

Place a side plate on the left of the centre guide, leaving sufficient room between it and the centre guide for more than one piece of cutlery. Now put the knife and fork for the main course into position on either side of the centre guide. Tlle knife and fork should be far enough apart for a main course plate to be placed between them without be seeming cramped. They should be about 1 cm. in from the edge of the table. Note that you should hold cutlery so that finger prints do not show, the best place is usually the neck of the knife or fork where the blade joins the handle.

A side knife is usually put on and to one side of the side plate, to allow room for a bread roll. A wine glass in put about 2 cm. from the point of the main course knife. Salt and paper shakers and an ashtray are put where they can be reached easily by all diners.

A simple table decoration, often of flowers or candles, is placed in the middle of the table. It should not be so large that the diners cannot see each other comfortably. Finally, a folded napkin in placed in the middle each place setting.

As seen later, the cover for each customer is adjusted after their order have been placed. For example, they may need soup spoons or fish knives which do not form part of the usual basic cover.

Napkins

There is a wide variety of napkins available to choose from for any style table setting. Paper napkins offer an enormous range of colours an different qualities. Although they can only be used once, they are cheaper then linen napkins which require daily laundering.

There is no need to the number of ways in which napkins can be folded. Complex and elaborately impressive folds are usually be avoided, but each restaurant will have its own policy on what appropriate.

Back-up Preparatory Tasks

These will vary in detail from restaurant to restaurant, but typical tasks include:

(a) Preparing Cups and Saucers. These have to be made for coffee and tea. They should be polished like other crockery. Sometimes they are warmed in a special warmer.

(b) Preparing the Coffee. There are different styles of coffee and coffee making machines, so the details of what needs to be done will very considerably from place to place. Filtered coffee machines have to be switched on with cold water available nearby. Espresso machines also have to be switched on, and the supply of pulverised coffee checked. Powdered chocolate or cocoa must be made ready to 'garnish' the cappuccino.

(c) Preparing Accompaniments for Coffee. Cream, milk, sugar (often sugar crystals) are served with coffee and need to be organised. Coffee is also often served with after dinner mints or petit fours, which should be arranged ready for service on small plates.

(d) Preparing Condiments. Salt and pepper shakers must be checked and filled regularly, and their outsides cleaned daily. Containers for oil and vinegar must also be cleaned and refilled.

(e) Preparing Rolls and Butter. Sometimes bread rolls are put into a warming oven, sometimes they are just arranged in baskets. Butter dishes must be prepared, with the butter arranged in pats or curls as management requires.

(f) Preparing Tea. Different styles of tea require different preparation. Dark Indian 'teas are served with milk and white sugar or lemon slices. Green 'China' teas and herbal teas usually have no accompaniment, through sugar is often served with them. Just in case a customer should want it. Find out how the tea is served and prepare accordingly.

Receiving and Seating Guests

How customers are received is very important indeed. It sets the mood for the meal. It is very difficult to recover from a bad first impression, no matter how good the food and service may be.

Customers should be greeted in a warm and friendly way. Smile and ask what you can do to help. Only when you have established that the new arrivals want a table, do you ask whether they have booked, and then check the booking diary. It is most off-putting for customers if the first thing they are asked is, in a rather hostile manner, Do you have a reservation? In a bigger restaurant the greeting of guests and showing them to their table is usually done by the head waiter, but any waiter must be ready to greet and help new arrivals.

When the guests have been shown their table, they are seated. Sometimes they seat themselves, sometimes the waiter seats the women but not the men, sometimes the waiter seats all the guests. It depends on the style of restaurant and the wishes of the guests.

If you are seating a guest, move the chair so that he or she can stand by the table. Place the chair behind the guest's knees and move it in under as he or she sits down, using a knee as well as your hands to keep the chair steady. Let the guest settle, and be prepared to ease the chair further if required.

The napkin must be moved before food service can begin. How this is done varies. Some diners will take their own napkins and place them on their laps, others will expect the waiters either to take the napkins and place then on their laps or hand them to them. Most restaurants will have their own rules about what the waiter should do.

Water and break rolls are then offered, and butter is placed on the table.

Premeal Drinks

Some licensed establishments have a separate cocktail bar where diners go to have a drink before their meal, and where they can look over the menu at their leisure. If there is no separate cocktail bar, the first thing the waiter does after presenting the menu' is to offer the diners a premeal drink, a cocktail, or to make some other suggestion.

Presenting the Menu

A la carte menus, which offer a large number of courses, with each dish priced individually, are used in most circumstances. Table d'hote menus are usual at functions and banquets, and for set specially priced 'business lunches'.

Menus of all types can be presented in different ways. Common styles of presenting menus include blackboards, placemats, single cards and folded cards (sometimes in a cover). Obviously the style of the menu must affect the way in which it is presented.

When presenting the menu, the waiter should tell the guests if there are any alterations, and describe any special dishes not listed. You must also be ready to answer questions. Now your knowledge of the menu comes fully into play and you have a chance to use you sales skills.

The Wine List

In a licensed restaurant the wine list is brought to the table soon after the menus have been presented so that the customers can choose wines to suit their food. If there is a special wine waiter he or she will present the wine list, but often this is the table waiter's job. Only one copy of the wine list is used. It is presented to the host (if the host is obvious). Wine and other drinks are dealt with later, but it is worth noting here that if you can take the wine order when you take the food order you will save time. Many customers, through, like to look through the wine list at leisure after they have chosen their food dishes and they must be given time to do so.

Taking Orders

Waiters must be able and ready to give advice and make recommendations. If you are asked what is good, try to assess the kind of food the customer would like and make a recommendation. Never say simply that 'Everything is good'. Describe the dish you are recommending in some detail, with its sauces and side dishes.

Assume that customers will want all courses. Do not say, Would you like a starter?' but recommend one or more of them: May I suggest the duck terrine? It's one of our chefs specialities. When the main courses have been cleared and you are taking orders for sweets, make suggestions or bring up the sweets trolley, don't just ask if your customers would like sweets. Sell by suggestion.

Often you will have been told by the chef or the manager that there are certain dishes it is particularly important to sell-'must move' items. For example the chef may have bought a quantity of an excellent fish on good terms so that the profit margin or it is particularly good. Selling items of this kind is a subtle technique, and they must never be forced on people who seem unlikely really to enjoy them. Selling must never be heavy-handed.

Taking orders is an important skill which must be learnt. It is not easy as to might seem to make sure that your customers each receive exactly what they have ordered, and that they are properly billed for what they have had.

Guests need'some time after they have been presented with the menu to make their choice. Knowing when to approach them again to take the orders is a subtle business. They must neither be rushed nor kept waiting. Usually they will want between 5 and 10 minutes to choose, but you must be alert to any sign that may be made to indicate that they are ready to order or want help. It might be a simple closing of the menu or an attempt to catch your eye.

The precise technique used varies from restaurant to restaurant, according to the style of service offered and the method of billing, but there are some general principles common to all. Orders must be clear so that:

1. The kitchen staff prepare the right dishes.
2. The right dishes are served to the right people in the order they are wanted.
3. The bill is made out completely and correctly.

Each restaurant will have its own particular system for achieving these things, and you must make sure that you understand the order-taking system in the place where you are working before you attempt to serve anyone. Here are some of the different ways of taking orders.

Triplicate Checking System

This system is used mainly in traditional hotels and restaurants. This is a pad full of checks with three copies and their own serial number. The top copy is given to the kitchen to order the food, the second copy goes to the cashier who compiles the bill and the third or 'flimsy' is kept by the waiter for reference. For complete control the four corners must be completed by the waiter/waitress.

At the beginning of the meal only the starters and main course are written on the first check. A new check is made out for the sweet after the main course has been eaten and as coffee comes from the 'skill room' a further check is written and the top copy left in exchange for the beverage.

For a la carte menus where dishes are individually priced and cooked to order, the price should also be put on the check. Some restaurants also indicate the time that the order was taken, so that the kitchen can cook and issue the meals in the sequence in which they received them.

The bill is a top copy and duplicate and is usually folded so only the host sees it and it is presented on a small plate.

If the guests are staying in the hotel their room number is clearly written on the check and is signed by them so that they can pay for everything on one bill at the end of their stay.

Duplicate Checking System or Bill Book System

This order taking tool suits places with a limited range of menu items such as table d'hote menu, a family restaurant or fast-food establishment with a quick turnover.

The top copy goes to the kitchen to order the food, the second copy becomes the bill. It is therefore very important that all items served are entered on to the check.

The top copy is made up of a number of perforated slips which tear off as each course is ordered. The slips are serial numbered. Other information on the pad includes the waiter's initial or number, the table number, number of persons, and space for the total addition.

When the customer requires the bill the waiter checks that all has been entered and makes the addition. The guest may then pay the waiter or pay at the till on leaving the restaurant. A receipt is then given.

Computer-aided system can analyse which dishes sell the best, and exactly what individual waiters and waitresses sell, which as very useful to aid sales and promote incentive schemes and identify certain training needs.

Liquor Ordering

The order pad is usually pink and in duplicate.

Rough Copy System

The first thing to do is to draw up a plan of the table, noting the host and numbering the guests clockwise around he table, with the person to the host's left as number one, and the host last. And a clue to who the host is her hat, his bow tie or whatever strikes you as memorable. Add a cross to show where you were standing when you took the order. Note what each guest orders against their place in the seating plan. This is a rough note for your own use only.

If the party is particularly large, say more than six, it may not be possible to note what each person has ordered on the seating plan itself. You must then draw up a separate rough order using the seating plan to number each guest. This is best done using columns for each of the courses.

When everyone has ordered, you take away your seating plan or roughs order and write out the order on a duplicate docket. One copy is used by the kitchen staff and the other by the cashier. Note that on the duplicate order the number of each dishes required is simply noted with no attempt to record which particular customer ordered. For example, if two people have ordered tropical fruit nests, the duplicate docket will note simply 2 tropical fruit nests or an abbreviation like 2 nests which has been accepted by the kitchen.

After the orders has been taken, you must thank the host and collect the menus from each of the guests.

Adjusting the Covers

After the orders have been taken and passed through to the kitchen the waiter must adjust the covers so that each customer has the right cutlery for the particular dishes he or she has ordered. You will remember that only a basic cover was set in each place.

The principle is that each customer should have the correct cutlery for the dishes he or she has ordered, starting from the outside and working in as the courses follow each other. How the covers would have to be changed if the orders were for the four guests we noted previously.

You must learn what cutlery each dish on the menu requires. It may depend on how the dish is served. For example, avocados require a teaspoon if they are served in their shells, but an hors-d' oeurve or fish knife and fork if they are served sliced on a plate out of their shells. Certain foods require special tools to enable the diner to eat them, such as snail tongs and oyster forks.

Serving the Food

Food has to be served in order. Just which order will depend on the circumstances, in particular how formal the style of service is.

In a formal traditional situation, the role is to serve the woman on the host's right first, and then the remaining women in clockwise order followed by the men also in clockwise order, with the host last.

The host is the person who is paying for the meal. He or she may sometimes place all the orders, and usually selects and orders the wine. The table will probably have been booked in his or her name.

It may not be clear who the host is. Indeed there may be no 'host' if group of people has come to eat together and the bill will be shared. In that case you must decide who you will treat as 'host' and plan the order or 'sequence of service' round that decision.

In an informal eating placc it is probably not necessary to serve the women before the men, and all the customers can be served in whatever order is most convenient. Unless there is a very good reason for doing things otherwise, such as serving cold food first, this will probably be to serve everyone in clockwise order regardless of sex, with the person you have decided to treat as host last. You will have to find out what is expected in the place where you are working.

While the custom is for food to bc served clockwise, wine and other beverages are usually served anti-clockwise, also starting from the host. In this way the waiters serving the food and the wine are less likely to get in each other's way. Food takes precedence because it will go cold.

Collecting the Food

When all the dishes in each course are ready the waiter collects the food from the kitchen or an extension of the kitchen called the servery. In some restaurants there will be a sideboard in the dining rcom, ideally one for each waiter's station. If there is a sideboard you collect the food from the kitchen on a tray and put it on the sideboard before unloading the tray and taking the dishes to the table by hand. In smaller informal restaurants all the food is brought from the kitchen directly by hand.

It is very important for the kitchen staff to be considerate of the waiter so that the food is served efficiently and looks attractive. The plates should be presented to the waiter in the right order and on the correct plates for the type of service. Care should be taken over the appearance of each individual plate. In some restaurants extra care is given to the plate of the host, who will be paying the bill, but you should aim to achieve as high a standard as possible for all your customers.

Portions must be of equal sizes, and not only for the sake of cost control. Imagine the embarrassment of the waiter when the customer complaints that his wife's portion is larger than his own!

Another potential pitfall that kitchen staff can make for the waiter is if there is any spillage or if sauce drips across the plate. A smear of gravy on the top of the plate ruins the appearance of the meal. A smear on the bottom will dirty the waiter's cloth or could cause the plate to slip. A plate with a dirty underside will leave an ugly circle of grease on the tablecloth, which will be revealed as the poor waiter collects the plates.

How to carry plates

An experienced waiter can safely carry up to four plates with food arranged on them. This take practice. Don't try carrying three plates on one arm until you are completely at ease carrying two.

Carry plates in front of you and, as far as possible, within the width of your body. This makes it less likely that they will get knocked by accidents as you move through the restaurant.

Plate and Family Service

With plate service, the food is arranged on the plate in the kitchen and simply placed in front of each guest by the waiter. The left hand and arm are used to carry the plates, leaving the right hand free to place them in front of each guest from the guests' right unless that is inconvenient because of the position of the table. In family service the vegetables are brought separately and placed on the table for the diners to help themselves. It is not important whether the vegetable dishes are put on the table from anyone's left or right. Disturb the customers as little as possible and try to put the dishes in a place where they can easily be reached.

Silver Service and Semi-silver Service

Plates are put in front of each diner from their right as in plate service. In semi-silver service, plates have the main item (usually meat or fish) on them and in full silver service the plates are empty. (Make sure that the plates are hot if you are serving a hot dish and cold if serving a cold dish.) The vegetables or, in the case of full silver service, all the food is then served to each diner individually by the waiter.

You stand at the customer's left-hand side, holding the serving dish on your left hand and arm, and serve the food with your right hand using a spoon and fork. This takes practice! It is done from the left for convenience (assuming a right-handed waiter); the right hand is used for the tricky business of managing the fork and spoon in one hand. The serving dish should be held well forward, slightly above and overlapping the customer's plate. If you are left-handed you still stand on the diner's left.

Accompaniments

Different dishes have different accompaniments. For example, deep fried fish is often accompanied by tartare sauce, and roast pork by apple sauce. A range of mustards may be offered with a steak. Those accompaniments are served after the main dish has been served. The kitchen staff must take care to produce any special accompaniments they have made promptly so that the customers are not kept waiting with their main dishes growing cold in front of them. Accompaniments are served from the customer's left, in the same order as the main dishes have been served. In informal plate service restaurants, they can be simply placed on the table for the diners to help themselves.

Sometimes the accompaniment can be almost as important as the dish with which it goes, and presenting it gives you the opportunity to be slightly theatrical and create a sense of occasion. For example, if a customer has ordered a steak, you can bring a range of mustards on a tray and say, 'Would you like some mustard, Sir We have English and French.' The mustard chosen can then be spooned onto the plate beside the steak with a stylish flourish. Whether or not theatrical presentation is encouraged where you work, customers should not have to ask for the standard accompaniments for the dishes they have ordered. The correct accompaniments must be offered automatically.

Finger bowls are usually offered whenever diners actually touch the food with their hands or when it is likely that they may get their fingers greasy.

Some of the most common accompaniments are:

Storters	
Crayfish, prawns. mussels	Finger bowl and lemon wedges
Calamari (deep fried)	Tartare sauce and lemon wedge
Minestrone soup	Grated parmesan cheese
Oysters	Brown bread and butter. lemon wedge. peppermlll. tabasco sauce
Pate malson	Fingers of toast
Smoked salmon	Brown bread and butter. lemon wedge. peppermill

Main courses	
Curries	Mango chutney, lime pickle, sambals, poppadums
Deep fried fish	Tartare sauce
Roast beef	Mustards, horseradish sauce
Roast pork	Apple sauce
Roast turkey	Cranberry sauce
Steaks	Mustards (range of)

These are, of course, standard accompaniments. Every chef will have dishes for which special accompaniments are required, and you must get to know them and how they should be presented. Getting to know the accompaniments is as much a part of learning about the menu as learning about the main dishes.

CLEARING THE TABLE

Plates should not be taken from the table until all the diners have finished the course. The usual sign that people have finished, even if there is food left on their plates, is that they push the remaining food to one side df the plate and place their knife and fork together.

Not all customers will give this signal, unfortunately, so you must be alert. They may simply stop eating nd lean back in their chairs, or perhaps light a cigarette. If you are in doubt whether someone has finished or not, the only thing to do is to ask them.

Remove plates from the table by taking them from each customer's right. Take the first plate with your right hand and transfer it to your left hand, gripping the handle of the fork with your thumb. Place the knife so that it is firmly wedged under the fork.

Now move clockwise round the table to behind the second customer and take the plate from his or her right with your right hand. Before lifting the plate, move the knife and fork together and put your thumb on them so that they do not slip when the plate is lifted.

Standing behind the customer, balance the second plate on your left arm, with your right hand use the knife to scrape any leftover food onto the first plate held in the left hand below it. Do all this as discreetly and quietly as possible.

Put the second knife and fork onto the first plate, so that the second plate is completely clear. Move behind the third customer and repeat the process, stacking the third and subsequent plates on the second plate and transferring all the leftover food and cutlery onto the first plate.

If there are not too many half-eaten bread rolls on them, you can remove the sideplates at the same time, stacking them on top of the empty main course plates.

Sideknives go with the other cutlery on the first plate, the knives held firm under the forks.

Butter plates and the salt pepper shakers should be removed at the same time or as soon as possible after the dirty plates. With practice, you can learn to stack the butter plates on top of the empty plates, and take the salt and peper shakers in your right hand. The objective of taking so much at once is to reduce the number of times you have to go back to the table, and to disturb the customers as little as possible.

Disposal of Dirty Plates

Some dining rooms are provided with convenient sideboards to which you can take the stacked plates for sorting, but very often you will have to take them directly to the kitchen. Routines will vary from restaurant to restaurant, but everything will have its proper place. Usually it will be your job to scrape the dishes clean and put them in the right racks in the dishwasher. Cutlery, after any heavy debris has been scraped off, is sorted onto the dishwasher baskets. Untouched butter will be stored in a suitable container.

Crumbing Down

After the main course has been removed, the table should be 'crumbed down', Brush the crumbs, using a clean service cloth, onto a clean side plate held just under the edge of the table.

Ashtrays

If your customers smoke during the meal, make a point of changing the ashtrays before each new course is served. The main thing to remember when changing ashtrays is that ash must not be allowed to blow or fall out of the used ashtray onto the table. The technique is to bring the fresh ashtray and place it upside down on top of the used one. Lift both ashtrays with one hand onto a tray or a clean service cloth. Remove the clean ashtray and cover the used one with a folded service cloth to prevent the ash escaping. Plate the clean ashtray on the table.

Wine and Beverage Service

If a restaurant is licensed to serve alcohol, all waiters must know how to open and serve bottles of wine. Any waiter dealing with wine must know the wines on the wine list and be able to make sound recommendations, just as the food waiter must know all about the dishes on the menu.

Wine orders are normally placed on pink check pads so that they are easily distinguishable from food orders.

The Wine List. The wine list is a sort of menu. Although it is called the wine list, it usually lists all the beverages available wines, beers, spirits, liqueurs and non-alcoholic drinks. The wines are usually grouped into wines of a similar type to help the customer choose; most obviously white and red wines are listed in separate groups. Usually they are several groups, for example wines from different countries may be separately listed. There are usually separate section for still table wines, sparkling wines (like champagne) and fortified wines (like sherry, madeira and port).

Waiters dealing with wine have to be able to make recommendations. This of course means that they must know the character of each of the wines on the list and must be able to describe it in items the customer will understand. It also means that they must know which wines go well with the various dishes on the menu. An excellent wine may be a very poor recommendation if it is to go with an unsuitable dish.

This book cannot even attempt to describe the huge variety of wine available. There are plenty of wine appreciation courses available in the larger cities, and there are innumerable books on the subject. Table and Bar by Jeffcey Clarke, published by Hodder & Stoughton is a good, modestly priced, introduction to wines, beers, spirits, liqueurs and cocktails, and helps the reader cope with the vast amount of information on the subject.

What Wine to Choose? There are no hard-and-fast rules of what wine goes with what food, except that: The customer is always right. Never allow yourself to look surprised or disapproving no matter which wine your customer selects.

There are, however, some rules of thumb which usually apply, and it is useful to know them. For example, it is usually to drink white wine with fish and white meat (like chicken) and red wine with red meat (like lamb or beef). It is also usual to drink dry wine before sweet wine, light wines before 'full' (heavy and strong-tasting) wines, and young wines before old / wines. If the dish has a light and delicate taste (as many fish dishes do), the wine which goes with it should also be light and delicate, or the taste of the wine will overwhelm the taste of the food. Similarly, strong meats, like roast beef, need a full-bodies wine to go with them or the flavour of the wine will be lost.

The wines chosen should complement the food they accompany, and if more than one bottle is being taken, the wines should change in character as the meal progresses. Just as the dishes in a meal should vary in colour and taste, so should the wines chosen to go with them. But don't forget the customer is always right!

Presenting the Wine List. The wine list is presented to the host by the wine waiter (if there is one) soon after the menu has been presented to all the guests. This allows the host to select wines which will go well with the dishes that have been chosen by his or her guests. For this reason the wine order is usually taken after the food order.

Remember that the waiter will have suggested a pre-dinner drink, an aperitif such as a dry cocktail or sherry, before the menu was presented. The diners, therefore, probably already have something to drink while they choose their dishes and the wines to go with them, and wait for their first course to be served.

Many people appreciate advice and recommendations when choosing wines. The waiter taking the wine orders must therefore be at hand, ready to give advice, when the wines are being chosen. This is, of course an opportunity for suggestive selling. Recommend suitable wines, being careful not to suggest the most expensive wines on the list as this is more likely to upset and offend the customer than to be thought helpful!.

The Waiter's Friend. Any waiter who has to open a bottle of wine should have a professional corkscrew, usually known as a 'waiter's friend'. This invaluable piece of equipment consists of a corkscrew, a knife, a lever and (usually) a champagne cork lever. You should always have your waiter's friend on you. Take good care of it, and do not lend it! Keep it tucked in your skirt, belt, commerbund or apron. Do not keep it hanging out of a pocket where it may easily get caught on things.

Still Table Wines. The technique of opening and serving bottles of wine is different for still table wines than for sparkling wines. Sparkling wines (champagne for example) are effervescent or bubbly, and have a different kind of cork from still wines. There are also differences in the way red and white wines are served because they are served at different temperatures. Red wine should be served at 'room temperature' (about 18°C), while white wine should be served cool, but not too cold (about 6°C).

If the wine is white, a wine cooler should be put on the table or an ice bucket and stand should be put beside the table before the bottle is opened, so that it can be kept cool.

Different glasses are often used for red and white wines. If there are two different glasses, the red wine (which does not need to be kept cool) is served in the larger glasses and the white wine in the smaller ones.

Red wine is often opened a while before it is going to be served so that is has time to 'breathe'. Red wine may be opened at the beginning of a meal even if it is not going to be served before the main course.

The steps for opening and serving still wines are:

1. Present the wine on a clean service cloth so that the host can see the label clearly. Announce it saying, for example, 'Your Chablis, Madam'. Do not begin to open the bottle until the host has approved. Open the bottle in full view of the customer.

2. Using the knife on your waiter's friend, cut the foil neatly just below the lip of the bottle, remove the top of the cap and put it in your pocket. Your knife must be kept sharp to cut the foil easily and safely. Wipe the top of the bottle clean with your service cloth.

3. Close the knife on your waiter's friend, and open the corkscrew. Put the point of the screw carefully in the middle of the cork, making sure it is straight, and then press the point into the cork. Turn until only one twist of the screw can still be seen.

4. Keeping the screw straight, draw out the cork. The thumb of the hand pulling the cork out should be used as a pivot. Make sure that the lever is held straight and firm on the lip of the bottle by the other hand.

5. When the cork is almost out, ease it with your thumb and forefinger so that it does not come out suddenly with a pop. Clean the top of the bottle again with your service cloth to get rid of any mould or cork. In some restaurants,

where expensive wines are served, it is the custom to put the cork onto a saucer to show it to the host. (The corks on many good wines are branded by the bottler and the brand is evidence that the bottle has not been wrongly labeled.) The cork can also be indicative of the wine's condition.

6. Place the lever onto the lip of the bottle, holding it in place with a finger of the left hand (if your are right-handed).

7. Pour a little wine into the host's glass for the host to approve. The host may take a little time testing its 'nose' by sniffing it, and its colour as well as its taste. When the host has approved the wine, fill all the glasses, moving round the table anti-clockwise. Each glass should be filled to about two-thirds. Remember to fill the host's glass last. Make sure that the wine's poured into the right glass, *i.e.* red in the larger glasses if there are two different sizes.

8. If the wine is white, put it into the wine cooler or ice bucket. If it is red, place it on the table within reach of the host.

9. When you are pouring wine hold the bottle a little above the glass so that you do not touch the rim of the glass with the bottle. When there is enough wine in the glass, lift the mouth of the bottle and at the same time give it a slight quick twist. This will stop drips.

These steps nevertheless should not be taken as hard and fast rules as the situations may differ from host to host, environment to environment and so on.

Champagne and Sparkling Wine

There is considerable pressure from compressed carbon dioxide gas in a bottle of champagne. Because of this the bottle is particularly strong and the cork has to be held into the bottle by a wire muzzle. The following technique is followed.

1. If champagne glasses are being used, place them on the table. (Champagne glasses are usually tall and narrows 'flutes' which preserve the sparkle in the wine). The bottle is usually brought to the table in an ice bucket. It is announced and shown to the host for approval just as its done for a still wine. When the host has approved it, the bottle is put back into the ice bucket.

2. Cut the foil neatly just below the muzzle (called in French the muselet).

3. Hold the bottle so that it is not pointing at yourself or at anyone else, occasionally the cork is forced out by the pressure and can cause a nasty accident.

4. Put your thumb firmly on the cork and untwist the wire ring on the muzzle.

5. Remove the muzzle, while keeping a thumb firmly on the cork (and making sure that the bottle isn't pointing at anyone).

6. Take the bottle gently from the ice bucket. Then, gripping the bottle in one hand and the cork in the other, twist the bottle and the cork in opposite directions, easing the cork from the bottle. Hold the bottle as still as possible so that the champagne is not shaken up. The cork should come out of the bottle with a mild pop (there should be no violent explosion) and remain firmly in your hand.

7. Pour a little wind into the host's glass taking care to pour slowly because champagne can fizz over if you pour carelessly. When the host has approved the wine, fill all the glasses in the same way as for still wines. When you have filled the host's glass, put the bottle into the ice bucket.

Refilling and Selling Additional Bottles

As the meal progresses, you should keep an eye on the glasses and refill them when they are nearly empty—unless requested not to by the guests. If the meal is far from over and the bottle first ordered is nearly empty, suggest to the host that you should bringing another. This is a moment for suggestive selling. Say something like, 'shall I bring another bottle, Sir, or would you like to choose a different wine this time?'

BILLING

It is important that customers are billed in a way which does not spoil their meal; it is easy for all the good work which has gone before to be spoiled if there is a mistake in the bill or if it is not brought when it is wanted.

Presenting the Bill. Be sensitive to what your guests want. If the bill is presented too soon, customers may be offended, feeling that you are trying to push them out. On the other hand, it is extremely annoying for diners, if they have limited time, to be kept waiting for the bill. This is particularly so at lunch time when office workers and business people must get back to work quickly, and the early evening when your customers may be going on to the theatre or some other engagement. Delay with the bill is one of the most annoying, and one of the commonest, failure in good service.

The waiter must be alert to signs that the bill is wanted. If you are not surc, go to the table and ask, 'Is there anything more I can get you?' People will usually be ready for the bill as soon as they have finished their coffee.

When the bill has been asked for it must be brought quickly. There should be no long delay while the amount is calculated. How this is to be done depends on how the bill is prepared.

In some small establishments the bill may simply be a duplicate copy of the order, with the amounts added and totalled by the waiter. When it is clear that the customer is not going to order anything more, the waiter should total the bill so that it is ready as soon as it is asked for. In other cases the bill will be prepared by a cashier. In those cases it is the waiter's job to warn the cashier that the bill for a particular table is likely to be wanted soon, so that the cashier can have the bill ready. This takes teamwork.

There are various ways of presenting the bill, and you must find out what is done where you work. The most usual ways are to put it (folded) on the table, to present it (also folded) on a clean saucer, or to present it in a credit card folder. However it is presented, the amount to be paid should not be visible until the bill has been opened by the host, or whoever is paying.

There must be no mistake about which bill goes to which table, so it is usual for the bill to be folded in such a way that the table number shows clearly at the top. This is for the waiter to check before placing the bill on the table.

The bill should be put on the table in a place convenient for the host. This will usually be discreetly at his or her right-hand side. Be careful not to present the bill to a man if a woman is clearly the host. Present the bill to the host, who will almost invariably be the person who asked for it.

Do not stand about waiting for your customers to pay; leave them alone so that the host can check the bill. (Be sure it is right!) But be alert so that you are ready to deal with any queries and to collect payment when the host is ready to pay.

Collecting Payment. When the host has checked the bill, he or she will put money or a credit card on it for you to collect. Just as it is important that there should be no delay in presenting the bill when it is asked for, so it is equally important that you should collect the money, or more commonly, the credit card, promptly. It is maddening for customers to have to try to catch your eye to tell you to collect the money or their card. As always you must be alert. This takes effort at the end of a long shift.

If the bill has been settled in cash, take it away from the table and check that there is enough money to cover the amount due. Do not leave the room until you have checked this, and, if the amount is not sufficient, discreetly point this out to the host before you take it to the cashier. This saves time and embarrassment.

Credit Cards. Bills for meals are very commonly settled by credit cards usually Access. Visa, Diner's Club or American Express. Not all establishment will accept all these cards, so you must know which cards are acceptable where your work.

The credit card will usually be checked by the cashier, but it may sometimes be the waiter's job. There is a routine to be followed with credit cards which may vary in detail according to 'house rules,' but generally is:

1. Check the card. Is it valid or has the expiry date passed? Has it been signed? Does the number appear in the warning bulletin (issued by the card company)?

2. Next check that the amount due does not exceed the 'floor limit'. If it does you must phone the card company to get them to authorise the transaction. (The floor limit is the amount up to which the credit card company says your establishment can accept without checking. If you do accept a payment over this and the card is being misused the restaurant and not the card company is liable for the money. Checking for larger amounts not only helps to guard against fraudulent use of lost or stolen cards but also checks that the customer has not exceeded his or her credit limit with the card company.)

3. If all is well, and you are using vouchers, run the card through the machine with a fresh voucher. Check that the details of the card have been properly printed on the voucher.

4. Some restaurants now have special computerised terminals for dealing with credit card payments. These are often connected to the till and you will receive training on how to use the particular system in your establishment.

5. Retain the card and present the voucher, with the bill and a good clean ball-point pen, to the customer for signature. The voucher and the bill are often presented in a special

folder provided by the card company. The folder allows only the person paying the bill to see how much it is for.

6. Write in the service provided (usually 'meals') and the amount to be paid on the voucher. It is usual not to fill in the total in case the customer should want to include a tip.

7. When the customer has signed the voucher, collect it and the bill. Then check the voucher. Is the total equal to (or more than) the amount due? Does the signature match the one on the card?

8. Return the customer's copy of the voucher and the credit card to the customer.

9. Put the card company's and the restaurant's copies of the voucher in the cash drawer.

10. If the amount is more than the amount due, the balance is probably intended as a tip. There may, however, be a mistake. If what as written is much more than could possibly be excepted as a tip, say more than 25 percent over the amount due, check with the customer to make sure the total is really intended. And, of course, if the total is not sufficient to cover the amount due, point this out discreetly to the customer.

Tips and Tipping

Different customs for tips and tipping cause more embarrassment to travelers and tourists than almost anything else. In America substantial tips are excepted for all sorts of services which in Britain no one would think oftipping. On the continent of Europe the customer is sometimes given no choice about tipping: the meal is charged for 'service compris' (service included) and the charge for service can be substantial! In general the British are not comfortable giving tips. To many of us giving tips seems patronising, and taking them seems servile.

It is nowadays becoming more usual to show appreciation of good service by tipping waiters. However, not everyone tips, even if they are perfectly happy with the service, and a tip must never be expected. A waiter has no right to a tip.

When bringing cash change to a customer, bring whatever change is most convenient to the customer. Don't try to bring change which will improve your chances of a tip. That can be very annoying.

Never, ever, show any sign of disappointment if you are not tipped. Never hang around expectantly hoping for a tip. If you irritate or embarrass customers by some indication that there should have been a tip, or a bigger one, you won't see them again, so your chance of a tip next time will be lost forever!

The job of the professional waiter is to make sure that the customers leave the restaurant after their meal happy and content. Some embarrassment over a tip can destroy the effect of everyone's good work through the meal and permanently drive away a good customer. Customers pay your wages; you have no right to except them to tip you as well.

Saying Goodbye

This is your last chance to make sure that your customer leave feeling content that they have had a good experience. Have hats, coats and umbrellas ready to give them.

When the customers are ready to go, help them from their chairs, and give them all the things they brought with them. Quickly check round the table to make sure that nothing has been left behind. If they have costs or raincoats, help them into them. Check that on one has left a hat or an umbrella behind.

Lastly, accompany your guests to the door, thanking them for coming. Just how this is done will depend on the style of the place, and how formal it is. In one place 'Good evening, Mrs. Roberts. Thank you very much for coming' would be right, and in another 'Thanks for coming, Cathy. See you again soon'.

No matter how formal or informal, saying goodbye is a good opportunity to use your customer's name. You have probably just been reminded what it is by the credit card; if not, check the booking if you have not managed to remember it. Try to remember it for the next time.

Cleaning up and Resetting

At the end of each shift the restaurant must be prepared for the next shift whether it is the same day or the next day. This involves:

(a) Cleaning the tables;

(b) Rearranging the tables to suit the booking for the next shift;

(c) Resetting the tables with the appropriate covers;

(d) Restocking the sideboard;

(e) Dismantling and storing food and wine displays (if necessary);

(f) Checking that everything is clean and tidy.

Good waiters will always leave their stations clean and tidy, with the tables rearranged and rest ready for the next shift.

❐

15

Menus and Menu Planning

The term menu refers to the list of food and beverage items served or the list of alternative items available for selection. if is usually in written from and often includes description and/or illustration and prices of the items or group of items served. Menus are the focal point around which all components of a foodservices system are centered. The success or failure of a foodservice operation primarily depends on the menu and how foods on it are selected and served. Profit-ability of an operation may also be dependent on the menu Because menus play a key rol in any foodservice system they must be very carefully planned. Menu planningis the process by which menus are planned, taking into consideration all factors such as food preferences of the clientele, nutritional qualities of foods, operational aspects involved in preparing and serving menu items, foods costs, and labour costs. it involves selection of food and beverage items that are acceptable to both management and consumers.

Basic Considerations in Menu Planning

Careful menu planning will result in consumer satisfaction, employee motivation, and management success. The numerous factors that should be considered prior to and while planning menus may be considered from two aspects: the management's viewpoint and the consumers' viewpoint, as shown in Table 1.

Management Viewpoint Considerations

Organizational goals and objectives. The primary consideration in menu planning is whether the menu conforms to the goals and objectives of the operation. For example, the menus planned for a hospital will be entirely different from the menus planned for a restaurant.

Budget. Budget is an extremely important factor in menu planning. The amount of money that can be spent depends on the income from food sales and the relative food cost percentage. In turn, the income from food sales depends on consumers' available disposable income (ADI), the location of the facility, the type of service, and several other depended factors. Menu planning requires careful consideration of the relative costs of food, labor, and equipment. Careful planning with a blend of imagination, efficiency, and creativity is an important attribute for success in menu planning.

Efficient utilization of all the available resources is essential for success in planning menus.

Table 1

Factors to be Considered in Menu Planning

Consumer	*Management*
Food characteristics and sensory attributes	Organisational goal and objectives
Food habits and preferences	Market conditions
Nutritional requirements	Budget
	Facilities and equipment
	Personel skills
	Production types and service systems

Depending on the type of foodservice, budgets are normally projected *(1)* on the basis of estimated costs for serving an actual number of residents, *(2)* by per capita allowances for the expected number of consumers, or *(3)* by forecasting the number of consumers during a specific period of time. The food cost percentage is also a very valuable tool in determining budgets. Also, precosted standardized recipes, when updated from time to time, help in the calculation of costs to be used in the formulation of budgets. Menu planning becomes very complex and difficult when a number of high and low cost items are included on a menu and when one or more of the items are offered as choices. Careful screening and selection of items are required in order to arrive at the desired combination that will result in a consistent average consumer check.

Food Market Conditions. Raw food products are subjected to seasonal fluctuations that have an enormous impact on the demand and supply. Favourable weather conditions may result in overbundance of a product and result in lower prices. On the other hand, adverse seasonal conditions may cause severe food product shortages and consequently higher prices. This factor is of primary importance when menus are planned, particularly for longer time periods. Fruits and vegetables are the food items most commonly affected by seasonal fluctuations. Menus should be planned to take maximum advantage of the seasonal availability or non availability of the food products.

Physical Facilities and Equipment. The physical facilities and available equipment dictate the type of menus that may be planned. Not only the availability of certain pieces of equipment but their number play an important role in the selection of menu items. Efficient menu planning requires a well balanced approach toward the utilization of materials, equipment, and employees.

Available freezer and refrigerator space also determines the types of food items that can be stored prior to or after preparation.

Personnel Skills. Efficient equipment and its layout will be of little value without skilled employees to handle them. Elegant menu items requiring specific skills cannot be included if trained food personnel are not available to make them. Any temporary or permanent lack of skilled personnel therefore restricts the number and type of menu items. In most restaurants, chefs play an important role in the success and popularity of the operation. Employees' capability and availability should be considered when planning menus.

Types of Production and Service Methods. Time lag between production and service and the time required for service are very critical. In a conventional food production and delivery system, where foods are prepared, held at serving temperature, and served on the same day, relatively many choices may be included on the menu. On the other hand, in systems where food is cooked and chilled or frozen, there are limitations on the type of foods that can be prepared and served, Thus a menu item that is suitable for one foodservice operation may not be appropriate for another.

Consumer Viewpoint Considerations

Nutritional Requirements. Meeting nutritional needs of the consumers in such institutions as hospitals, nursing homes, and schools, is extremely important and should be given top priority when planning menus. Commercial foodservices are also now beginning to give nutrition serious thought in the meals that they offer. An essential guide that is necessary for nutritional planning of menus is the table of Recommended Daily Dietary Allowances (RDA). Percentage of the daily RDA values should be taken into consideration when planning nutritionally well balanced menus. On the basis for RDA, United States Recommended Dietary Allowances (USRDAs) are defined; they are primarily based on the average requirements, without taking into consideration the age or sex of the individuals. USRDAs are used primarily for nutritional labeling. Nutritional labels are printed on food packages and give information pertaining to calories per average serving; the amount of carbohydrates, proteins, and fats; and the percentage of nutrients provided in significant quantities by the specified normal serving of that food. The growing nutritional concerns among consumers warrants careful review of the portion sizes and the percentages of the RDAs derived from menu items. The salt, sugar, fiber, and overall carbohydrate contents provided by menu items need careful assessment when planning menus. Consumer's food preferences should also be taken into consideration since nutritional content alone does not guarantee a popular menu. The nutrient content of meals provided by school foodservice menus is restricted by the requirements of the National

School Lunch Act, which provides guidelines for the nutritional adequacy of school lunches.

Providing nutritive foods by careful menu planning becomes absolutely necessary for hospital patients and nursing home residents. Closely associated with the selection of the items based on their nutrient contents are the different food groups, the most important of them being *(1)* meats, *(2)* fruits and vegetables, *(3)* milk and milk products, and *(4)* cereals and breads. The U.S. Department of Agriculture (USDA) has published various handbooks and tables that can be used in the calculation of the nutrient values of different foods.

Food Habits and Preferences. No matter how sophisticated preparation methods are or how attractively foods are served, a menu is of little practical value if the foods in it are not liked by the consumer. In menu planning, food preferences and habits play a very important role. Food preferences may be defined as the selection of food items from choices available among acceptable foods. Patterns of food selection may emerge as a consequence of temporary or permanent food preferences. Food habits may be defined as the way in which individuals, in response to social and cultural pressures, select, consume, and utilize portions of the available food supply. Food preferences are based on sensory, social, psychological, religious, emotional, cultural, health, economic, preparation, and other related factors.

Intrinsic factors are those that are directly associated with food such as appearance, colour, odor, texture, temperature, flavour, and quality. The manner in which food is presented (with both desirable or undesirable attributes), the way food is arranged on the plate, and the temperature at which it is served, all have an impact on food preferences. Standardized large-quantity food production may lead to a different food preference ranking than if similar foods are prepared at home. Variability in these intrinsic factors affect food preferences.

Extrinsic factors include the direct external factors that can affect food preferences as follows:

(a) Environment. Food preferences are affected by the environment in which the food is served. A good example is the hospital environment, which has a market effect on the selection of food. On the other hand, the effect that a candlelight environment in a restaurant has on food preference compared to that in a fast-food restaurant is obvious.

(b) Situational Expectation. The quality of food one expects is a function of the situation in which it is to be consumed. Food is expected to be good when it is associated with social, ritual, or religious occasions. Thus, the food served at a banquet or wedding party carries with it the expectation of something outstanding, in keeping with the occasion itself.

(c) Advertising. It is evident and many studies have proved that advertising can influence one's attitude toward food. Many foodservice operations use this vehicle for attracting consumers. Also, the consumers are tempted to try new food when it is properly advertised. Many places advertise the specialties on their menus.

(d) Time and Seasonal Variations. Food selections appear to be somewhat immune to the influence of certain natural phenomena such as seasonal variations, outdoor temperatures, and the day of the week. In addition, biological, physiological, and psychological factors can have a profound effect on food preferences by changing the appreciation, perception, or appetite toward food.

The individual and personal attributes that affect food choice are:

(a) Level of Expectation. This has been shown to have a definite effect on food preferences and selection. For example, patients in hospitals have a low expectation regarding hospital food. When these patients find food better than they expected, the preference ratings are favourably affected. On the other hand, the level of expectation is much higher when dining at a restaurant. If the food is of lower quality than expected, the ratings can be adversely affected.

(b) Priority. This factor is indirectly related to the level of expectations. Airline foodservices or hospital foodservices are good examples of the consumers' priorities to reach their destination or recovery and well-being, rather than to have outstanding gourmet meals. Thus, other aspects are more likely to be critically evaluated than food.

(c) Familiarity. The conditions (both environmental and social) under which a person initially experiences food has an impact on acceptance behaviour.

(d) Influence of other Persons. Friends, relatives, and family members can influence food preferences. Even those being served on a cafeteria line can influence the food selection of a person behind them in the line.

(e) Appetites, Moods, and Emotions. These represent a complex intermingling of preference factors. A careless server may be spared for bringing cold food to the table when the consumer is in a good mood; the same may not be true if the consumer is in a bad mood. Moods are unpredictable and constantly change, which causes problems in planning. Moods and appetites are also influenced by physiological disorders, as well as such factors as satisfaction or dissatisfaction with work and salary.

(f) Family Influence and Educational Status. The impact of socio-economical, cultural, and religious factors on food selection is evident and should be considered in planning menus.

The above-mentioned factors seldom have an impact singly. They are interrelated and therefore are very complex.

Food Characteristics. Probably the most important factor to be considered in menu planning is the food itself. Characteristics of foods, which include their organoleptic properties, play an important role in their acceptance. The most important aspects related to food characteristics are:

(a) Colour. Interesting and coordinating colour combinations are very desirable and help in the acceptance food and to an extent (indirectly) in stimulating appetite. Planning and arranging foods so that there is a good colour combination, whether on a plate, tray, counter or salad bar, are very important aspects of menu planning. Colour also emphasized the variety available for selection. When planning menus, different coloured items should be included, and too many items with similar colour should be avoided. In some printed menus, the visual aspects of the foods are enhanced by providing colour pictures.

(b) Texture and Shape. These characteristics of foods also affect consumers' preferences. Certain foods are preferred because of their hard texture and some because of their soft texture. A desirable combination between the soft and hard-textured items on the menu is essential. "Soft," "hard," "crispy," "chewy," "smooth," "brittle," and "grainy" are some of the adjectives used to describe food texture. A variety in texture in foods is highly desirable. Certain food items go well with a difference in texture. Soups are preferred with crispy crackers, soft-textured potatoes go well with chewy steaks, and cases roles are desirable with crisp vegetables. Food in different colours and shapes add to the attraction of the menu as well as to eye appeal when the foods are served.

(c) Consistency. Consistency refers to the degree of viscosity or density of a product. Like texture, consistency provides for variety among the menu items. "Runny," "gelatinous," "pasty," "thin," "thick" "sticky," and "gummy" are the most common adjectives used to describe consistency. Food items on a particular menu should have varying consistencies. As a rule, items that have a hard texture should be complemented by items having a thin consistency. Relatively hard textured meats go well with thin gravies while nuts in thin items add a desirable combination of textures.

(d) Flavour. It is obvious that the flavour of foods is a very important consideration when planning menus. Simply stated, foods can have sweet, sour, bitter, or salty flavours, which can be present alone or in combination. In addition, there are various off-flavours or undesirable flavours sppcific to foods. A desirable blend of flavours is essential for creating uniqueness in the menu. The predominance of anyone flavour is often undesirable. A contrast in the types of flavours and their intensity adds to the acceptability of menu items. Bland foods may be made more appetizing by adding pungent sauces or a blend of sweet and sour flavours may be added to a menu. The right combinations of spices and condiments are therefore essential in order to develop the right kinds of flavours.

(e) Method Of food Preparation. Consideration should be given to the method of preparation in menu planning. Food items can be prepared in several ways, and a variety in the methods of preparation is desirable. These methods include frying, baking, broiling, boiling, steaming, grilling, braising, or a combination of these methods. In each of these types of preparation, there may be variations based on the sauces or gravies used or the equipment used, such as flame broiled chicken with barbecue sauce or roast duck with gravy. Front the management point of view, it is essential that there be a uniform distribution of the methods selected for food preparation. Optimum use of employee skills and equipment demands that there be a balanced distribution in preparation methods.

(f) Serving Temperature. This component is probably the least complex in planning menus based on food characteristics. Temperatures for food preferred by individuals vary with age and other personal factors. Both hot and cold foods are desirable items to be included on the menu. A chilled gazpacho appetizer is desirable with hot entrees a cold salad may go well with hot bread, or a cold sandwich may be more desirable with hot food items.

(g) Presentation Method. The final appearance of food-whether on a plate, cafeteria counter, serving tray, take-out package, buffet table, or a display case is a very important aspect in the final selection of the item. A threedimensional appearance of the food adds to the attractiveness of the menu whether on paper or in actuality. A combination of tall, flat, and other shapes, when arranged in a symmetrical pattern, is eye appealing and should be considered when planning menus.

Menu Patterns and Types of Menus

A menu pattern is the outline of food items and choices to be included in each meal. Menu patterns are based on the types of foods to be included on the menu, considering all different factors. There are different kinds and styles of menus used in foodservice operations. However, menus may be divided based on the patterns into three principal types.

1. A static or fixed menu is one is which the same menu items are offered repeatedly. Many restaurants have static menus with a few limited choices. In many of the franchised restaurants static menus are offered.

2. Cycle menu refers to a series of menus, offering different items for a predetermined time period. The time period (daily, weekly, biweekly, monthly, quarterly, or other period) for which menus are planned may range from a few days to several weeks and is referred to as menu cycle. Menus are carefully planned and are rotated at selected fixed intervals of time. An advantage of using cycle menus is that they provide for changes based on seasonal variations. The food items selected should be adequately balanced throughout this cycle. The cycle may be short or long. Short cycles may be of three weeks'. duration or less. Long cycles may range over an extended period of time, such as six-week cycles within a year or more. Cycle menus are commonly used in institutional foodservices, particularly hospitals and nursing homes. Where consumers are likely to utilize foodservices for a short period of time such as hospitals, shorter menu cycles are very appropriate. On the other hand, cycle menus may cause problems and may create monotony due to repetitions.

The advantages of the cycle menus may be summed up as follows: *(1)* if menus are carefully planned, cycle menus reduce the need for planning menus frequently, which avoids this tedious procedure and also frees much needed time for other management functions. *(2)* The frequent use of menu items in the cycle helps in standardizing production and service procedures. *(3)* The work loads of the employees and the equipment used may be evenly distributed on a long-term basis and can be uniformly balanced. *(4)* food purchasing and inventory control are facilitated, since purchase orders are easy to make and the inventory can be controlled accordingly. Also, well-planned and formal methods of food purchasing may be utilized since the long-term needs are known. *(5)* production forecasting and control becomes relatively easier. *(6)* Comparative evaluations of the costs of production can be made between menu cycles as well as between set periods within the cycles. *(7)* It is easy to make changes and troubleshoot any problems.

Certain disadvantages are associated with the use of cycle menus. The greatest problem is that the food items may become monotonous because of the lack of variability over a period of time. Also, if the cycles are not very carefully planned, the errors or problems keep repeating. Shorter cycles may result in too frequent repetitions and monotony. If the cycle is too long, planning and management may become too difficult and complicated. Therefore, the length of the menu cycle is extremely important and should be carefully assessed before and after its implementation.

Once the cycle menus are carefully planned and evaluated, they become established and provide all the above-mentioned advantages. Their proper use results in considerable savings, increases profitability, and facilitates overall management.

3. Single-use menus are planned only for special days or occasions and are not repeated.

Menus can also be categorized by choice(s): No choice or non-selective menus do not provide any choices among menu items. Limited choice menus provide selections for some menu items but offer no choices for others. For example, only a choice of entrees may be offered. Choice menus or selective menus offer a wide variety of choices among the items offered.

Mechanics of Menu Planning

Menu planning is one of the most important responsibilities of management. Thus the person(s) planning menus should be aware of all aspects of production and service.

Reference Materials

Some of the reference materials that should be readily available for menu planning include:

* Standardized recipe files, showing in detail method of preparation, portion sizes, portion costs, and nutrient content
* Copies of previous menus, if available
* Cookbooks
* Pictures of prepared foods, if available
* Food preference data, if available
* Market statements
* Consumer comments, if available
* Food delivery schedules
* A comprehensive list of menu items, preferably with their prices
* Food sales records
* Production records
* Professional and trade journals
* Organizational manual
* Other pertinent publications

An example of a menu planning form used on a weekly basis is shown in Table 2. These menu forms, which may be modified to suit individual needs, are very useful since the food items selected are based on the type of the items included on the preceding day and the succeeding day. These interrelations should be considered one day-to-day and week-to-week basis. A menu form should include meal pattern(s), number of meals, days of the week, and types of food items. When planning menus, care should be taken to avoid food leftovers as much as possible. In cycle menus, it will be difficult to utilize any leftovers until the cycle is repeated. It is advisable to keep a record of the leftover items and consider that when planning menus. The leftovers are also indicative of the non popularity of those items or the preferences for other menu choices.

Steps in Menu Planning

It is advisable to follow a sequence every time a menu is planned. The steps in menu planning, which have proven successful for many foodservice operations, are summarized on the following pages as examples.

Step 1. Select entries, or main courses, of meal selection for entire menu cycle. In most cases, this selection would be dinner entries, meat items, or their alternatives. These should preferably be selected first because *(1)* other food items for each meal are selected to complement the entree choice, *(2)* they are often the most expensive items on the menu, *(3)* good balance among the menu items may be maintained by planning food items that complement the entree, and *(4)* Their cost will be indicative of the average meal price that can be expected. It is also recommended that the entree selection be based on the cost of the item, maintaining a good balance between the high and low-priced menu items. If the menu pattern does not provide for choices, a weekly menu should be planned using different entree items from meats or meat substitutes, such as beef, chicken, fish, pork, and organ meats. Care should be taken to see that the same type of meat is not repeated on the preceding or succeeding day of the week, even if the preparation methods are different. If there are several choices provided for the same meal, combinations may be selected on the basis of consumer preferences. Variations in preparation methods should be provided for various days of the week. All factors discussed for menu selection should be taken into consideration.

Step 2. Select entree for second most important meal of the day. In most cases this will be the entree for lunch, except in the case of certain foodservice operations where the elderly or the employees are served. (In these cases, lunch is the most important meal of the day.)

Most people prefer salads or light meals for lunch, and therefore these should be included on the menu. If choices are provided, there should be a balance among these items. Variety among type of meat, preparation methods, texture, and colour should all be considered. Also, a balance should be maintained by selecting high-cost and the low-cost entrees. For example, if a highcost entree was selected for dinner, a relatively low-cost entree may be selected for lunch, and vice versa.

Table 2

Sample Suggested Form for use in Menu Planning of all Meals for a Week

Dates: From *Through* *Name of the Operation*

Meal and Food Items	*MON.*	*TUE.*	*WED.*	*THU*	*FRI.*	*SAT.*	*SUN.*
(1)	*(2)*	*(3)*	*(4)*	*(5)*	*(6)*	*(7)*	*(8)*
BREAKFAST							
Cereal							
1.							
2.							
Meat or Meat alternative (s)							
1.							
2.							
Breads							
1.							
2.							
Beverages/Fruit							
1.							
2.							
3.							

(1)	(2)	(3)	(4)	(5)	(6)	(7)	(8)
LUNCH							
Appetizer							
1.							
2.							
Entrees/salads							
1.							
2.							
3.							
Vegetables							
1.							
2.							
3.							
Breads							
1.							
2.							
Desserts							
1.							
2.							
3.							
Beverages							
1.							
2.							
3.							
DINNEIR							
Appetizer							
1.							
2.							

(1)	(2)	(3)	(4)	(5)	(6)	(7)	(8)
Entrees							
1.							
2.							
3.							
Vegetables							
1.							
2.							
3.							
Breads							
1.							
2.							
Desserts							
1.							
2.							
3.							
Salads							
1.							
2.							
Beverages							
1.							
2.							

Step 3. *Select starchy foods.* Starchy food such as potatoes, rice, pasta, and yams should be selected to complement the entree, since they will provide variety in colour, texture, consistency, shape, and flavour. These starchy foods should be coordinated with the entree. If the entrees are relatively dry, moist and creamed dishes should be selected; on the other hand, if the meats have drippings or juice, bland foods such as mashed potatoes should be included to complement the flavour. Creamed or steamed items provide moistness when included with entrees that tend to be dry. Care should be taken to see that there are only a limited number of starchy items on the menu. It is quite possible that the entree may be a casserole with starchy foods such as rice or potatoes; under these circumstances, this step should be totally excluded from the planning process.

Step 4. *Select vegetable(s} for lunch and dinner.* Vegetables should complement the entree items and should be selected on the basis of colour, shape, size, texture, preparation method, and flavour. The food characteristics discussed earlier should all be taken into consideration. In addition to contribution nutritive value, vegetables play a very important role in making the total meal attractive and appealing. The versatility in the types of vegetables that can be planned add to their desirability. Their colours, texture, and preparation methods provide for various possibilities and alternatives for the menu. They may be served as whole, halved, quartered, sliced, diced, cubed, julienne, or carved into attractive shapes. Carrots, broccoli, peas, cauliflower, beans, and other vegetables provide rich colours and interesting combinations. They may be prepared by using various methods such as steaming, boiling, and sauteing. Vegetables served should complement the entree of the day. Highly seasoned entrees should be complemented with mild-flavoured vegetables and vice versa. From the nutritional point of view, vegetables are a very important food group and more than one type of vegetable should therefore be included in anyone menu.

Step 5. *Select salads.* Salads may consist of one or more combinations of vegetables, fruits, meats, fish, cheese, and gelatin molds. They may be accompanied by different kinds of dressings and garnishes. As in the case of vegetables, salads also add colour, flavour, and texture to the meal. In the selection of salad items, entrees and vegetables for the meal should be considered in order to avoid any type of repetition. In general, if salads complement the entrees, smaller serving sizes are usually adequate. Although salads do not require elaborate equipment for their preparation, a good deal of hard labour is involved in their prepreparation, preparation, and arrangement. Aiso salads require more storage space as well as careful handling during holding and storage.

Step 6. Select soups and appetizers. Like salads, there are numerous types and kinds of appetizers and soups from which to choose. These items precede entrees or the main items of the meal. As is evident from their name, appetizers are for stimulating the appetite. Soups, to a great extent, serve the same function as appetizers. Since these foods are included to whet the appetite, it is essential to select recipes for soups that would increase the appetite for the main course of the meal. Soups and appetizers can be light or heavy based on their ingredients. A light appetizer should therefore be planned when heavy and filling entrees are offered and vice versa. Light entrees or sandwiches may be complemented by heavier soups. Leftover vegetables, juices, and drained syrups from canned foods may be effectively utilized in soups. Soups for the succeeding meal should be planned with consideration of possible leftovers and their utilization.

Step 7. Select desserts. Since the bulk of the menu items for the meals have already been selected, it should be easier to plan the desserts. It is always preferable to keep the dessert selection to the end. Desserts are very important since many patrons look forward to desserts, which not only add a final touch to the menu but also provide a lasting impression of the meal. Careful menu planning is therefore essential, as a well-planned meal may be spoiled by an unappealing dessert. It is primarily the taste of the dessert that is important rather than the quantity. A tasty small serving of a dessert sufficient to leave a lasting impression of the meal. Desserts may consist of fruits (whole, part, or combination), cakes, pies, cheese, puddings, ice creams, and cookies. Many interesting combinations are possible with desserts. Since there is much concern regarding caloric value, it is important to consider that factor in menu planning. As in the case of other menu items, a light dessert should be planned with heavy meals and vice versa. There should be no duplication with any of the foods already included in the menu. The colour, consistency/texture, and shape should be considered. A hot, spicy, entree may be followed by an intensely sweet dessert, or a hot meat item may be followed by ice cream. Sweet and soft desserts also go very well with filling entrees.

Entrees and desserts are usually the main items that the food patron considers when selecting items from the menus, and so they should be planned very carefully. Appearance of the desserts is very important when they are displayed on the dessert cart or in display cases. Nuts, condiments, and syrups add to the appeal of the desserts.

Step 8. *Select bread items.* Breads can be of nrany different kinds and shapes. Their preparation methods and final texture also vary considerably. Breads complement the entree item and should be planned accordingly. Among the many varieties of breads are yeast, quick, sweet-dough, sourdough, flat, and several other specialty breads. Bland types of breads may be included when spicy and/or juicy items are on the menu. Breads may also be used in entree items such as cheese rarebit on rye bread. In these situations bread duplication should be avoided. Also the shape, size, and texture of the bread should be taken into consideration.

Step 9. *Select beverage.* This is probably the easiest step in menu planning as there are several hot and cold beverage that are usually included on the menu. Beverages may be selected from alcoholic or non-alcoholic beverages, carbonated beverages, fruit juices, lemonade, coffee, milk shakes, hot tea, iced tea, and various types of milk products.

Step 10. Select breakfast menu. Breakfast items are relatively simple to plan. Normally, there are fixed breakfast items that need to be included on the menu, although variations in the preparation method are desirable. Juices, cereals, toasts, eggs, sausage, ham, and biscuits are among the popular breakfast items. Too much duplication and repetition of the items should be avoided as much as possible.

These steps outline the recommended procedure for menu planning. A final check is essential, taking into consideration all above-mentioned factors. Enough flexibility should be built into the menu to accommodate future changes and/or unexpected conditions. Examples of possible final checklists are provided.

Computers in Menu Planning

Several types of computer programms are available for use in menu planning. The menu planning process becomes extremely simplified if a computer is used. However, all factors should be considered and all applicable data should be included in the menu planning process. Data pertaining to consumer food preferences, food characteristics, production time, labor needs, nutritional quality, overall costs, selling prices, inventory control, and/or forecasting are needed. Careful programming t.o include all of this information as well as the handling of data is necessary; this requires both skill and experience. The major advantage of using a computer for menu planning are:

1. *Storage of a Voluminous Amount of Data.* Inventory records, lists of recipes and ingredients, cost of ingredients and prepared menu items, serving sizes of menu items, nutritional and food preference data may all be stored in the computer and recalled for use in planning menus.

2. *Financial Savings.* Computers may save significantly the costs incurred in planning menus.

3. *Simplified Calculations.* Using a computer with stored data, it is relatively easy to calculate the cost of the menu items or the nutritional value of the menu.

4. *Selection of Menu Items.* Menu selection or choices at random can be facilitated if a sequential rating/ranking is provided.

5. *Avoidance of Human Bias.* Bias related to us of menu items and employee scheduling can be avoided by using computers.

6. *RDA Calculations.* RDAs provided by meals can be very easily calculated by computers.

7. *Cost Calculations.* Cost of the items, food cost percentages, selling price, percent: profit, and other such calculations can be easily made.

8. *Forecasting.* Forecasting can be done by using the stored data.
9. *Consumer Related Data.* Popularity of the menu items can be calculated from consumer demand data.
10. *Illustrations.* Graphs, charts, bar diagrams, pie diagrams, and tables produced almost instantly by computers are easier to interpret than raw data and can help in decision making.

Menu Design and Display

Menus can be written in two different formats for foodservice personnel and for consumers. Menus written for foodservice personnel are supplemented by such pertinent technical information as recipe file number, name of the recipe, production schedule (if not included separately), equipment usage, and prepreparation schedule. From the consumers' viewpoint menus are designed to "sell" and therefore menu items are described to attract consumers' attention. The descriptions are planned to create an appeal for the items served. Since the purpose of the menu is to communicate with the consumer, a good menu format is one that is effective in communicating the message to the intended consumer.

Menu design primarily depends on the type of the menu and foodservice facility. Menus that are a la carte allow for the selection of food items by the consumer from a list of foods presented on the menu with prices. Table d'hote menus offer complete meals at a fixed price. There may be choices provided in one or more categories. There are different sets of menus in hospitals for regular meals as well as for modified diets. Cafeteria and fast-food restaurant menus usually consist of a listing of items on a menu board or printed sheets. Some restaurants prefer to have two different sets of menu, one with prices to be given to the principal host and one without prices to be given to the rest of the customers in a party. Many places prefer adding special clip-ons to the menus. Foreign terms are often used in naming menu items.

❐

16

Guidelines for Room and Food Services

Mostly, foods are served in the restaurants. Depending upon the hotels, the types and numbers of restaurants vary. In big hotel there are a number of restaurants and some are known as speciality restaurants. In the speciality restaurants speciality items like Italian foods, Chinese foods, Indian foods, French foods etc. are served with typical atmosphere and service style. In general, most of the places we have only one restaurant serving more or less a mixture of food items like Indian, Continental and Chinese. The hotels are also required to arrange service of foods in the rooms and also in the conference halls and in other locations like bar, roof tops etc. Under special circumstances, in all such cases foods are supplied from the kitchen and pantry. In the restaurant foods are served under certain procedures universally accepted. However, because of the style of the restaurant and because of other conditions, such rules and styles are not possible always to maintain but it is essential to have clean, decent and methodical service in small or big restaurants. The following are some of the example of the typical restaurant services followed in different parts of the Globe.

1. French Service. The table is set up for hors d'oeuvre, soup, main course and sweet.

The food is fully prepared and portioned in the pantry. The portioned food is put on the platters.

The waiter picks up the food platters and carries them with serving plates to the restaurant.

He places plates before the guests and picks up the food platter from the side board and presents the main dish to the host. Serves each guest using service spoon, and fork to transfer the food. The rule of service is to set empty plates from the guest's right moving clockwise round the table. Serve food from the platter from guest's left moving clockwise. Clear dirty plates from right.

Only one waiter is needed in each station. It is less expensive than Russian Service. It is much faster than English and Russian Service. In this service there is comparatively less wastage as unused food goes back to the kitchen to be served again. It gives personal attention.

2. English Service. In restaurants, the dish is presented to the host. The waiter portions the food on the side-board, plates the food and sets the completed plates in front of the guests, serving the host last. The portioned out food is placed in front of the guest preferably from the right and cleared from the right hand side.

3. American Service. Portioned food is plated in the pantry by the kitchen staff. The preplated, pre-portioned food is brought by the waiter and served from the guests right. Serve solids as well as beverages from right and clear from right too.

4. Russian Service. All food served is finished in front of the guests on a guerdon trolley. The guerdon trolley is equipped with a small stove or heater which is used to keep the food warm and for the preparation of small items. The service is carried out by Commis and chef-de-rang. Food is partially prepared in the kitchen and finished in the restaurant.

Semi prepared food is brought on platter to the restaurant by the commis.

Chef-de-Rang takes order and finishes the food by carving, preparing and garnish and flaming the dishes. Commis-de-rang holds the guest's plate below to receive the food. Chef-de-rang using service spoon and service fork transfer the food from the platter to the plate.

Once the food has been arranged in a plate the commis take the plate in his right hand and serve the food.

5. Breakfast Service. Breakfast service is also equally important lunch or dinner service in the restaurant. This service are of two types *i.e.* food item for breakfast are pre-arranged on the service tray and delivered in the rooms as per guest's orders—room service breakfast. The orders may be booke in the night before the service in the following morning. The food items usually are limited but guest's may order for items of their choice in big hotels where there are arrangements for morning shift cooking. There are some typical breakfast items internationally used. European breakfast consists of bread, honey, butter, tea, jam, coffee, milk and eggs. Cold meat can also be served. Anglo American breakfast includes hot toast, rolls, muffins, butter jam, marmalade, honey, tea, coffee, fruit juice, other items like kippered herrings, cornflakes, porridge, milk, fried or grilled fish, bacon, ham, sausages, egg preparations, cold meat etc. are also served. Puri bhaji, parantha, halwa, kachori, jalebi are popular Indian items served for breakfast in restaurant. Tables are laid after dinner and before the close of the restaurant but in some places the early morning time is utilised for the purpose. Table layout should be in the following lines. Breakfast tables are usually laid the evening before without cups which are brought warmed up to the table with the order. A breakfast plate with a folded napkin on top is laid for each cover with a small knife on the right side, for the Anglo American breakfast often a knife and spoon, sometimes a fish knife and fork and a jam spoon. The saucer is placed on the right side of the plate, when the cup is brought in it is placed on the saucer with the handle to the right and the spoon parallel a little higher than the cup and above this the cream and the water jug. Marmalade, jam or honey, butter, sugar and salt may be placed immediately behind the cover and rolls in the center of the table. Toast or griddle cakes are brought in fresh on demand, and hot breakfast dishes are best served directly on hot plates and not on a dish. After the breakfast plates have been removed, an ashtray is placed in front of the guests who would like to smoke.

6. Banquet Service. This is a very formal sit down service organised in special occasions like marriage, ceremonies in honour of VIPs, during visits of Head of the States etc. Special attentions are paid to the sitting arrangements and for suitable floral decorations. The shape of the table depends upon the size of the room, it may be T-round, oval horse-shoe or block-shaped. For a banquet consisting of hors d' oeuvre, dear soup, fish, a main dish with a service plate, a large knife and fork, a dessert spoon for the soup, fish and dessert knives and forks, a bread plate with a small knife, a water, a wine and a champagne glass. Formerly it was customary to place five glasses on the table at banquets, now the glasses are changed if more than one wine is served. Plates for the hors d'oeuvre are laid, cups for the soup and plates for the fish and the main dish are kept in the hot cupboard ready for use. A soup ladle, saucers for the soup, plates to place under the saucers and dessert plates are kept ready for use on a separate service table. Cocktails or a glass of champagne are usually served in the lounge before the start of the banquet. At a wedding the service always starts from the center with the bridal couple, at banquets the most important guest is served first. The first course is served from right to left, the second from left to right, the other courses alternately. If ladies are present they ought to be served first, but this is not customary everywhere.

7. Indian Sit down Service. This is a mixture of Anglo-American style. In comparatively less expensive places eating plates are mostly of China and stainless steel but other service implements are made up of stainless steel only. All purpose knife, fork and a spoon, side plate, napkin, water tumblers are laid pn the table with a set of dessert knife and fork. Foods are brought from the kitchen and served to the guests from donga and the donga with unserved helpings are kept on the table in front of the guests. Guests may himself take food from the donga or the waiting staff serves the food and takes away empty dongas. Indian thali meals are served on thalis. Additional helpings are served from, multi donga unit with a handle carried by the waiting staff. Price includes additional helpings of selected items like rice, dal, sabji etc. These services are very popular in South India and also in restaurant run by vegetarian Marwari Basas.

8. Coffee & Tea Service. For the utmost guest satisfaction certain salient points for the preparation of tea and coffee may be followed.

Coffee—Best coffee should be used. Proportion of coffee and water should be measured and the water must be on continuous boil as in case of tea before pouring over the coffee. Fresh grinded coffee are far better flavouring than grounded coffee. Coffee should be properly stored in air tight container in cool place. Coffee must not be reheated and coffee service should be prompt. Coffee machine should be regularly cleaned before coffee preparation.

Tea—should be made in China pot out of good quality tea only. The pot should be warmed and the water should be on continuous boil before pouring over the tea. Use approximately 2 gms. for one cup of tea. It is not advisable to use boiled or hot milk for the tea.

9. Wine/Cocktail Service. Wine service with food is gradually gaining popularity in Indian eating places. Hard drinks like whisky, gin, and beer are frequently served in restaurants and in Indian bars. During parties and cocktails mixed drinks are also made on order. A separate table with drinks glasses filled with alcoholic beverages of approximately one peg each are arranged for guests who help themselves with their choices and mix the drink accordingly with ice, water, soda etc. which are also kept handy for the guests. Sometimes, waiter carry tray with glasses filled with alcoholic beverages and soda, water, ice etc. to the guest who picks up glass and advise the waiter to add other ingredients of choice. A strict supervision and account should be kept particularly for the consumption of alcoholic beverages.

10. Buffet and Cold Buffet. Here foods are displayed in chaffing dishes or in other suitable containers of various style and origin and guests pick up items of their choice. Waiter may also help in the service foods to guest's plates behind or from the front of the buffet table. Buffets are also arranged for various occasions and for large number of guests. Buffet for convenience, has been gaining popularity. The buffet can be for hot food as well as for cold foods. Cold buffet is particularly popular in Western countries. Convenience of the guests, space arrangements, guest movements prevention of over crowding at stations, decoration etc are to be carefully considered in this type of service.

PLANNING OF MENU

By Menu planning is meant to compose a series of dishes for a meal. A good menu is an art and it needs careful selection of dishes for the different course, so that each dish matches with each other. The planning of meals in commercial catering establishments is based more on economic considerations and reputation of the establishment. The dishes produced are intended to please the eye and the plate. The menus planning for school feeding, industrial canteen, hostels etc. has a different aspect and well balanced foods according to budget are to be considered. It is essential to have knowledge about the sequence of courses in Western menus, because for Indian menus all the dishes are served at one time in a that. The modern trend is to give about 4 to 6 courses. A sampler list of various traditional courses has been given under:

Sequence of Courses

— Hors d'oeuvres

— Soups

— Fish

— Entree

— Releves

— Sorbet

— Roasts/Grills

— Vegetables/Salads

— Sweet

— Savoury

— Dessert, coffee is almost always served.

There are mainly two different types of menus: Table d'hote, and A la carte special party menu for banquets, buffets, and formal parties etc. can be tailor made.

Table d'Hote

A fixed menu planned for a complete meal at a fixed price. It is a meal of three or four courses with a limited choice of dishes and it is cooked in advance. It is changed daily or may be used in rotation. It is set in the classical sequence starting with hors d'oeuvres or soups and soon.

A La Carte

A la carte means the presentation of a menu of varied sequence of dishes and courses. Each dish is individually priced. Dishes are cooked to order and the portions are often larger than a table d'hote menu. This type of menu is normally permanent, until either prices or change of management makes it out of date in a restaurant.

Banquet

Usually the menu is composed for a number of people and it is necessary to know the reason for the banquet. It is usually a formal affair and dishes should be compiled to suit the occasion. The dishes chosen should be such that will not require last minute dressing. The menu is elaborate and of a high class quality. It is fixed menu, with no choice. The sequence may be as follows:

First Course—Fruit cocktails, hors d'oeuvres or soups.

Second Course — Fish.

Third Course — Entree Roasts, grills or cold meats with vegetables and potatoes or salads.

Fourth Course — Sweet dishes with emphasis on the hot variety.

Fifth Course Cheese and biscuits.

Coffee.

Buffets

There are two main types of buffets in western eateries *e.g.* the light buffet and the Fork Buffet. The buffet table is attractively displayed. The food served is colourful and attractive, tastefully decorated. A large variety of dishes are offered, for everyone to choose.

Light buffets are given for various reasons to augment a long function *i.e.* late in the evening, also could be given for tea dances and supper dances etc. in western countries.

The Fork Buffet will also provide a variety of dishes and the food item can be easily eaten with a spoon or fork, while standing.

The modern trend is buffet lunches or dinners. The elaborate well decorated dishes are displayed. The price is fixed. Western and Indian dishes also are displayed together and the guests can take both or either. The dishes displayed may be:

Salads, soups, roasts, fish fried, vegetables, potato dishes, and puddings of different kinds. The Indian dishes are pulaos, biryanis, kormas, roghanjosh jhalfarze, bhajees, bhurtas, raitas, papad, pickles, salads, nans, bhaturas, chhole, tandoori chicken, seekh kababs, assorted sweets etc. There could be table arrangements for guests who like to take the food of their choice and then sit and comfortably eat.

Cocktail

The main ingredients are actually drinks. Very tiny savoury snacks are also served, such as stuffed olives, gherkins, walnuts, salted almonds, sausage, bacon rolls, cheese fritters, cheese straws, canapes, shami or goli kababs, mini seekh kababs, aloo ki tikis, fried prawn etc.

IMPORTANT POINTS FOR MENUS

1. Type of Meal. The different types are—Breakfast, luncheon, dinner, supper, tea etc.

Breakfast

There are three types, Continental, English and Indian. Continental is a light breakfast, comprises of bread, croissants or French loaf, jam, jelly or marmalade and coffee or tea.

(i) Indian. Popular breakfast comprise stuffed paranthas and curd or vegetable bhajee and poories, or besan cheelas and curd or dosas and chutney and pickles and beverages like tea, coffee, lassi or milk.

(ii) English. It is on a larger scale and comprises fruits-fresh or stewed, cereals, bacon and eggs to order, or fish breads and beverages.

Luncheon Menus

Lunch Menus are usually shorter than dinner menus with less courses and simpler dishes. The emphasis is placed on stews, roast joints, grilled meats, cold buffets and steamed puddings in western style. Luncheon is a quick affair and dinner taken more leisurely. A six course sequence of dishes is given.

Sequence of Dishes

First course — Appetiser. Fruit or shellfish cocktails, delicacies, such as caviar, oysters etc. Smoked fish or hors d'oeuvres.

Second course — Soup—Thin or Thick soups.

Third course — Fish—The fish could be steamed, grilled or fried.

Fourth course — Meat/Chicken—Stews, blanquettes, fricassees, goulash, cutlets, rechauffee dishes, braised or roasted meat. Served with vegetables and potatoes. Salads can also be served.

Vegetables—A choice of vegetable dishes is given for vegetarians such as: augratin, cutlets, vegetable bombe, kievs etc.

Fifth course — Sweet—Hot puddings, pancakes, pies, flans, milk puddings, ice cream, fruit salads, bavarois, cold souffles etc.

Sixth course — Dessert—Fresh fruits, nuts etc. Coffee.

Dinner Menu

Dinner menus comprise highly garnished, classical dishes. Here one has a scope of showing one's skill of compiling menus with a choice of the exotic dishes. Large joints could be carved in the restaurant in front of the customers or flambe dishes could be served.

Dinner Menu Courses

First course — Appetiser: Cocktail, caviare, oysters, snails etc. Smoked salmon, hors d'oeuvres.

Second course — Soups:-Consomme, cream soups.

Third course — Fish—Deep poached salmon, trout with sauce and garnishes. Grilled lobster, lobster thermidor, fish meuniere with garnish for sole, turbot, trout, salmon. Fried whitebait. Cold fish always in aspic.

Fourth course — Entrees/Releves—large joints, chicken pole, grilled beef fillet, chicken en casserole, encocotte, served with vegetable and potatoes.

Fifth course — Sorbet—In a long menu dinners refresh their appetite, with a light sherbet, flavoured with champagne or liqueur.

Sixth course — Roast—Roast game and poultry served with a salad.

Seventh course Sweet—Cold or Hot-souffles, pancakes, crepesuzettes, melba ice-cream, baked alaska.

Eighth course Dessert—Fresh fruits and nuts.

Coffee

Indian Menu

There is no much clear cut difference between lunch and dinner menus. All the courses are served together on a thali. A list of Indian dishes is given to make the planning of menus easier:

Vegetarian — Malai kofta curry, aloo dum, paneer, jhalfarze, paneer pasanda, paneer matar, gobi, aloo, tinda masala etc.

Rice disches — Tomato and coconut pulao, biryani, kashmiri pulao, keema pulao, lime rice, curd rice, aloo-ki-tahari, pea pulao etc.

Meat — Chicken masala, chicken badam, chicken tandoori, gosht mutton korma, roghanjosh, keema matar, mutton koftas, pork vindaloo, lamb curry.

Lentil disches — Rajma shahi, urd dal makhana, khatte chhole, peshawari chhole, besan kadhi, sambar.

Atta/dishes malda — Nans, paranthas, roomali roti, tandoori roti, bhaturas, kulchas, luchi etc.

Sukhi Sabzi — Aloo matar, bhindi masala, karela stuffered, brinjal sag, aloo and tomato, bean mixed masala.

Fish dishes — Fish Patiala, patiya, masala machi, machi jhal, Goan fish curry, hilsa with mustard etc., fish kalia.

Raitas — Mint, potato, tomato and onions, boondi or pine apple, chatni.

2. Type of Establishment. Menu will vary according to the type of establishment: *(i)* Hotels; *(ii)* Restaurants; *(iii)* Hospitals; *(iv)* Industrial canteens; and *(v)* Hostels.

The menus for restaurants and hotels will be generally a la Carte, buffet, banquet, or table d'hote. The dishes will please the eye and palate and will be determined by the customer's appetite and pocket. On the other hand the hostels, hospitals and canteens will generally have a set pattern and will offer meals to provide nutritionally balanced diets within a limited budget. As there will be no choice and food will be eaten daily. A variety given will break monotony.

3. Occasion. Special dishes for certain days or time of the year should be considered. For example, roast turkey at Christmas, special eggs for Easter, halwa for Baisakhi, sweet rice for Basant, Semia for Id are the seasonal and occasional.

4. Type of Customer. Customers can affect the type of food served because of age, sex, occupations etc.

5. Kitchen Equipments. While planning the menu, it is important to see that the kitchen is well equipped to cope up with preparation of various dishes.

6. Seasonal Availability of Ingredients. Season is important in the choice of food. Crisp and fresh foods are ideal in summer. For the cold weather, heavier, richer foods high in calorific value are welcomed. These days foods are available all the year round because of storage facilities. Foods in season should be included in menus, as they are fresh plentiful, and the colour and flavour are good. Foods selected should be easy to obtain locally.

7. Kitchen Staff Capabilities. The kitchen staff's capabilities have to be taken care of. Whether they will be able to cope with the high class cookery, whether they are experienced and have the skill and the knowledge. If the staff is not capable, it will be difficult to produce good meals. Equally important is the serving staff, if they are efficient, the well dressed and garnished dishes can be served in presentable manner. Varied and sophisticated dishes can only be given if the waiter is highly skilled.

MAIN SERVICES IN HOTEL

Counter Service

1. Type of Service. Like coffee shop service, counter service, emphasizes speed and simplicity of service. Check averages are usually low, eat turnover high, selections limited and a near round-the-clock service provided.

2. Mise-en-Place. Place mats, paper napkin, fork, coffee spoon and water glass are placed at each seat. For breakfast, cup and saucer, knife, coffee-spoon and water glass are placed on the table. Sugar and bulk creamer, salt and pepper shaker and ashtrays are placed on the counter, along with the bulk jam container.

3. Menu. The guests select their own seats and place their order at the counter. The menu features simple items such as sandwitches, salads, egg dishes, hamburgers, steaks, soups, appetizers, desserts, ice-cream, soft drinks beer, coffee, etc. if the counter is a self contained unit. If all food comes from the kitchen, a limited coffee shop menu can be offered.

4. Service. Service consists of politely placing the dishes on the counter, and removing them as the guest finishes his meal. In all food service personnel are wen groomed, with a pleasant disposition as they are closely interacting with guests.

5. Bill. Bills are written directly as the order is taken. When the guest has completed his meal, the check is totalled and he pays the cashier directly.

Guidelines for Room Service

1. Taking the Order. The person who takes the order answers the telephone promptly, in a polite manner. He thanks the guest at the end of the conversation. Room service sales volume is directly related to the sales ability of the telephone sales clerk in the room service department. The clerk must learn to pick up the name of the guest ordering along with the room number and use the name throughout the conversation. The order is taken on his order check in legible letters and is repeated to the guest to avoid a possible misunderstanding, making certain the room number spelling of the name and the number of covers to be served. The order is taken in triplicate and time stamped. The original is given to the waiter so that he can place the order with the check. The waiter retains a copy one copy is kept by the order taker to write out the bill. For control purposes, the bill number is inserted on the order slip. The order is then handed over to the waiter-in-charge. If there are several waiters working in one shift, each waiter receives an order in regular rotation. Room number and service time, be it a tray or a table is entered on the clearing chart.

2. Preparation for Service. For breakfast, a regular room service tray is covered with a clean tray cloth including the necessary service materials. Every item placed on this tray is checked to see if it is cleaned and polished.

(a) For a Continental breakfast, the following items are necessary: Small plate, butter knife, cup and saucer, sugar cubes, coffee spoon, napkin.

Ice water is not filled to the brim of the glass since water will be spilled while being carried to the guest's room. The Continental breakfast comprises the following:

Sugar—2 or 3 wrapped cubes per person.

Butter—20 grams per person

Bread & Roll—3 for the first person, 2 for each additional person. If toast is specified (always wrapped).

Jam—If possible, choice of 2 jams or honey each portion not exceeding 25 grams. Beverage—As ordered. Coffee must be served in thermos to keep hot.

Tea served with a pot of hot water chocolate served in pot with cover, and large creamer of hot milk, juice is a la carte.

(b) To serve a full course luncheon, dinner, or American breakfast for more than one person the service table is used. This tablecloth, and set up with the following items: Knife and fork, bread and butter plate with knife, napkins, service spoons and fork, water glass, dessert, soups, coffee spoons, salt and pepper shakers ladle, fish service, loose sugar, entrement service (as order dictates) table removal sign, candle light lamp for dinner/supper, if supremes are available, they must be used for juices, ice creams, shorbat & cold soups.

(c) Depending on local hotel policy, newspapers may be included at no extra charge with continental and or American Breakfast room service orders.

3. Service. The cold food items are placed on the prepared table or tray. All hot food and warm plates in the hot food container, and the solid fuel alcohol is lighted to keep this container hot. Care is taken that the food is not burned or dried out from the heat in the warmer. The bill is picked up from the cashier and double checked to make certain that the foods on the table or in the food container, are those listed on the bill. The captain in charge checks all orders before they are released for service. Missing foods or service items aggravate the guest and slow down service. All tables are covered with a plastic cloth or disposable plastic sheets prior to being wheeled into the guest's room. The waiter knocks on the guest's door, and enters at the guest's request. He greets the guest by name, deposits the tray on the table making sure that the cover faces the chair. If table/service is used, the table is wheeled in an open area and the chair and silver, glass and china arranged at each setting. The guest is asked if he wishes to be served, and if not, the fuel is extinguished before the waiter leaves the room. If a bottled beverage is served, the bottle is opened. After the guest signs the check, the waiter explains the use of the table removal card, and asks if he may be of any further assistance before leaving the room. The guest is allowed approximately one hour to eat, and then the tray/table is taken away by the waiter. The clearing chart indicates which rooms have to be called on for removals. When the tray/table is removed, the entry is marked off on this chart. It is the responsibility of the room service department not house-keeping to remove all trays/tables and other room service equipment, from guest rooms and guest floors. The signed bill is handed to the cashier, and any irregularities are reported to the captain in-charge immediately.

4. General Information. A detailed chart of glassware, china and silver needed for each menu is prepared and placed in the room service area for the waiter's information. If there is language barrier, it is important that the waiter fully understand the guest's requests or call the captain in charge to follow up on the guest's wishes. Flowers fruits, baskets, etc. are sent according to the local management policy.

Formal Dining Room Service

1. Type of Service. Service in the formal dining room is elegant. Use French service and appropriate service equipments taking full advantage of the trained skills of the Maitre d'hotel. In a speciality restaurant, the particular dishes or 'specialities' are emphasized, merchandised, and presented in an unusual and sophisticated manner.

2. Mise-en-Place. Before the restaurant is opened, all tables are covered with fresh, clean table-cloths and the 'cover' properly placed. The 'cover' consists of: service plate, bread and butter plate with knife, knife and fork, water glass and napkin. A salt and pepper shaker, an ashtray, a flower or candle decoration, and perhaps, a table number complete the table setting. Plates, silver and glassware are polished by the waiters prior to placing them on the tables. Napkins are folded in a single manner, to avoid contact with the waiter's hands. A decorative display may be placed at the entrance, featuring appetizing items such as, fruit, flower, wine or speciality food items. If this is done, it must be continually checked and kept appetizing.

3. Each guest entering the dining room is received at the door by the headwaiter or his assistants, in a cordial manner and courteously seated. Chairs are held out for the lady guests, and gentlemen, if need be. The headwaiter distributes the work load evenly between the various stations, however, he inquires if the table which the guest has chosen is agreeable, prior to his being seated. If all guests cannot be accommodated, they should be asked whether they wish to wait in the bar until a table is available, or have their meal in one of the other restaurants in the hotel. Ideally, somebody accompanies the guest to the other facility to ensure that they will be taken care of properly.

4. Taking the Order. While the headwaiter hands a menu to the guests, he inquires whether they wish to order an aoeritif or cocktail. The guests are given sufficient time to study the menu, and not hovered over and rushed in their ordering. Orders are taken by the headwaiter or captain. In a pleasant manner he suggests those dishes which are 'menu specialities' that evening. Care is taken to avoid recommending expensive items merely for the sake of a higher average check. Basically, the headwater's duty is to direct the guests in such a way that they will be satisfied with their selection.

5. Beverage Order. The food order taken, a polite query is made as to whether any wine is desired. The person taking the order is knowledgeable about the wine list, and knows what type of wine is suitable for the particular menu ordered. It is unnecessary to employ an aggressive approach, the guest must be given a chance to order only a plain glass of water, if he wishes, without feeling intimidated.

6. Completion of Cover. The 'cover' is completed according to the order, and if the guests are accustomed to it, ice water is served. Bread and butter is offered.

7. Wine. Wine is served shortly before the food, and at the correct temperature and observing the rules of good service. The opening of the bottle at the guest's table may have some merchandising effect, if proper showmanship is displayed. While wine service is speedy, care is taken that the bottle, particularly red wine and champagne, are not shaken. White wine, rose and sparking wine bottles are cleaned and placed in a wine cooler. Red wine bottles remain dusty as they come from the cellar and are placed label upwards in the service basket.

8. Opening the Wine Bottle. The guest who placed the order is first shown the bottle's label. The foil on the bottle is then cut at the first groove and the small piece of cut foil removed, as the wine must not touch the foil when poured. If the mouth of the bottle is soiled, it is cleaned. The cork is then extracted and the bottle mouth is wiped carefully, to avoid any cork particles falling into the wine. A champagne bottle is kept at 45° angle, and opened in such a manner that the extraction of the cork does not create any undue disturbance in the dining room for other guests.

9. Serving Wine. The wet bottle is wrapped in fresh napkin, label showing prior to the service. The waiter pours a few drops of wine into the host's glass, so that he can taste it and give his approval.

10. Wagon Control. Strict controls are maintained on all items displayed, when served from a table or wagon. Extremely expensive items are not displayed, and only the headwaiter or trancheur responsible for all food items in the restaurant, is allowed to cut the meat. If expensive items, such as smoked salmon, prosciutto, etc. are served from a buffet or wagon, they are weighed by the chef prior to issuing them to the restaurant and again after they are served. The quantity consumed matches the number of portions accounted for as served. Also, the consumption of items from the pastry wagon is controlled. In some restaurants, it may prove desirably to designate a cook to do all carrying and serving from the wagons and buffets. He must be extremely presentable at all times. A selection of flambe desserts is offered. Also where feasible some meat or fish items can be prepared at the table.

11. Cleaning the Table. The table is cleared when all persons at the table have finished their meals. Plates are removed from the right side of the guest. Before the dessert is served all dishes and the salt and pepper shakers are removed, and crumbs cleaned from the cloth. Ashtrays are checked and replaced as necessary. They are covered before removing them from guests.

12. After the Meal. Coffee and liquor are offered. Coffee is poured at the table from individual pots. While the coffee pot is kept hot after the first service sugar and cream are left on the table for self service. If the management decides to have a wagon offering liquors and cognac circulating in the restaurant, only one captain or a sommelier is in charge of handling the wagon, so that accountability is assured. If cash register slips are in use, the person in charge collects the slips and replaces an empty bottle from the service bar, turning in the proper amount of cash register slips. If order checks are used, they are stamped by the cashier, as an acknowledgement that the drinks have been billed. After dinner, mints and a hot towel are good ideas to round off the service with a flair. Also an open package of foreign or local cigarettes can be presented. The bill is presented only upon request. And it is placed face down on a small silver tray or plate. Change is also presented on this plate. If appropriate, the check may be placed in a decorative envelope or cover prior to being presented.

Coffee Shop

1. Type of Service. Service in the coffee shop is speedy and economical, using the simple American type of plated service. The mise-en-place is identical to that of the formal dining room, except that service plates are not used, and filled sugar bowls are on the table. In most coffee shops, place mats are used instead of table-cloth. Table-cloths may be used on special occasions, holidays, etc. Less expensive china, glass, linen and silver are used.

2. Seating and Order Taking. The guest is received at the door and seated by a headwaiter or hostess. This procedure is identical to that of the formal dining room, except when two ladies are seated, an enquiry should be made as to whether they wish separate checks.

The order is taken by the hostess or it can be taken directly by the waiter, if they are capable of performing this task. Again, the procedure is the same as in the formal dining room, except that emphasis is placed on quick service.

3. Completion of Cover. The "cover' has to be completed according to what has been ordered and, if the guests are accustomed to it, ice water should be served at this point and both are generally put on the same plate, by the waiter and placed to the guest's left side.

4. Serving the Food. The waiter receives the food items from the kitchen in a plate, and places the plate in front of the guest, crest up, using his right hand and serving from the guest's right side. Elaborate dishes requiring time-consuming preparation and serving, and any flambe dishes, are not offered in the coffee shop. Pastry can be served from a tray, or from a small pastry wagon.

5. Clearing the Table. The table is cleared when all persons at the table have finished their meal. Plates are removed from the right side of the guest. Before dessert is served, all dishes are removed. Crumbs are cleaned. A cup of coffee or espresso and dessert is offered after the meal. The coffee is poured from a large coffee pot, making certain that it is hot. Cream is served in a portion-controlled individual creamer. Guests are asked, prior to the coffee service, whether they prefer cream or milk, since the cost of these items can be eliminated if the guests desire their coffee "black'. The bill is presented, after the guest is finished with dinner or has requested the bill. The bill is, placed face down on the table near the host. It is not necessary to use a plate.

6. Breakfast. Breakfast service emphasises speed, and it is usually offered only in the coffee shop, snack bar and room service. Mats, where available are used with paper napkins. Small-sized cloth napkins are used only if they are less expensive than paper. Before the coffee shop opens, the covers should be placed on the tables, with ample replacement kept at the service stands. This breakfast cover consists of: cup and saucer, medium-sized knife, fork, coffee spoon, napkin and water glass. A salt shaker, pepper shaker, ashtray and perhaps a flower decoration and table number complete the table setting. The guest is received at the door, and seated by the person in charge. The order may be taken directly by the waiters if capable of performing this task, and orders are written directly on the bill. When breakfast is ordered, the cover is completed according to what has been ordered. If the guest is accustomed to ice water, it should also be served. Fruit juice is well chilled and served on an underliner. However, chill cups are not used. Care is taken to use specified glasses, so portion controlled quantities are guaranteed. Hot coffee is poured from a large coffee pot. Cream is served in a portion controlled individual creamer. Tea and chocolate are served in individual pots. Milk is poured from the individual container into a glass which has been placed at the guest's right. Bulk milk is served in a large creamer. After the service is completed, the bill is placed face down on the table-together with a pencil. The bill may be placed on the table without the guest's asking for it, as an expedient. The table is cleared, except for the cups, cream and sugar when the guests have finished their meal. The guest is asked if he desires more coffee. Generally, coffee shop service requires the guest to pay to the cashier directly.

Candle Light Service

In order to upgrade and merchandise room service dinner/ supper service, some hotels use a candle light service and the procedure for this is as follows:

When a dinner/supper order is taken, the service table includes a hurricane lamp. Each hurricane lamp is numbered and before the table is taken to the guest's room this lamp is entered on a control chart, as well as on the check. The waiter is now responsible for the return of this lamp. When the waiter enters the guest's room, the candle is ignited and the lamp placed on the service table. These hurricane lamps are always kept in a serviceable condition.

Buffet Service

A buffel provide an opportunity to display high standards of cuisine, but proper control is exercised to maintain a reasonable food cost. There are a number of points to consider about buffets.

1. The buffet table is situated where it receives maximum attention from arriving guests. It must have easy access

from all tables and be practical to service from the kitchen or pantry areas.

2. The table set-up itself may take some sort of interesting form which can be accomplished through the use of half round and quarter-round tables.

3. Buffet tables can be made interesting by tieing the tables, or making several levels through the use of boxes or crates. The table itself can be decorated with candelabras, silver platters, greenery, leaves, flowers etc.

4. The centrepiece is important, and could be an ice carving, sugar piece floral decoration or some other large eye catching presentation. Height is extremely important in buffet service and often spectacular effects are created with a little imagination.

5. The buffet is artistically set up with decorated pieces.

6. The service line areas are individually defined, so that smooth service pattern and flow are established. If a large group of people congregate on the buffet line at one time, with no control of line formation, the result is chaotic. This is especially true for banquet buffets where the guests arrive together.

7. When the buffet platters, bowls and other food containers are depleted to a point where they are no longer eye appealing, they are replaced on the table so that the buffet retains its effectiveness.

Guidelines for Waiting the Service Table

A primary objective of food and beverage departments is to sell the products. Good food and beverage with good presentation and service will help catering establishments to increase its sales. To perform a proper food service some procedures are to be followed during waiting at the table. These techniques are as follows:

(a) That the cutleries, crockeries, glassware etc, are perfectly-cleaned before use. The dining hall should also be equally clean including its personnel with clean and nice dress,

(b) The menu of the meal be carefully studied before offering it to the guests,

(c) That the side board (dummy waiter) is completed and ready for the service session,

(d) Waiter should not make any misleading statements about the quality of any food or drink,

(e) When waiter is about to take order or to serve and if the guests are busy in talking among themselves, the waiter should in a polite and gently tone say, 'Excuse me Sir/ Madam' or 'I beg your pardon SirlMadam' which will inform the guest that the waiting staff is ready to take order or to serve. After having served the food, stand at a reasonable distance away from the table but watch for the need and call of the guest,

(f) While taking orders, do not rest your hand on the table or on the back of the chair. Always avoid having your face coming into close contact with the guest,

(g) That the articles of silver dropped on the floor must not be used at the table without wash,

(h) That never use a chipped glass or plate and avoid serving from any such imperfect articles,

(i) That articles such as teaspoons, menu cards or lumps of sugar should never be kept in waiter's dress,

(j) That avoid filling glasses, cups etc. upto the brim. Do not put fingers inside the glasses when lying or removing them. For service of ice, use spoon or an ice tong,

(k) The waiter should never put the spoon in the guest's soup, tea, coffee, and

(l) That for wiping plates, glasses, etc. never use soiled or used napkins or table cloth. Waiter's cloth is to be used for the purpose.

General Tradition for Service. Place clean plates and glasses from the guest's right. Serve food from the guest's left. Serve drink from the guest's right. Preplated food is served from the right. However, these rules may depend on the house custom of the establishment/country. Salt, pepper, and other cruete should be remove a from the table just before the sweet is served. Wine should be presented to host for approval by the host. Serve guests host last. White wine is served chilled and red wines at room temperature. Beer must be chilled and served in large glasses or jugs. Some more details of alcoholic and non-alcoholic beverage service are described separately elsewhere.

GUIDELINES FOR GUEST RECEPTION IN RESTAURANT

The procedure for receiving a guest from the moment he or she enters the establishment till he or she leaves is mentioned. This is just a sample procedure and the style and character vary from place to place and from country to country. When a guest enters the restaurant he or she should be received and shown to a suitable seat-usually by the head waiter.

Reception by Head Waiter

In large, first class establishments, there is one or more head waiters exclusively engaged on receiving guests. This reception head waiter takes advance bookings and enters them in the restaurant reservation book. He receives the guests at the door with properly. Having received the guests the head waiter leads the way to a suitable table. If he gestures towards a table or to indicate a direction he should do so with open palm to avoid any impression of pointing. He then helps the ladies to be seated and calls the head wine butler and the section head waiter or station waiter to attend to the guests.

Reservations

Allocation of tables, particularly in busy and reputed restaurants starts before guests arrive. This is because many guests reserve their seats, usually by telephone in advance. Reservations are normally registered on register reserved for the days' lunch and dinner parties. In such cases regular guests or those making reservations who are known to the restaurant are likely to be given priority and to have their wishes met in regard to their seating. It is vital not to let new guests or less favoured guests be aware of any priority given to the others for the interest of the business.

Choice of Tables

The actual location of the seating depends on the number of vacant places at the time of entry, the size of the party and as far as possible others to be near an orchestra or by a window and so on. It is the duty of the head waiter to ascertain the wishes of guests. The assessment of guests and their wishes is acquired by long experience only. A group of guests should not be placed at different places as far as possible. If the restaurant is busy the waiter should therefore know just when tables will be vacant or be ready to extend the service to other people on waiting.

Guidelines for Setting a Dining Table

During setting a table the food and beverage service staff should follow some procedures which will not only help them to serve food and drinks rightly and smoothly but will give a good look of his/her serving table also. The following guidelines for setting a dining table:

(a) Before laying the table cloth you must ensure that the tables and chairs are in their correct position.

(b) See that the chairs and tables are perfectly clean and perfect.

(c) Some kind of flower arrangement should be provided at the table. The flower arrangement shall be on a low vase and heavily scented flowers should be avoided.

(d) Each cover should form a balanced definite unit. It must not be overcrowded. An ordinary cover will require 24" length and 18" width while in case of banquet it should be 27" x 18".

(e) Place only the required silvers needed for the particular meal. The sequence of silvers should be from outside to inside and from upwards to downwards in the order they are to be used.

(f) The knives should be placed on the right hand side of the cover with the cutting edge towards the left. The forks are placed on the left hand side of cover with prongs turned up, spoons are placed on the right hand side of the cover but the spoons for sweets or cereals for breakfast for curry or for rice preparations are placed on the top of the cover with the handle towards the right. The fork for the sweets is placed at the top of the ocer with the handle towards the left. When serving farinaceous dishes *e.g.* spaghetti, macaroni, etc. in the typical Italian way spoon is placed on the left hand side of the cover with the forks going to the right hand side.

(g) The water glass or goblet, turned upside down is positioned just on the right hand sides useful to place them on left for service of Indian food.

(h) Place a side plate to the left of the cover, place a side knife on the plate.

(i) Butter dish should be placed on left. Butter knife must be on the dish with the handle towards the right.

(j) The napkin (serviette) should be placed either in the centre of the cover or on the side plate.

(k) All the cutleries crockeries should be placed half an inch away from the edge of the table.

(l) Salt and pepper cruets are always placed on the tables in the case of a long table allow one set for each two covers.

(m) A void handling of cutleries etc. in bare hand as far as possible.

Reception at Table

When the guest reaches the table the waiter of that table should always greet him/her with a smile and in a courteous manner. 'Good morning Sir' to a gentleman 'Good morning Madam' to lady. If the guest is known the first greeting may be addressed as 'Good morning, Mr John' but thereafter he should be addressed as 'Sir'. A waiter aims to make sure that guests feel welcomes and gain the impression that staff are glad to look after them. However, a waiter should be guided by management and his supervisor before developing informality. When the head waiter has shown the guests to the table he should see that they are properly seated, he may do this himself, if necessary the assistance of the station waiter or he may leave it to the latter while he attends to new arrivals. If there is one guest only the waiter will stand by the chair and move it slightly to make it convenient for him to sit down. If there are several guests in the party the waiter will attend first to lady guests unless the gentlemen accompanying them do so. Similarly at the end of the meal when they are ready to leave the ladies should be assisted again and the chairs should be pulled back. The head wine butler now comes forward and after giving the appropriate greeting will enquire if an aperitif is wanted. When the aperitif order has been given, the section head waiter or the station waiter approaches the host from the left, and offers/places menu in front of him.

ORDER TAKING

The waiter should know what is on the menu and be able to advice accordingly. He will approach the guest from the left and enquire 'May I have your order, Sir (Madam)?' He should wait patiently facing the guest until the order is completed. When the menus are long and varied it is advisable to allow guests a few minutes before asking the order. During this time, the waiter may provide bread rolls butter etc. (in special restaurant) and fill water glasses. It is also usual for a waiter to assist by unfolding table napkins, offering or helping to place them for guests while taking an order it may be necessary for a waiter to enquire about the preparation of certain dishes as boiled egg 'How do you like them cooked, Sir, half boiled, full boiled or under boiled?' as steak 'How do you like them cooked, Sir-under medium or well done?'

If in any doubt over the order repeat the order back to the guest to avoid error. While taking the order a good waiter should keep in mind certain factors such as:- *(i)* dishes ready for quick service to guests who are in hurry, *(ii)* items suitable for children, *(iii)* suggestions for vegetables, salad etc. for roasts grills, main coursesm, and *(iv)* suggestions for sweet dishes.

Guidelines for Taking an Order

In recording an order, a waiter should fold his service cloth into a neat pad on which to rest his book. The orders taken should be recorded on K.O.T. (Kitchen Order Ticket) or service papers with information about waiter's number, table number, number of guests, date time details of dishes (using abbreviation) etc. The writing should be clear as it has to be read by other people. This waiter's book of K.O.T. is made out in duplicate. The original being given to the kitchen clerk or any responsible person in the kitchen before he will transit the order to the chef or staff concerned. The carbon copy is retained as the waiter's own record. It may serve additionally as the bill that will be presented to the guest at the end of the meal. Sometimes two carbon copies are made out, the original for the kitchen clerk, one for the preparation of the guest's bill and the other for the waiter.

Guidelines for Wine Order and Service

By the time food order has been taken the wine butler should attend the guest. This type of functioning is not generally found in most of the restaurants of our country. The wine butler then returns to the table and presents the wine list to the host from the left and must be ready to answer any queries and if required advise the guest on the choice of wines. While the station waiter will serve the food the wine butler serves that particular wine to match the food. He should always co-ordinate with the station waiter with skill and intelligence.

Serving the Meal

The waiter must know the order of service of dishes that his guest has ordered. He will therefore pass on the K.O.T. to the appropriate part of the kitchen or to the kitchen clerk or whoever is accepting the orders. In order to keep the guests waiting the first dish in course of the menu is usually kept ready for immediate service. Meanwhile, the dishes that are to follow are immediately put into preparation. Having served one course, the waiter goes to the kitchen for the next course which he will bring to the side table in time. He should check other tables at his station before leaving for the kitchen to ensure that no other guests are trying to attract his attention. Where a waiter has severaJ separate guests to attend at a time he must have a clear memory and service skills to bring and serve the dishes correctly and promptly.

Order of Service

In a party of two a lady and gentleman serve the lady first. In a party of four consisting of two ladies and two gentlemen, serve the lady on the right of the host first then the lady on his left, the gentleman opposite the host and finally the host. In a party of six, three ladies and three gentlemen the host and hostess will sit facing each other. The lady on the right of the host is served first then the lady on the left, then the hostess. Next the gentleman on the right of the hostess followed by the left of the hostess and finally the host. In a large party, if there is a top table, the top table guest is served first. During the service if there is any undue delay in obtaining an order, the guest must be informed by the head waiter with a suitable excuse.

Presenting the Bill to the Guests

The waiter must always check his bill before presenting to ensure that it is correct. Bills, can be paid in two ways. By the guest to the waiter or by the guest on leaving direct to the cash desk. But the present mode of presentation in a sophisticated restaurant is by using a bill presentation folder. The time for presenting the bill varies with the type of restaurant. In a quick service restaurant after the waiter has ensured that the guest requires nothing else, he can usually place the bill on the table. But in a more sophisticated restaurant or speciality restaurant more service may be required after the meal. So the bill must remain open until asked for. No time should be lost in presenting the bill once it is demanded. At no time should a waiter give the impression that he is trying to get rid of his guest either because other guests need the table or he want to go home. The bill with the money when paid should be taken to the cashier for encashment and the receipted bill with the change if any should be placed on the table at the left hand side of the host. Any tip left on the plate, of no matter what size should be picked up graciously with the plate with 'Thank you very much, Sir/Madam'. If the guest is on credit facility his/her signature has to be obtained in the bill and the same must be submitted to the cashier immediately for his action. For Credit Card prescribed formalities are to be observed without any inconvenience to the guests.

When the guest rises from the table in order to leave, the waiter must immediately come forward and help the guest to leave his/her seat by pulling the chair. He should also check that belonging to the guest has fallen under the table or is hidden under the napkin and finally at the end should say thank you very much Madam/Sir for your visit in the restaurant, see you again, etc.

MAINTAIN THE RESTAURANT FURNITURE

Within the restaurant, furniture varies according to the establishment. Floors may be covered with costly carpeting, polished wood or, in simpler restaurant, with linoleum or plastic floor covering. Chairs similarly vary in upholstery and covering according to the degree of luxury. Items such as curtains, decor, table lamps and other light fittings are similarly variable in quality and design and local flare. Theme of the restaurant if any is also important for the decoration.

Special functional qualities (of the furniture should have): *(a)* durability, *(b)* ease of storage, *(c)* ease of cleaning, and *(d)* functional suitability for restaurant.

Table height varies a little according to choice but does not usually exceed 2½ ft. Lower tables sofa etc. have greater serving problems to a waiter because of bending. Table tops may be of wood or sunmica covered with glass of plastic materials or marble and other contemporary products. Tables should be stable and with legs well spaced to afford minimum interference to a guest. In good restaurants, each party of customers has its own table and two parties are never, made to share. Oval tabling are suitable for seating larger parties. Round tabling with rotating inner elevated portions are also used for serving Chinese food. In more popular restaurants, square or rectangular tables of uniform size are generally used. Advantage of square table is that two or more can be put together quickly during service to accommodate large parties who have not reserved table in advance.

Cover Space at Table

Table sizes should allow a length of atleast 2 ft per cover for simple plated service and upto 2½ ft per person for silver service.

TABLE 1

Guide to Table Sizes and Seating Capacity

Shape	*Seating*	*Approximate size Feet*
Circular	2 persons	3 to 3-1/4 dia
	4 persons	3-1/4 dia
	6 persons	4 dia
	8 persons	5 dia
Rectangular	4 persons	4 × 3-1/4
	8 persons	5-3/4 × 3-1/4
	10 persons	9½ x 3-1/4

Sideboard

For efficient service, waiter needs his own sideboard in the restaurant. This furniture is also described as dummy waiter, or station service table. It normally consists of an upper shelf on which a waiter effects all his preparations during service. A hot-plate may also be accommodated on the top surface. Under the side board top are drawers with compartments, open or partially open at the front. All the silver (cutlery) available is arranged here. Below the cutlery compartment there is usually another shelf for storing plates of various sizes and usages. Second lower shelf is space for spare linen, including table cloths, slip cloths, service cloths and napkins. Sometimes the sideboard has a cupboard for temporary storage of used linen. The side board is indeed the focal point of service. Cutlery stored in the compartments usually comprises table spoons, forks, dessert spoons, small forks, knives fish knives and forks and any special cutlery or serving implements. Small knives, Stacked under the cutlery compartments are the various plates coffee saucers, coffee cups will be obtained as required from the hot cupboard. Pickles, finger bowls, tooth pick etc. are also kept in the side board. Following is a broad guide to furnitures for a good restaurant for 100 covers:

1. Reception cum billing desk
2. Buffet table
3. 50 tables
4. Sideboards with hot plates
5. 100 chairs
6. 1 liquor Trolley
7. Trolleys for service of appetiser & dessert.

Linen

Table-cloths, napkins and other textile items of tableware are usually described in hotels and restaurants as linen. Whether or not they are actually made of linen. Table linen may be of materials mixed with linen and cotton, or mixture of synthetic fibres with cotton or linen. Damask is a form of seaving in which the weave produce a selfpattern. Dasmask is traditionally but not necessarily, white. The self pattern can be simple, elaborate or even incorporate a restaurant's name or creast. Textile company's produce good quality damask in India.

Linen Sizes

Table cloths are available in variety of sizes. It is also made out of large cloth roles by cutting tin to desired sizes for a standard table sizes *i.e.* 60" × 40" or 60" × 80".

Chairs

From serving point of view, a chair style is important in the restaurant. It is important to guest to have comfort and intimacy, Management is concerned with durability, ease of movement and stackability. A customary chair height (seat to floor) is about (18 inches) and should not touch nor press against the table cloth Wherever possible, chairs, should be placed in the manner so that table legs do not obstruct seated customers.

Napkins

Varying from small to large:

12" ×12"	(Tea)
18" × 18"	(Lunch)
20" × 20"	(Dinner)

Trays

Trays are chiefly used by waiters for breakfast tea/coffee service where a rectangular type is appropriate. Wine waiters use salvers (or small trays) at all meals for the service of drinks served in glasses and whisky, gin, aperififs, beer, minerals etc. and for removing dirty glasses from tables. Square or rectangular trays are sometimes used for carrying food from kitchen to sideboard during meal service and also for clearing the dirties from the restaurant.

Cutlery

The principal cutlery and their uses are:

Soup spoons for soup when served in soup plates.
Fish knives and forks for fish and hors d' oeuvre.
Large knives and forks for main course
Dessert or sweet spoons and forks for all sweets served on plates.
Small silver fruit knives and forks for fresh fruit.
Small knives for side plates.

There can be other varieties of fork, knife, and spoons for specific purposes.

Sundae spoons: may be provided for ice cream.

Coffee spoons: for coffee: tea spoons for tea, cheese knife etc.

Service spoons and forks are used for serving all food orders from the serving dish on to the plate. Examples of some varieties of fork, spoon, knives:

Silverware

As all table fabrics are called linen in restaurants, so sliver is used to describe cutlery and metal flatware and hollowares. In fact, restaurant silver is often of stainless steel. Even when not stainless steel, cutlery and other items used are not made of solid silver, but of electro plated nickle silver (EPNS). Stainless steel is increasingly used instead of silver plated items for reasons of cost and maintenance. Its stain resistance is due to chromium being incorporated into the iron. Knife blades are usually made of a harder type than other stainless material and are therefore tough and tain resistant.

Glassware

In all the eating establishments some quantity of glass wares are used except in very small places where all the implements are of stainless steel origin. The quality of glassware, their design and variety sometime change the whole ambience of a eating place. More sophisticated use of glasswares lead to more careful use and extreme attention to its up-keep. The glasswares are also generally known as China or Crockery. Bone china is very fine quality of porcelain and very expensive also. Depending upon the policy and budget of the management, the crockeries are to be selected for any hotels. Crystal and cut glass items are also used in very class restaurants.

Dishes and plates are of different types used for different purposes so are the wine glasses. Following is a rough guideline for estimating crockery need of a restaurant.

Dinner plate (Full plate)	2-3 times the number of restaurant seats.
Small plate (Half plate)	3 to 4 times the number of restaurant seats.
Quarter plate	4 times the number of restaurant seats.
Soup plate	3 times the number of restaurant seats.
Tea cups	3 to 4 times the number of restaurant seats.
Saucer for the above	3 to 4 times the number of restaurant seats.

Because of limited wine service in India hotels and restaurants, we practically do not come across the varieties of wine glasses. Otherwise specified glasses are used for specific wine and cocktails. Beer is served in large glasses or in beer mugs.

Some typical glasses used in restaurants are given below:

Care of Crockeries, Cutleries and Glasses

The best of restaurant services and restaurant reputation not only depends on the food but also on the sparkling clean and choicest crockery, glass and cutlery. Appropriate methods need to be introduced for proper removal of dirty item, cleaning them and storage for repeated use. A separate washing area of washing room use the process quite a lot. One must be trained to take meticulous care in the whole process otherwise heavy breakage of china and glass may occur. Selection of glass and crockery are also important. Because very fragile and delicate china or cutglass implements may only be introduced considering factors of trained staff. Washing, storage;

facilities etc. as well as considering the nature of customers following are some important guidelines for cleaning and caring various implements of restaurant Glass: In India we now have many good glass manufacturing companies. Glasses are usually purchased in gross or in dozens. Because of limited wine service in the country, only long lasting plain all purpose glasses are used in majority of hotels. Decent, light weight and moderately thick rom glasses are preferred for wine. The general glass sizes that are used have capacity ranging between 200 to 300 ml.

Due to fragile nature of Glass selection and care of handling of glasses particularly that of wine glasses is very important. Glasses should be held from the base and should not be picked up with rims between fingers. All glasses should be washed in hot water and cleaned with glass cloth. Some cleaning agents like 'Teepol" is particularly good for glass cleaning. Clean glasses may be lifted and can be examined for the cleanliness against light. For hotel rooms glasses are first cleaned and wrapped in cleophone or similar papers. Very special care must be taken to see that there is no chipped rim or crack in any glass for the use of customers. Crockeries: Large and small plates comprise the bulk of the crockeries used in majority of average Indian hotels. These are generally hand washed in soap solution, rinsed and dried. Warm water (65°C-75°C) is reported to be very ideal for crockery wash. Strong surface abrasion because of careless scrubbing etc. spoils the design and decorations. If the dishes are washed in dish washing machine particular care must be taken for the proper use of the machine as per instructions. The cleaned plates are usually kept hot in plate warmer till the time of service. Before offering to the guest checking must be made regularly for chipped or cracks in plates. Should there be any, those must not be used.

Cutlery. Hotel cutleries are mainly of metallic origin. The most common metal is stainless steel. The hotel silver are simply items silver plated over a base metal (copper, zinc, nickel alloy). The life of silver plating depends upon the thickness of silver coat, washing methods and atmospheric conditions. Sulphurous connection either from food or other sources damage the silver through chemical interaction. Egg and onion very sharply react with silver plated cutleries. Appropriate polish like silvo, or polish powder etc. should only be used by trained people for cleaning the silvers. Stain on stainless steel is very rare and implements made out of this metal in relatively easy to clean and keep. Electrical machine cutlery washing machine is now available in the country. Apart from service of food and cleaning duties the restaurant staff are also responsible for care of glasses, china and cutleries used in restaurant. The cleaning and arranging of the restaurant at the time of opening and organising things at the closing time are also part of restaurant stff duties. The golden rule for the restaurent staff is to arrange, clean and keep the place in proper order and per policy of the proprietor.

□

17

Equipments in Kitchen

ROASTING AND BAKING

Roasting is defined as cooking (especially in the case of meat) by exposure to open fire or in an oven; baking is cooking by dry heat in a closed place or on a hot surface (not by direct exposure to fire). Cooking by an open fire is rarely used nowadays, and so the terms roasting and baking are to a certain extent interchangeable. They are both used chiefly to describe cooking in a closed and heated space-that is, an oven. In the oven heat is transferred to the food partly by conduction through the metal runners or sheets on which the food is placed, but mainly through: *(i)* direct radiation from the oven walls and *(ii)* convection currents of heated air.

The circulation of heated air within the oven may be increased by the use of a fan, which forces air round the oven chamber. In the days when meat was roasted in front of an open fire a rotating spit was used, and the spit was turned by hand, clockwork mechanism or other means. Nowadays, for obvious reasons of efficiency and cleanliness, the oven has taken the place of the spit in nearly all circumstances. Where spits are used they rotate inside an oven, the heat source is an electric element, and the spit is power-driven. This sort of rotisserie is used on a limited scale for poultry, game and small joints. Usually meat is roasted by standing it in a tin containing hot fat inside an oven, and certain vegetables are cooked in the same way. The term baking applies when the oven is used for cooking bread, cakes, pastry and made-up dishes, and it applies also to the use of bakestones and girdles (chiefly for domestic purposes) to cook scones and other small items. In both baking and roasting an attractive external appearance is given by exposure to dry radiant heat in an enclosed space (or in the case of a girdle by contact with a heated surface), which causes chemical changes to take place on the surface of the food. This is fundamental to the process.

Ovens for Roasting and Baking: The Basic Structure

Ovens are usually made of metal, but in special cases they may be brick. The source of heat may be either inside or outside the oven chamber. Examples of the former are ovens with gas burners inside; an example of the latter is a solid-fuel oven where heat is obtained from the fire and from hot gases passing through flues. There are also ovens where the heat source is partly external. For example, in a gas oven the burner or burners may be under a metal plate called a sole. Hot gases then enter the oven round the edges of the sole plate, or through vents in and over the oven's inner wall.

Questions of Dimensions and Temperature

In the processes of roasting and baking the distribution of temperature within the oven is significant, and convenient automatic or manual controf is necessary to ensure suitable temperatures for various kinds of foods and dishes. Uniformity of temperature throughout the oven is important where large numbers of like items are to be cooked, and when products such as bread, tarts and buns are baked a uniform appearance will not be achieved unless the same temperature is maintained throughout the oven during cooking. One way to achieve this is to have a shallow oven, with the minimum clearance between floor and top: another way is to circulate the heated air by means of a fan. When an oven is used for general purposes, and not just for baking batches of similar articles, different considerations about temperature arise. When several different foods are in the oven together, each may need a different cooking time and temperature. In this case variations in temperature in different parts is an advantage, and the ease with which some items may be removed and replaced while other dishes are left undisturbed is an important consideration. The traditional general purpose oven with a relatively high chamber and several shelves meets these needs, and it may, because of its greater height, occupy less floor space in relation to its capacity than does the traditional baker's oven, but this will not necessarily be so if the baker's oven has several decks.

Some 'Design Considerations

1. Ease in Loading and Unloading. Except where there are special devices for loading and unloading, the operator must be able to reach easily those dishes that are at the back of the oven, and he will not be able to do this if the oven is too deep. The design of the door must be such as to allow easy access. A hinged drop-down door may cause burns if its dimensions are such that the cook is liable to catch his arm on the open door when he reaches into the oven. Burns may also result if side-hung doors cannot be opened to an angle of more than 90 degrees, because freedom of movement when tins are manipulated will be restricted. The oven's height from the ground is another point to be considered. The most convenient height for loading and unloading is waist level, and shelves positioned not more than 0.6 m above or below this height are reasonably convenient. If the shelves are lower than this, a great deal of bending and lifting is involved. If they are higher work becomes difficult and dangerous, especially since hot dishes and liquids are involved. Shelf heights between 440 mm and 1660 mm are usually convenient.

2. Efficient Performance. The user of the oven is entitled to expect an even distribution of temperature over each shelf, and in the case of forced-convection ovens the temperature should be even throughout. If this is not so, the matter should be taken up with the manufacturer or other technical expert. Oven insulation has an important bearing upon efficiency. Ovens are usually built with a double shell, the inner forming the walls and the outer affording protection and good appearance. The space between the two is usually filled with insulating materials such as mineral wool or urethane foam: these materials must also be heat-resistant, since otherwise they would deteriorate.

3. Hygiene and Durability. An oven should be designed so that it may be cleaned effectively with the minimum of effort, and the materials from which it is built must stand up to working conditions. The high temperatures involved in cooking, and the nature of the materials being cooked, combine to make oven-cleaning difficult. It is therefore essential that the inner surface should be smooth, hard and nonporous, and it must not deteriorate when it is constantly subjected to high temperatures. Stainless steel and vitreous enamel fulfil these requirements, but one disadvantage of the latter is that it is sometimes damaged during transit or installation, and as a result chipping occurs. The inner surface of the oven is not the only part needing careful cleaning.

In order to make cleaning easy, some gas catering cookers are designed so that they may be heated to especially high temperatures, at which deposits of soil are burned away. These ovens are known as 'self-cleaning' or 'helping to clean themselves'. Others have drainage notes and plugs in their bases, so that if they are cleaned by highpressure jets water from these jets may readily drain away.

The Range (Gas and Electric)

This is the most traditional piece of equipment found in kitchens. It consists of an oven (or a unit of two ovens) with a boiling table mounted on top. The ovens may be general purpose or forced convection. Sometimes they are fitted with upstands, and these serve as splashbacks, and also as supports for eye-level grills. Typical external dimensions for a single-oven range are: 900 mm wide x 778 mm deep x 850 mm high, with an oven capacity of 160 litres. Smaller models are available. There is a considerable variety in the make-up of boiling table tops for ranges. Gas ranges may have either open boiling rings or solid tops with graduated heat (the centre is the hottest part). Electric ranges offer the choice of: a solid top with tapered heat: individual solid boiling plates; and radiant rings. Griddle plates may be substituted for boiling rings or boiling plates. One disadvantage of the range is that the oven is too low to be ideal for loading and unloading; this is because of the need to have the boiling table at a convenient height. If the boiling table is higher than 910 mm, it becomes difficult to lift pans on and off the range top. The traditional range is a versatile and compact piece of equipment, by means of which almost all traditional cooking processes may be carried out. A single unit is capable of producing up to 50 meals without ancillary equipment.

Heat Storage Cookers

Heat storage cookers have many of the characteristics of ranges. Operating on heat-storage principles, they burn continuously at a low rate. Except for recovery periods after intensive use (and refuelling in the case of solid fuel models), they maintain a constant temperature and are available for instant use. Their use is almost entirely restricted to small residential establishments, and they are not considered suitable for large-scale catering. Heat storage cookers have fast and slow hotplates with insulating covers to prevent heat loss when the plates are not in use. They have two or more ovens suitable for roasting and baking, slow cooking, and plate-warming.

The General Purpose Oven

These ovens are usually mounted on legs or stands to give a convenient height for use. Sometimes one is placed above another, and, while this has the advantage of being economical in floor space, it means that several shelves are at inconvenient heights. Also, depending upon position, they may block the light or the view across the kitchen. Oven dimensions and capacities are similar to those of ovens forming part of a range. Doors may be either drop-down or side-hinged, and double doors are necessary for wide ovens.

The Pastry Oven

These shallow ovens with drop-down doors often consist of several decks mounted on a stand. Each tier has its own heating element or burner, so that different temperatures for each oven may be used, or, in the case of some gas ovens, all decks are heated by a single burner system. Gas ovens are externally heated, and this is an additional aid in ensuring the even temperature that is characteristic of this type of oven. Oven heights range from 127 mm to 305 mm.

Baker's Oven

Ovens for yeast goods are similar in many respects to pastry ovens, but there may be provision for steam injection. Steam is necessary when French bread and rolls with crisp crusts are baked. To obtain this finish the bread when first placed in the oven must be exposed to a steamy atmosphere that cooks the outside but leaves it soft and moist. The process is completed by cooking in a dry atmosphere to give a crisp, brown exterior. Bakers' ovens are not usually found in catering establishments.

The Reel Oven

In this type of oven, trays swivel between two wheels and the operator stops the mechanism when he wishes to unload. Some models have glass doors. They are designed to give a high output of one commodity at a given time.

The Forced-convection Oven

The special feature of these ovens is the recirculation of convection currents of heated air by means of an electric fan. The fan may be inside the oven, or, in the case of a semi-externally-heated gas oven, below the oven chamber and above the source of heat. The forced-convection oven was originally developed for the regeneration of frozen foods, and it is a standard item of equipment in finishing kitchens. It is, however, suitable for cooking processes, and it is now widely used for general purposes. A list of points of comparison with general purpose ovens of the traditional type is given below:

(a) less time is needed to heat the oven to the appropriate cooking temperature;

(b) the oven is heated evenly throughout;

(c) food cooks more quickly;

(d) meat shrinks less during cooking;

(e) as pre-heating and cooking times are less, output is greater;

(f) it is generally possible to cook at lower temperatures.

When forced-convection ovens are used for frozen food, the continuous movement of hot air takes away the humid air that develops round frozen food when it is first placed in an oven, and allows heat to penetrate more quickly than would otherwise be possible. The variation in temperature through the oven is not more than 3.5° Celsius, and this means that food is reheated evenly throughout a batch, and cold spots do not occur. It is convenient to load and unload batches of frozen food with like reheating times by means of a trolley. For this purpose, oven shelves are designed as a capsule that can be rolled en bloc on to a specially-designed trolley. Forced-convection ovens are available in a very wide range of sizes (oven capacities from 60 litres to 280 litres). There are several counter-top models, which are suitable for use in snack bars and very small kitchens.

Microwave Heating

When food is heated by microwaves, high-frequency radiation waves penetrate the food and cause water molecules in it to vibrate, and thus generate heat. Microwaves penetrate to a depth of up to 35 mm, and because of the depth of penetration food is heated very rapidly. No surface browning takes place, because the temperature in the oven is lower than that of the food being heated, and the food is not exposed to radiant heat. However, there are special heat-absorbing plates that may be used for browning purposes. Microwave ovens heat food in about one-seventh of the time taken by a conventional oven, and are ready for almost instant use. Microwaves are particularly suitable for reheating chilled food. Where frozen food is concerned, because ice absorbs microwave energy less rapidly than does water, the rate of rise in temperature is slower than for thawed food. If full power is maintained for long enough for frozen food to be reheated, results may be unsatisfactory; by the time that all cold spots have reached a satisfactory temperature, some parts will be overdone. Hence it is common practice to allow food to defrost beforehand. Food is withdrawn from the cold store and placed in the refrigerator for this purpose. Another method is to heat frozen food in the microwave oven for a limited period, and then to allow it to rest for a similar period, during which time the heat that has been generated will be distributed evenly through the food. This process is then repeated until the required temperature is reached. Some microwave ovens have pulse control, so that ovens are switched on and off automatically for suitable periods to allow frozen foods to be defrosted and heated in this way. Recently, sensing devices have been developed by means of which the cooking cycle is automatically adjusted according to the state of the food during the defrosting and heating processes. When food is heated by means of microwaves it should not be heaped, as this would cause uneven heating.

The Microwave Oven

Typical components of a microwave oven Microwaves are generated by means of a magnetron, guided to the oven by means of the waveguide and distributed evenly by means of the mode-stirrer. Oven doors have at least two separate interlock systems to ensure that the supply of microwave energy power is cut off when the door is opened. In some models the oven will not operate if the interlock system fails. British Standard 5175 specifies safety requirements for microwave ovens.

Because they heat foods quickly and convert electricity into heat efficiently, energy costs for microwave ovens in relation to output are low. Microwave ovens are small, and external dimensions range from 1381 mm x 578 mm x 438 mm to 612 mm x 596 mm x 485 mm. When these ovens are used for large-scale operations, several magnetron units are joined together to form a tunnel, and food passes through them on a moving belt.

Except for the tunnel variety, microwave ovens are not suited to heating food for large numbers. Their chief uses are as follows:

(a) As an ancillary in large-scale catering for providing extra items on a small scale, as, for instance, when a few extra portions are needed at short notice;

(b) For regenerating prepared meals (chilled or frozen) for those wanting meals at awkward hours;

(c) For regenerating food for small groups of people (as in a hospital ward);

(d) In snack bars, where chilled dishes are regenerated as called for by customers;

(e) In conjunction with vending units to provide a 24-hour meals service.

Grilling

Grilled food is cooked by radiant heat. In the traditional charcoal grill, where food is cooked over an open fire, the source of heat is red-hot fuel. In the cases of gas and electric grills, heat usually comes from red-hot metal or healed refractory bricks. In electric grillers, elements are of either wired or rod type. Some grills combine radiant heat with infra-red heat. Small pieces of meat (chops, steaks, beefburgers, etc.) and fish are the principal foods cooked by grilling. It is fundamental to the process that the finished product is tasty and succulent and of attractive appearance.

Underfired Grill

A disadvantage of this type of grill is that melting tat and juices from the meat when they drip below may cause burning smells, and also cleaning difficulties.

Overfired Grill or Salamander

This type of grill may also be used for making toast, and for browning dishes such as cottage pie. The position of the grilling tray or hearth is adjustable. A channel below the hearth collects any drips of fat and juices.

Dimensions of Grills. Typical dimensions for the grill area are 610 mm × 495 mm, with overall dimensions of 710 mm × 690 mm × 610 mm. It is essential that the grilling tray is at a convenient height for the operator—that is, between shoulder and waist level.

Toasting

There are two types of equipment used solely for toasting bread:

1. Rotary Toaster. This is designed for toasting on a large scale. Bread is fed into racks that pass in chain between radiant heating elements that toast both sides of the bread at once. The finished product is delivered into a tray. The colour of the toast may be controlled by varying the speed at which the racks pass between the elements. Output is up to 9 slices a minute.

2. Pop-up Toaster. These automatic toasters are similar to domestic models, and are available to take 2, 4 or 6 slices. The degree of browning may be controlled by a built-in time switch. Models are available with a red light and a bell to indicate that toast is ready and the next batch may be inserted.

Frying

When food is fried, heat is conducted to it by means of hot fat or oil, in which it is either partly or totally immersed. Transfer of heat is very rapid, and, although the temperature of the frying medium is much lower than that of the elements used in grilling, the temperature at the surface of the frying food may be as high as that of grilled food. The frying medium is maintained at a temperature ranging from 1500 Celsius to 1900 Celsius according to the type of food being fried.

Deep-fat Frying

The simplest form of fryer that can be used for deep-fat frying, where food is totally immersed in the frying medium, is a round or oval pan about 150 mm to 200 mm deep, sufficiently thick and strong to withstand the weight of oil and the high temperatures to which it will be subjected. But this sort of equipment is unsuitable for large-scale operations. Large pans of oil are difficult to move, and when the oil is hot they are potential sources of danger. In all large establishments, and in small ones where there is a steady demand for fried food, it is customary to install one or more fryers in fixed positions, with their own sources of heat. Deep-fat fryers create certain problems in kitchens, in that frying smells are very penetrating, and also oil tends to sublime during the cooking process and as a consequence grease may be deposited on various surfaces in the kitchen.

Shallow Frying

When food is shallow fried (that is, partly immersed in fat or oil or cooked in its own fat—for example, bacon), a shallow metal pan of stout construction is used. The food rests on the bottom of the pan, and must usually be turned at least once to complete the cooking process. There are several pieces of equipment suitable for shallow frying. Pans similar to, but larger than, the ordinary domestic variety may be used on the top of boiling plates and rings. Very shallow frying may be done on a griddle, which is a metal plate heated by gas or electricity. Griddles may be separate items of equipment, or they may be mounted over a cooker, or they may be included in a boiling table.

Design of Deep-fat Fryers

1. Size and Dimensions of Pan. When a fryer is to be used chiefly for frying chipped potatoes, which are cooked in batches in baskets, a narrow, deep pan is suitable. For items such as fish and doughnuts, which rise to the top when cooked, wider, shallower pans are better. Deep pans maintain the quality of the oil better than shallow ones, because the oil does not oxidise to the same extent. (Oil deteriorates through oxidisation.) Another point to be considered in relation to pan size is the amount of food to be cooked in one batch. Pans should not be too large for the size of the batch, since this again leads to excessive deterioration of the oil. Two small pans are more useful than one large one. This is partly because they are more flexible in use, but also because pre-heating times are shorter; it has to be remembered that oil deteriorates rapidly during any period when it is hot, but frying is not taking place. Fryers are often designed in units of one, two or more pans.

2. Cool Zones. Nearly all fryers are of the cool-zone type. Small particles of food that break away during frying fall into the cool zone, and are thus removed from the main body of the oil where they would carbonise, causing the oil to deteriorate and impairing the appearance of the finished cooked food through the deposition of carbonised particles.

3. Controls. Fryers are fitted with thermostats to control oil temperature; these may be adjusted to a maximum of 1900 Celsius. Such control is essential for a good end-product; it is also an important safety factor, since overheated oil is a fire risk. For safety reasons some gas fryers incorporate a second cut-off device which, if the thermostat should fail, comes into operation at a temperature of 2150 Celsius. Electric fryers sometimes have a second thermostat bonded to the heating element, which is effective if the main thermostat becomes defective. This prevents damage if the fryer is accidentally switched on when there is no oil in the pan. Cooking timers, usually with bells, are often fitted. When a gas fryer is chosen, the controls should be checked for ease and safety in lighting.

4. Capacity. The capacity of fryers is reckoned in output or chips (raw state, not blanched) per hour.

Continuous Deepfat Fryers

The way in which these fryers operate. Because items are automatically fed into the fryer in small amounts, incoming food does not perceptibly affect the temperature of the oil; hence a temperature about 10 per cent lower than usual is used, and as a result oxidisation is considerably reduced and the oil's life thereby lengthened.

Oil Clarifiers

After each day's use it is necessary to strain frying oil to remove particles of cooked food. This may be done manually, or a mobile oil clarifier with an electric pump may be used.

When the processes of boiling, stewing and steaming are compared with those of roasting and baking, two main differences are found. First, food is cooked under moist conditions rather than in the dry atmosphere described in the previous chapter. Second, cooking temperatures are much lower. In boiling and stewing, and in steaming at atmospheric pressure, temperatures do not rise above boiling point 100° Celsius. But in baking temperatures up to 260° Celsius are common.

Boiling and Stewing

When food is boiled it is immersed in water maintained at boiling point, and heat is transferred from water to food by conduction and convection. The outside of the food, which is in contact with the boiling water, quickly reaches a temperature of 100° Celsius, but the cooking is not complete until the required temperature has been reached throughout the mass of the food. This temperature is not necessarily 100° Celsius, for it may be that a lower temperature is enough to cook the food. Boiled potatoes are an example. They are completely cooked when they are soft throughout, and this condition is reached when there is a temperature at their centres of 65° to 71° Celsius, which is sufficient to burst the starch grains and soften the cellulose. But when meat is boiled not only must the temperature throughout be raised to 100° Celsius, but it must be held at that point for some time in order to soften the fibrous insoluble collagen in the meat and convert it into soluble gelatin. The length of time needed for this varies according to the size and quality of the meat being cooked. The stewing process is similar to boiling, but in this case the liquid in which the food is cooked is maintained at a slightly lower temperature, and the amount of liquid used is kept to a minimum. Because the temperature is lower, the transfer of heat is more gradual, and the movement of the liquid is less violent. These are important points in the cooking of certain foods. For example, fruit needs this sort of cooking if it is not to disintegrate.

Equipment for Boiling and Stewing

The basic requirements for boiling or stewing small quantities of food are simple. All that is needed is a container that will hold water and withstand heat, and that has a lid to prevent undue loss of steam. It is not practicable, however, to use very large portable containers for this purpose, mainly because of the weight of liquid involved. If it is remembered that 1 litre of water weighs 1 kilogram, it will readily be appreciated that portable pans of more than about 14 litres are unsuitable. Saucepans of this capacity and under can be accommodated on the boiling table of the range, or on free-standing boiling tables. Where food is to be cooked in larger batches than a 14 litre pan will hold, equipment is needed that can be filled and heated without being moved. It is interesting to trace the development of equipment for this purpose.

The Soyer Boiler

During the Crimean War, complaints were received about the quality of food served to the troops, both in the field and in the hospitals, and one of the main causes was bad cooking. A chef of that period, Alexis Soyer, whose name became world famous, had already achieved renown for his exhibits at the Great Exhibition of 1851. Soyer agreed to go to the Crimea to investigate the problem, and he quickly realised that one of the main difficulties in providing wellcooked food for the troops was the lack of suitable equipment in which large quantities of food could be cooked at one time. Very quickly he designed, made and put into use for the first time the boiler that was the forerunner of those used in catering today. An improved design of Soyer's boiler, still bearing his name, is used today in the army for field exercises, and is available for use in civilian emergencies. During the World War II it proved its worth for emergency feeding of the population in many British cities after heavy aerial bombardment. The Soyer boiler is a round, open-topped vessel made of iron with a diameter of about 0-76 m, with a rounded base and a capacity of 45 to 90 litres.

Boiling Pans

1. General Description. Boiling pans used today are similar in principle to Soyer boilers, but they have many refinements and modifications. Rustless metals and surfaces provide durable, hygienic and easily-cleaned finishes. Stainless steel is usually used for the inner casing of the boiler and for the lid. The outer casing also may be of stainless steel: vitreous enamel is an alternative finish. The lid is usually hinged and counterbalanced to facilitate lifting. Taps with swivel arms are fitted near by so that the boiler may be filled easily with water for cooking or cleaning.

2. Capacity and Dimensions. Boiling pans are available in capacities from 45 to 180 litres, but the sizes most often chosen are 45 and 90 litres. Caterers usually prefer to have several smaller boilers rather than one or two very large ones, for three reasons. First, more flexible arrangements are possible with several boilers.

Second, because smaller quantities of food need shorter cooking times, vegetables suffer less loss of nutrients. Third, because less weight of water is involved, certain foods, such as potatoes, are less likely to break up during cooking. There is, however, the disadvantage that several small boilers occupy more floor space than a few large ones. Typical dimensions for boilers are: diameter 760 mm for both 45-arid 90-litre pans; height 680 mm for 45-litre and 760 mm for 90-litre pans. Modular boiling pans have square or rectangular casings so that they may be fitted *en suite*. The height of the boiling pan is important to the operator, especially when the pan is to be used for dishes such as milk sauces that need frequent stirring.

3. Facilities for Emptying. Solid foods are lifted out of boilers either before or after liquid has been drained off. It is possible to have mechanical means for doing this, in which case food is cooked in a wire basket with a handle; this is removed from the boiler by means of pulleys. This sort of apparatus is, however, rare. Liquids are usually drained off by means of a draw-off cock, and the outlet is protected by a removable strainer so that it does not become blocked with particles of food. It is usual to provide a waste outlet gulley underneath the outlet, so that waste water may run directly into the drain. Removable anti-splash funnels are hung over the outlet tap while the boiler is being drained.

Types of Boiling Pan

Single Boiling Pan. These are heated directly by means of a gas burner or electric element. They are used for cooking vegetables and meat, but are unsuitable for foods such as milk and thick liquids that are liable to burn, because there is a concentration of heat at the bottom of the boiler near the burner or element.

The Jacketed Boiler. The jacketed boiling pan has an outer jacket of steam or water, which ensures even heat distribution. In kitchens with facilities for live steam, boilers have jackets into which live steam is injected. Another type of boiler has a jacket from which air has been evacuated. There is a small sump in the jacket, which, when heated by gas or electricity, produces steam. The sump does not need refilling, and the boiling pan has automatic temperature control. A simpler type of boiling pan is the one with a water jacket. Some water-jacketed pans are dual-purpose, with an inner pan that is removable so that food may be cooked directly in the outer pan.

The Tilting Boiling Pan. This pan is carried on trunnions, and is provided with a large cog wheel that engages with the pinion. Turning a handle on the pinion shaft causes the large wheel, which is rigidly connected with the pan, to rotate, carrying the pan with it. This leverage makes the process of tilting easy to carry out, and the rate of pouring is always under control.

The Tilting Kettle. This is a small, floor-mounted piece of equipment with a tilting mechanism operated by a lever, and with immersion elements as the source of heat. It has a quick heating-up period and a rapid recovery rate. It is particularly suited to batch cooking, and to cooking frozen vegetables. A typical capacity is 40 litres, and typical overall dimensions are 762 mm × 495 mm (back to front) × 1015 mm high. A space of 230 mm is needed for tilting.

The Bratt Pan. The bratt pan is a shallow pan that may be used for boiling, and also for frying and griddling. It usually has a tilting mechanism similar to that of the tilted boiling pan. Its characteristics are versatility, and a rapid heating and recovery rate. It is particularly useful for those meat and poultry dishes that require meat to be partly cooked or seared by dry heat before it is cooked in a liquid medium, because the whole cooking process may be carried out in the same piece of equipment. The tilting bratt pan is emptied by means of a broad lip to facilitate the flow of liquid and to avoid drips.

Continuous-boiling Equipment. In this type of equipment foods such as vegetables or rice are loaded automatically into small containers that pass in chain through a bath of boiling water. Because the amount of food in each container is small, cooking time is short, and hence the quality of the finished product is good. A continuous supply of freshly cooked food is available, and it is not necessary to keep it warm for any length of time before service. A device at the end of the cooking chain for rinsing farinaceous foods, such as rice, to separate the grains. Sophisticated equipment of this type is suitable for large establishments only.

The Stockpot Stand. This is a boiling table with one ring only, designed specifically to take a stockpot. The stockpot has to be filled from above, and is emptied through a draw-oft' tap, so the height of the stand has to be suitable for both purposes; a typical height for the stand is 450 mm. Stockpots have capacities of 45 litres or more.

Steaming

As a cooking method steaming has a great deal in common with boiling and stewing, but the essential difference is that, although boiling water is used, food does not actually touch the water but is cooked in the steam it generates. When the steam used for cooking is generated at atmospheric pressure, temperature conditions are similar to those for boiling. Where steam is generated at a higher pressure temperatures are higher, and in consequence the cooking time is reduced. At a pressure of 103 kN/m^2 the temperature is about 1210 Celsius.

When food is steamed there is no weight of water as there is in boiling to cause food to disintegrate, and leaching of soluble constituents does not take place, so that two of the disadvantages of boiling, which apply especially when large boilers are used, do not apply to steaming. One disadvantage is that certain foods sometimes discolour, this can happen with potatoes. There is no cooking liquor with this process.

Equipment for Steaming: Simple Steamers

The essentials of equipment for steaming are: a vessel in which water may be boiled to generate steam; a stand upon which food may be placed so that it is in steam but out of the water; and a lid to ensure that there is no unnecessary loss of steam. Instead of being placed on a stand, food may be put in a container connected with the vessel holding the water, which will serve the same purpose. In one type of simple steamer water is put into a round or oval pan into the top of which fits a covered vessel., with perforations in its base, for holding food. In another type a vertical pipe connects the two compartments and leads steam from the lower to the upper compartment, delivering it through a hole in side near the top of the vessel. Additional tiers may be used with both these types of steamer; three is usually regarded as the maximum. Larger steamers are usually oval in shape, up to 500 mm long, and have three tiers. This type of equipment has disadvantages. The base is heavy to lift, and the top tier difficult to reach. The steamer needs topping up with boiling water from time to time, and there is always the possibility that this will be forgotten, and it will boil dry.

□

18

Problems and Prospects of Hotel Industry

For many, the term marketing conjures up images of selling and advertising. Because of this long-standing and common belief, selling and advertising are often called traditional marketing. Although they are important subsets of marketing, they are only subsets. All phases of marketing derive from the customer. This concept of marketing permeates both the traditional and non-traditional elements of marketing.

Today's lodging marketing executives and today's hotel managers should understand that their properties run as a system. Demand is balanced with the ability to produce. Marketing plans and strategies strike a balance between the needs of the marketing mix (product/service, price, distribution, communications) and the external needs, wants and willingness to pay of the target markets.

The Two-fold Purpose of Marketing

The only valid definition of business purpose is to create a customer.

> It is the customer who determines what a business is. For It is the customer, and he alone, who through being willing to pay for a good or for a service, converts economic resources into wealth, things into goods. What the business thinks it produces is not of first importance-especially not to the future of the business and to its success. What the customer thinks he is buying, what he considers 'value',

is decisive—it determines what a business is, what it produces and whether it will prosper.

Creating a customer does not mean simply making a sale. It means creating a relationship wherein a buyer wants your product before that of the competition. In addition to creating a customer, the purpose of both marketing and business is also to keep a customer once he or she has been created. A business purpose and marketing's purpose, in fact, are really one and the same. Any definition of marketing must emphasize that the creation and keeping of customers is primary.

It should be clear then why marketing is defined as: Communicating to and giving the target market customers what they want, when they want it, where they want it, at a price they are willing and able to pay.

Any business that does this will fulfill its two-fold purpose of creating and keeping customers and, in turn, will produce revenue.

Solving Customers' Problems

There is a marketing premise that is even more basic than that already presented. Simply put, consumers do not buy something unless they have a problem to solve and believe that a purchase will provide the solution to the problem. It has been said that people do not buy quarter-inch drills, they buy quarter-inch holes. Another example, attributed to Charles Revson, founder of Revlon cosmetics, is, "In the factory we make cosmetics. In the store we sell hope".

In this sense, customers by solutions, nothing else. If you think of goods and services that you want to sell in this sense only, you are a long way on the road to successful marketing. Thinking this way forces you to stand. In the customer's shoes, to think like the customer thinks, and to understand what it is the customer wants, when, where, and at what price.

Consumers buy expectations at the same time that they buy solutions, both of which require a sacrifice. It then follows that the

greater the sacrifice, the greater the risk, the greater the expectation, and the more demanding the customer is of the solution. To put it another way, if the solution meets the expectation and the value justifies the sacrifice, the risk becomes more justifiable, and a higher level of satisfaction becomes more likely. The result is a higher likelihood that a customer has been created.

Marketing, of course, does not create the needs or problems associated with the need to sleep in a hotel. However, it does identify the needs associated with where to sleep. Marketing differentiates the available solutions through the creation of expectations. On the other side of the equation, having created expectation, marketing needs to reduce perceived risk so that the prospective customer perceives the expectation as worth the risk.

Naturally, the solution to any problem rarely exists in a vacuum. That is why marketing becomes far more complex. If a solution to the problem of needing a night's sleep was only a room and a bed at the right price in the right place, then there would be little need for marketing. Solutions are not that simple and include many, many needs other than a simple bed in a simple room. The instant that one hotel provides something different than another hotel, competition is created and the mettle of marketing is tested. Instead of "here's a bed" (solution to problem), marketing creates "here's this bed," the any solution to your problem.

The goal for marketers is to present the best solution to the problem as the lowest risk. Marketing, however, does not stop there, especially in the lodging industry. The creation of expectations might be classified as traditional marketing. It is now operations management's job to ensure that those expectations are fulfilled. Although this is surely operations management's responsibility, it also means that operations management is totally involved in the marketing effort: traditional marketing only brings the customer to the door, it is up to non-traditional marketing to create and keep the customer.

The Marketing Concept

If a company adopts the marketing philosophy as its orientation, then the development and implementation of that philosophy is based on what has come to be known as the marketing concept. The marketing concept is based on the premise that the customer is king; the customer has a choice; the customer does not have to buy your product. Thus, the best way to earn a profit is to serve the customer better. According to the marketing concept, an organization should try to satisfy the needs of customers through activities that at the same time allow the organization to achieve its goals. To do this it must be determined what will satisfy its target customers. With this information, the business can create satisfying products. This concept is called the product/service element of the marketing mix.

In the lodging business, the business must then get customers to its product/service. This element of the marketing mix is called distribution. It includes lo.cation, travel agents, tour brokers, and other ways and means getting the customer to the hotel.

In attempting to satisfy customers, business must consider not only short-run, immediate tasks, but also broad, long-run desires. Thus a business must try to satisfy current needs in a manner that will not produce adverse long-run effects that will cause strong customer dissatisfaction in the future. To meet these short and long run needs and desires, all activities within a firm must be coordinated. Production, finance, accounting, personnel, and marketing departments must work together. This is part of the pricing element of the marketing mix.

Finally, the business must communicate all this to the customer whether by personal selling, advertising, word-of-mouth, promotions, or whatever other means. This element of the marketing mix is called communications or promotion.

Lack of coordination of all of these marketing mix elements may lessen customer satisfaction or even cause severe dissatisfaction. The marketing concept consists of a willingness to recognize and

understand the consumer's needs and wants and a willingness to adjust any of the marketing mix elements to satisfy those needs and wants.

Practicing the marketing concept means putting yourself in the customer's shoes. It means selecting market segments that can be served profitably. This translates into profitable products and service that the company can produce, price, distribute. Practicing the marketing concept means positioning to those market segments in a way that creates an image, differentiates from the competition, and makes a promise to the customer.

Practicing the marketing concept means making the business do what suits the customer's interests. For management, it has implications of integrating and coordinating the research, planning, and systems approach of the firm. Practicing the marketing concept is a management approach to marketing that stresses problemsolving and decision-making responsibility to enhance the objectives of the entire firm.

Leadership

Many researchers have studied the qualities of effective leadership by observing the characteristics of men and women generally agreed to be successful leaders. Four major characteristics seem to be: A vision of the future, the ability to communicate that vision, an entrepreneurial spirit, and a constant quest for excellence.

These same characteristics can be applied to leadership in terms of the marketing concept. Marketing leadership accepts change as a constant. It not only recognizes needs and wants of the customer but it also recognizes that the customer changes; the customer is not in a static state and any successful company must change with, if not before, the customer. Marketing leadership envisions these changes through constant evaluation of the market.

Opportunity

Great success stories in business almost always include tales of visionary leaders who saw and grasped opportunity. Howard

Johnson, the founder, was certainly one of those. He saw the opportunity to give traveling Americans clean, inexpensive, dependable food and service from Maine to California. Kemmons Wilson, the founder of Holiday Inns, saw the opportunity to do the same with motel rooms.

Opportunities such as these are based on needs, wants, and problems of consumers that already exist, These men were visionaries with an entrepreneurial spirit. They did not create the needs, wants, or problems; they recognized them as opportunities. Practicing the marketing concept means constantly searching out opportunities. Very few opportunities are as grandiose as those above. To find the smaller ones, the marketing concept manager does not look for opportunities first; he looks for customer's problems because they are easier to identify.

Opportunity continues to be the lifeblood of successful marketing. It does not start with fancy drapery or upholstered walls. It starts with consumers' problems. Look for a problem, the real problem, and you will find an opportunity.

Planning

The third element of practicing the marketing concept is planning. Planning is defining what has to be done and allocating the resources to do it. It means proacting rather than reacting. It means shaping destiny. One writer summarizes the accomplishments attributed to good planning, as follows:

1. It leads to a better position or standing for the organization.
2. It helps the organization progress in the ways that its management considers most suitable.
3. It helps every manager think, decide and act more effectively for progress in the desired direction.
4. It helps keep the organization flexible.
5. It stimulates a cooperative, integrated, enthusiastic approach to organizational problems.

6. It indicates to management how to evaluate and check up on progress toward the planned objectives.
7. It leads to socially and economically useful results.

Planning in the marketing sense and in the sense of the marketing concept means planning with the customer in mind. While financial planning has become routine in many companies, marketing planning has yet to achieve that status. This seems strange if one accepts the premise that without customers there would be no finances to manage.

Control

Control is the last element of the marketing system quartet, but it is also the glue that holds the other three together and makes them work. when control is lacking in lodging firms, leadership and planning founders.

Control is the sense of the marketing concept means something quite different than cost control, although certainly marketers must be aware of costs and their impact on the bottom line. Instead, control in the marketing sense means control of your destiny through leadership, planning, and opportunity by control of the customer, the market, and the product.

Control is the feedback loop of the system that tells if the system is working and provides information to management on who the market is, who the customer is, and what are the customers' problems, expectations, perceptions, and experiences. Control is knowing whether perceptions equal reality, why the customers come or do not come, how they use the product, how their complaints are handled, and whether they return. In short, control in marketing is knowing and serving the customer. Control is also knowing your employees for every employee is an integral part of the marketing effort in a lodging firm.

Control in marketing means a good management information system, an essential element of practicing the marketing concept.

Why the Marketing of Lodging is Different

Lodging services are experienced, rather than possessed. There is no passing of title when purchased. The buyer has nothing to be displayed, to be shown to friends or family, to put on the shelf, or ever to use again. In sum, the buyer goes away empty-handed. He does not, however, go away "empty-headed." lie has an experience to remember and to talk about.

The intangibility of lodging has profound implications for the consumer, and thus for marketers. In the extreme, the buyer is not sure what he is buying or what he will get. Even if he has bought it before, he cannot go back and say. "I want one of the same" and show the seller what it is that he wants. The buyer cannot kick the tires, turn up the sound, choose the color, smell the aroma, measure the size, or taste the flavour.

The Consumer. It is the experience that helps create expectations for future experiences. This point demonstrates why each experience in a service rendered is a marketing effort. It is the only true way the consumer has of valuing the purchase and determining if it is worth the sacrifice. Even then he is not sure if it will be repeated in an identical fashion. These factors, in turn, increase the risk for the customer. Buying "blind" is indeed the riskiest of purchases.

Suppose, as may more often be the case, that the prospective buyer has not previously had this exact same experience. In this case the buyer may have to rely on similar experiences. If there have been none of these, then he or she may choose to rely on the experiences of others, either with the same experience or with similar experiences. If this information is not available, the buyer may have only the advertising, the "promise," or the seller on which to rely. Without even this he or she truly buying blind.

The Marketer. The marketer's job is to solve consumer problems, to create and keep a customer, so the marketer's task in the case of intangibles relates directly to the problems of the consumer that were just discussed.

The marketer must convince the prospective buyer that he or she offers the right solution to the buyer's problem. The first step, then, is to develop the expectation. Traditional methods of doing this are through advertising, personal selling, and public relations. In many cases lodging companies use these methods but there are inherent problems: How do you advertise or sell an intangible service? You can use words but often these are as abstract as the service itself and serve only to compound the intangibility (for instance, "the finest," "the ultimate").

What marketers really do is make promises; the greater the intangibility, the greater the promise, and the greater the risk for the buyer commensurate with the sacrifice that has to be made. The customer has no choice but to believe us and take our word, or not believe us and go somewhere elsewhere he or she will likely get the same promise and be faced with the same dilemma. Because of this quandary traditional marketing is only a small part of lodging marketing.

Simultaneity of Production and Consumption

The service characteristic of simultaneous production and consumption is probably the most unique of all service characteristics. It is also the strongest foundation for the premise that management is marketing in the lodging industry. This is so because in the case of simultaneous production and consumption, consumption depends on the participation of the seller, and the seller requires the participation of the buyer. The resultant effect is an interpersonal relationship between the buyer and seller that may supersede the service itself.

In lodging the customer is buying the service. One individual can totally personify the service of a particular establishment and cause a customer not a return. A friendly, smiling, call-you-by-your-name clerk is not enough. Each employee is literally part of the product because each employee is producing while the customer consumes.

Internal Marketing

Internal marketing means "applying the philosophies and practices of marketing to people who serve the external customers so that

(1) the best possible people can be employed and retained and *(2)* they will do the best possible work". The emphasis of internal marketing is on the employee as the customer and the job as the product Berry states: We can think of internal marketing as viewing employees as internal customers, viewing jobs as internal products, and then endeavouring to offer internal products that satisfy the needs and wants of those internal customers while addressing the objectives of the organization.

Careful perusal makes the case obvious: If the employees represent a major part of the hospitality product to the paying customer, then it is obvious that one of the first tasks of marketing and management is to have the employees believe in the product. Sasser and Arbeit (1976), in fact, suggest that "the successful service company must first sell the job to employees before it can sell its services to customers".

Viewed from this perspective, the job (or product) must satisfy the needs and wants and solve the problems of employees (the customers). If this is not the case, we will end up with dissatisfied customers (employees) who, in turn, will express, in one way or another, their dissatisfaction to the paying customers. Paying customers, in turn, find that their problems are not adequately solved so they go elsewhere. Clearly, this is not the way to create or keep customers.

What is practiced in the creation and keeping of customers of goods and services needs to also be practiced in the creation and keeping of employees. The elements of external marketing are just as appropriate and just as necessary in internal marketing. When we consider the tools of marketing such as segmentation, positioning, communication, product development, and research, we can see that they are just as essential to internal marketing as they are to external marketing.

As we separate customers according to needs and wants, so too should we choose employees. As we position a product to the marketplace, so too should we position the job to each employee. As

we communicate with customers, so too must we communicate with employees. As we develop new products, so too must we develop new job methods, rewards, and satisfactions. And as we research consumers, so too must we survey our employees to determine needs, wants, and attitudes.

Successful internal marketing considerable eases the task of implementing the second element of non-traditional marketing, relationship marketing, the primary task of keeping customers.

Relationship Marketing

Customers are assets, the most important assets a company can have. It is good management in business to protect your assets, but assets like buildings or a warehouse of goods, do not produce profits; the customer that buys the goods does.

Relationship marketing is defined as marketing to protect the customer base. It sees the customer as an asset. Its function is to attract, maintain, and enhance customer relationships.

Nowhere is relationship marketing more apropos than in the lodging industry. Relationship marketing is most applicable when:

* There is an ongoing and periodic desire for service by the customer.
* The service customer controls the selection of the service supplier.
* There are alternate supplier choices.
* Customer loyalty is weak and switching is common and easy.
* Word-of-mouth is an especially potent form of communication about a product.

These conditions are obviously quite prevalent in the lodging industry. We do not well one-time services and the consumer, especially today, has many choices. In an era of heavy hotel building,

any hotel is especially vulnerable to new competition. Most everyone likes to try a new place. The question is, will they come back? Do we offer a competitive product on dimensions that are meaningful to customers, solve customer problems, and are difficult for competitors to duplicate? This is what relationship marketing is all about and when the above conditions pertain, the opportunities to practice it are abundant.

Customer Complaints

If there is one place where internal marketing and relationship marketing come together it is in the handling of customer complaints. Customer complaints are a special case because they are one of the most misunderstood and mishandled areas of customer relations in the lodging industry. Customer complaints are:

* **Inevitable.** Nothing is perfect. The diversity of the lodging customer and the heterogeneity of the hospitality product absolutely ensure that there will be complaints.

* **Healthy.** The old army expression is, "if the troops aren't griping look out for trouble." An absence of complaints may be the best indication management has that something is wrong. Hospitality customers are never totally satisfied, especially over a period of time. Probably, instead, they are simply not talking The communication process is not working. The relationship is deteriorating.

* **Opportunities.** Customer complaints are opportunities to learn of customers' problems, whether they are idiosyncratic or caused by the operation itself. It is an opportunity to make it better, to be creative, to develop new product, to learn new needs, and to keep old customers.

* **Marketing Tools.** If marketing is giving customers what they want then the tool for doing that is to know what they want. All the customer surveys in the world will not tell you as much as customer complaints will tell you.

* **Advertising.** Negative, if you do not resolve the problems. There is nothing more devastating in the hospitality business than negative work-of-mouth. Positive, if you fix it. Research has shown that one of the best and most loyal customers is the one who had a complaint that was satisfactorily resolved. He or she loves to tell others about it.

Practicing relationship marketing through consumer complaint handling is not the easiest task in the world. Many discontented customers will not take the trouble to complain, yet these may be some of the best opportunities encouraging complaints becomes the necessary objective.

Research has shown that people do not complain for three primary reasons: *(1)* It is not worth the time and effort; *(2)* They don't know where or how to complain; and *(3)* They believe that nothing will be done about it even if they do complain.

Marketing's task is to overcome these obstacles by making it easy to complain, making it known where and how to complain, and truly doing something about it when customers do complain. This means setting up specific procedures. Such action will also constitute internal marketing; when employees see management taking complaints seriously they will feel more inclined to do likewise.

The benefits are clear: long-term profit from loyal customers and more positive, and less negative, word-of-mouth advertising. These are other ancillary benefits such as new product ideas, new product information, improved image, better educated customers, and higher productivity and service. For line employees there are also the benefits of less customer conflict, better image and word-of-mouth about the company, and better respect for the company and the product.

All told, marketing in the lodging industry is a complex process albeit a most essential one, in all its components.

Maintenance and Engineering

The hospitality industry provides services to the public or other clientele. For example, a lodging unit provides guest rooms and may

offer or provide food, beverages, meeting space, retail shops, and recreation facilities (this list is not meant to be all inclusive), These services require facilities and a building to house such facilities. The facility may be simple, such as cabinets and shelves in a retail facility; complex, such as a restaurant; or very complex, for example a full-service hotel. Facilities are housed in a building, a complex network of structural components, interior arrangements of space, finishing materials, utilities, life safety systems, and electro-mechanical equipment to provide an environment, all of which are blended together to provide a unique atmosphere. In the hospitality industry buildings and facilities require a large capital investment and if these are not properly maintained, the owners may never fully recover their investment.

Building maintenance and engineering management is physical asset management. The physical assets are the building and its facilities. Management includes policy making, decision-making, planning and organizing, control and communication, and human relations (workers and customers). This article reviews hospitality maintenance and engineering from its physical asset management role.

Hospitality Building and Facility Investment

Lodging investment per guest room (total facility investment divided by the number of guest rooms) has increased from $10,000 to over $300,000, and even over $750,000 for some recently purchased well-known hotels, during the past 35 years. Foodservice investment per customer seat has increased from $1,000 to over $10,000, and over $25,000 for selected foodservice units in recent years. Facilities cost of clubs have had similar percentage increases over the past two decades. If one considers a 500-guest-room hotel with an average cost of $100,000 per guest room, the total investment is $50 million. The owners would like to recover this investment and have the facility generate a fair profit. This is only possible if the facility is properly maintained and well managed.

Another way to look at facility cost is to review construction and furnishing costs per square foot of building area. Normal building

construction costs vary from $50 to $200 per square foot. Furnishings, depending on the building type, can vary from $50 to $100 or more per square foot. Relating these costs back to the previous lodging guest room data generates similar total investment costs. For example, a hotel with a gross guest room floor area of 500 square feet (total building square feet divided by the number of guest rooms) and a total facility cost of $200 per square foot generates a guest room average cost of $100,000. Or, review foodservice cost per seat: If the total space per restaurant seat is 35 square feet, and if the average cost of $200 per square foot is used, the cost per seat is $7,000. Buildings and facilities require continuous maintenance so that they can continue to provide desirable products a guest room that is desired by lodging customers, or a comfortable foodservice atmosphere and surroundings.

Maintenance Operations

The normal activities of a maintenance department are preventive, repair, corrective, and renovation maintenance.

Preventive maintenance includes inspections, standard comparisons, minor adjustments, replacement of low-cost components, and general lubrication, if required. A good preventive maintenance programme starts with scheduled inspections of facilities and the entire building. Some items may require daily inspections; others may only require annual inspections. The purpose of an inspection is to find possible problems. A simple fan belt (the driving linkage between an electric motor and a ventilation fan) wears with use and deteriorates with age. As the belt wears either more energy is required to move a specified amount of ventilation air or less ventilation air is delivered to a section of the building or to a room. An inspection detects a loose, worn belt. The corrective procedure is to replace the belt or at least to tighten an idler pulley to increase system efficiency until a replacement belt can be installed. The primary purpose of preventive maintenance programmes is to ensure the continuous operation of a system at efficient levels of performance and to minimize system breakdowns.

Repair maintenance is required when a system either stops or is not performing according to some acceptable standard. If an electric light bulb is not generating light, the simple repair maintenance procedure is to replace the light bulb. If a fluorescent light bulb is very dark at its ends and if it is only generating partial light, it is replaced, hence repair maintenance. Another example of repair maintenance is if there is a roof water leak, a section of the roof can be resealed to prevent that leak. Most hospitality industry maintenance is repair maintenance. Typical repair maintenance patterns are discussed later.

Corrective maintenance is frequently confused with preventive maintenance, hence the term may not be universally used in the hcspitality industry. Corrective maintenance could be a change in the preventive maintenance routine; it could involve a slight redesign of a component that frequently fails or replacement of a component with an upgraded unit; or it could correct a continuing problem. If an electric motor is frequently replaced on a compressor, the corrective maintenance procedure could require a motor with a higher mechanical rating or a different type of motor. Another example is a guest room toilet (water closet) with a flush tank attachment that is not supplying water at adequate pressure to completely flush the toilet bowl. In this case corrective maintenance replaces the flush tank with a water pressure valve. If paint continually peels from a painted surface, corrective maintenance may be to remove the surface, install a moisture vapor barrier, and replace the surface. The purpose of corrective maintenance is to minimize repair maintenance through redesign or component change.

Renovation maintenance includes redesign, removal of items requiring continual maintenance, and the replacement of components with items that require less maintenance, reduce operating costs, or upgrade product or service standards. Replacing a roof on a building is renovation maintenance. Refurnishing guest room facilities on a scheduled is an example of renovation maintenance. Replacing wood exterior siding that requires frequent painting with prepainted steel panels, aluminium siding, or vinyl exterior siding is renovation

maintenance. Covering painted dry wall in guest rooms with a vinyl wall covering is renovation maintenance.

The maintenance department in a hospitality industry building is involved with preventive, repair, corrective, and renovation maintenance. The percentage of time spent in each activity depends on several factors, including business activity level, type of building construction, number and types of facilities, the age of the building and its facilities, the geographic location of the property, management standards, past maintenance activities and practices, customer expectations, and availability and cost of technology.

Engineering Operations

Engineering operations includes energy management and building design and development criteria. Most maintenance departments are involved with energy management and some may be involved with the development of renovation design criteria. Very few departments have the on-staff experience for engineering design.

Energy management in the hospitality industry can vary from a minimal requirement of verifying utility bill charges to the complete development, implementation, and monitoring of an energy management programme for the entire building. At minimum, all energy charges should be verified by the maintenance department head. This usually involves reading electric, gas, and water meters and verifying purchased gallons (oil) or pounds (LPC or coal) of other energy sources. Energy meters should be read on a frequent schedule and compared to past records and business activity levels and any deviations must be investigated.

Some maintenance department heads may be required to suggest an energy management programme for a property. The purpose of the programme is to provide necessary energy for the successful operation of the property and to eliminate all energy waste, thereby reducing total energy consumption. For example, if a smaller wattage electric light bulb will provide adequate light for a necessary task, smaller bulbs should replace all larger wattage bulbs. Or perhaps guest bathroom hot water can be reduced from 140°F to 115°F. The

department head should meet with the other department heads to develop the energy management program for the total property.

Current engineering design is frequently related to energy management programs in the hospitality industry. For example, it is known that incandescent lighting systems are seldom over 12 per cent efficient (conversion of electric energy to light energy), so engineering design should develops fluorescent lighting replacement system that would include lamp sizing to provide the necessary lighting level, required changes in the electrical system, the conversion cost, the estimated energy savings, changes in maintenance requirements, and the development of a payback period. Engineering design may also include determining the cost of alternate plans for periodic guest room renovation, evaluating service contracts versus on-premise cost of doing the same work, determining the cost of alternate energy resources (natural gas versus electrical or oil), and evaluating energy management control systems.

Energy Management Systems

Currently available technology can significantly reduce property energy consumption. In addition, if an appropriate energy management system (EMS) is selected for a property, system capabilities are such that life safety, building security, and many maintenance record-keeping procedures can be included with the basic EMS. Some EMS computer software programmes are compatible with employee scheduling software and can be used to optimize employee activities.

The simplest EMS is a time clock. Time clocks can be connected to outside building and grounds lighting and some interior public space lighting. Normally lighting systems are activated 15 minutes before and 15 minutes after sunset and sunrise respectively. EMS load shedding is also available. Load shedding programmes can control maximum energy consumption during a specified time period for any type of energy resource (electric, gas, water or steam).

All equipment utilizing a specific energy resource is connected to a control center that limits the maximum consumption during a specified time period. If a unit of equipment not currently in operation

demands energy and if its energy requirement would exceed the maximum set energy level, this equipment is not activated until some of the currently operating equipment is shut off. Some systems automatically shut down some equipment if other equipment demands energy and has not been in operation for an extended time period.

Electric demand controllers only regulate maximum electric demand during a specified time period and operate very similar to load shedding systems. The current ultimate EMS is the computer-assisted system that can be used to replace the time clock, load shedding, and electric demand controllers. The computer-assisted system can also be connected to space occupancy sensors and hotel front office systems. Hotel guest rooms can be programmed for unsold-unoccupied status, sold-unoccupied status, or sold-occupied status with different room temperatures for each room status. Life safety, security, and employee staffing programmes can frequently be included with these computer-assisted EMS programmes. The maintenance head should be prepared to recommend an appropriate EMS for a property.

Maintenance and Engineering Management Functions

Maintenance and engineering management functions are policy making, decision-making, planning and organizing, communication and control, and numan relations.

Policy Making

Policy making as applied to the maintenance and engineering department is developing decision-making guidelines. Some policies are established by higher management, such as, the maintenance and engineering department head report to the property general manager, property president, executive assistant manager, or property manager. Another management policy may define the customer market segment that is being attracted to the property. These customers are attracted because of room rates, property facilities, or standards of service. The maintenance department head cannot change these policies, but can recommend policy changes.

The department head establishes decision-making guidelines that reflect these policies. For example, if a work order, (a request for maintenance department to do work) is received in the department, when should this work be done? As quickly as possible, of course. But what happens if two or more work orders are received at the same time? Or, if all workers are currently performing other activities, what activities are temporarily halted so that someone can be assigned to the new work request? A work order priority system that establishes department policy must be developed so that the correct decision can be made regarding work requests. Work orders are assigned one of these priorities; emergency, routine, or backlogged.

Emergency work orders have the first priority. An employee is immediately sent to handle a work request. In general, if guest or employees safety is affected, an emergency priority is assigned. Emergency examples include ice forming on the building entrance walks and roads, a leaking plumbing fixture flooding an area, or an activated fire alarm. The department had develops a list of emergency situations that serves as a general guideline for the immediate dispatching of workers. Examples of types of emergency work order requests are shown in Table 2 on next page.

Routine work orders-requests for work that does not require immediate action have a second priority. These work requests are scheduled on a first-in first-out basis in many cases. A normal procedure is to accumulate all guest room work requests by selected categories (plumbing, electrical, by floor level, or building section) and to give the work requests to a single employee to handle within a 2- or 4-hour period. Hence, an employee may be given six guest room work requests that the employee can be expected to complete in a 4-hour period. The employee may be required to call the dispatcher after the completion of each task and notify the dispatcher which task will be completed next. Table 2 shows typical routine work order requests for three hotels. All data is given in work orders per 100 guest rooms per day.

The figures in Table 2 show the effects of three different property management policies. Hotel C was built over 30 years ago

and management has established an excellent property renovation policy. The average of guest rooms, dining rooms, and public space is 5 years and a high percentage of maintenance activities is for preventive maintenance. Hotel B was built 25 years ago and the average age of guest rooms, dining rooms, and public space is about 7.5 years and an average of one employee per 100 guest rooms is assigned to preventive maintenance activities. Hotel A was build about 3 years ago, but guest rooms are renovated only as they becomes excessively worn, dining rooms are renovated only when food sales decrease, and public space is renovated when money is available. Hotel A has about 550 guest rooms and only two employees are assigned preventive maintenance activities. Each work order request requires about 0.55 work hours for guest room repairs, 1.00 work-hours for food and beverage repairs, and 1.50 work-hours for public area repairs. The effects of these different property management policies are clear.

Table 2

Work order requests per 100 guest rooms per day for three hotels

Origin of request	*Hotel A*	*Hotel B*	*Hotel C*
Guest rooms	6.77	4.77	2.12
Food and beverage	4.47	2.29	1.00
Public and other	4.04	2.06	1.05
Total requests	15.28	9.12	4.17

Table 3 compares the types of emergency work orders for the same three hotels. Data are expressed as a percentage of total emergency work requests for a 30-day period for the same three hotels. Hotel C has significantly lower lighting work requests because electric light bulbs are replaced on a set schedule based on estimated hours of operation in the three hotel areas. Hotel C still uses guest room keys, while Hotels A and B use plastic card computer controlled

guest room door locks, hence the difference between Hotel C and the other two.

Backlogged work orders represent a request for work that cannot be completed at the time of request because either replacement parts or skilled employees are not available. Employees may not be available because of vacation time or sick leave. This could happen if a property had only one on-premise television repair employee who was either ill, on vacation, or not on scheduled duty. Backlogged work orders are scheduled as routine maintenance when the replacement part becomes available or the employee returns to work.

Management Inspections

Another example of a management policy function is establishing a maintenance inspection schedule. The normal maintenance inspection team includes the manager, maintenance department head, and executive housekeeper. During the property inspection the team establishes property and facility standards. Property and facility standards refer to facility performance levels or acceptable appearance levels. An acceptable appearance level is easy to see, for example, when the outside lawn is 4 inches high, it will be cut to 1.5 inches. However, a dirty interior corridor painted wall could be washed or repainted. Wall washing is generaily a housekeeping task and painting is a maintenance task. The inspection team will havc to establish a policy regarding criteria for wall washing and criteria for wall painting.

Table 3

Types and percentage of emergency repairs for three hotels

Type of repair	*Hotel A*	*Hotel B*	*Hotel C*
(1)	*(2)*	*(3)*	*(4)*
Environment (heat cooling)	14.1	7.7	11.6
Door and locks	5.7	5.5	14.6

(1)	*(2)*	*(3)*	*(4)*
Drapes and rods	2.3	7.1	3.0
Electrical (non-lighting)	1.4	2.4	2.8
Lighting	34.1	32.6	8.3
Plumbing	21.1	30.0	31.9
Smoke alarms	1.4	1.9	0.6
Television	10.8	4.3	7.0
Other	9.1	8.5	20.2
Total	100.0	100.0	100.0

Sources: F.D. Borsenick. A Study of the Maintenance Department and its Management at the XXXHoter, unpublished. Howard Hughs Development Corporation. 1984; also extracts from various unpublished consulting studies conducted by ED. Borsenick In 1972, 1975 and 1982.

Facility, and especially equipment, performance guidelines are usually easier to establish. For example, when the combustion efficiency of the hotwater boiler drops to 75 per cent, the equipment and controls are adjusted to increase the efficiency to 80 per cent. If the efficiency cannot be increased to 80 per cent by normal adjustments, what is the proper action? Adjust the efficiency to the highest level above 75 per cent by normal procedures? Renovate the equipment with appropriate components to increase efficiency to some level, 80 per cent or higher? Or, replace the boiler with a new unit that has an efficiency of at least 80 per cent? The development of these decision-making guidelines is policy making.

One of the primary purposes of management inspections is to develop standards of acceptable appearance and performance. A secondary purpose of inspection is to determine the general condition of the property and as a result of the inspection to revise procedures to improve the condition of the property.

As a general guideline, lodging guest rooms should be inspected by the management team at least once year. This implies that 2 per cent of the total number of guest rooms should be inspected each week. Public areas should be inspected by the management team every two weeks. The back-of-the-house areas and facilities should be inspected at least 10 times per year. An inspection from that lists items to be checked must be developed. If during the inspections, the team agrees that the general condition of the property is satisfactory or exceeds their established standards, the number of scheduled inspections can be reduced. If established standards are not being maintained, inspection frequency must be increased.

❑